Anthem Popular American History

What I Saw in America

What I Saw in America

G.K. CHESTERTON

Introduction by Simon P. Newman

ANTHEM PRESS
LONDON · NEW YORK · DELHI

Anthem Press
An imprint of Wimbledon Publishing Company
www.anthempress.com

This edition first published in UK and USA 2009
by ANTHEM PRESS
75-76 Blackfriars Road, London SE1 8HA, UK
or PO Box 9779, London SW19 7ZG, UK
and
244 Madison Ave. #116, New York, NY 10016, USA

First published by Dodd, Mead and Company, New York, 1922

Introduction © Simon P. Newman 2009

British Library Cataloguing in Publication Data
A catalogue record for this book is available from the British Library.

Library of Congress Cataloging in Publication Data
Chesterton, G. K. (Gilbert Keith), 1874–1936.
What I saw in America / G.K. Chesterton;
introduction by Simon P. Newman. p. cm.
"First published in the UK by Dodd, Mead, and Company, 1922"—T.p. verso.
ISBN 978-1-84331-300-7 (pbk.)
1. United States—Description and travel.
2. United States—Social life and customs—1918–1945. 3. Chesterton, G. K.
(Gilbert Keith), 1874–1936—Travel—United States.
4. United States—Civilization—1918–1945.
5. National characteristics, American. I. Title.

E169.C52 2007
917.304'914—dc22
2007050840

ISBN-10: 1 84331 300 6 (Pbk)
ISBN-13: 978 1 84331 3 00 7 (Pbk)

1 3 5 7 9 10 8 6 4 2

Contents

List of Illustrations   ix

Introduction by Simon P. Newman   xiii

1. What is America?   1

2. A Meditation in a New York Hotel.   17

3. A Meditation in Broadway   29

4. Irish and other Interviewers   41

5. Some American Cities.   55

6. In the American Country   69

7. The American Business Man   83

8. Presidents and Problems 103

9. Prohibition in Fact and Fancy. 123

10. Fads and Public Opinion. 137

11. The Extraordinary American 153

12. The Republican in the Ruins 163

13. Is the Atlantic Narrowing? 175

14. Lincoln and Lost Causes 187

15. Wells and the World State. 197

16. A New Martin Chuzzlewit. 211

17. The Spirit of America 223

18. The Spirit of England 235

19. The Future of Democracy 247

List of Illustrations

Frontispiece New York City. Lower New York from New Jersey ferry II, by Theodor Horydczak.

Introduction Portrait of the author from 'Current Times.' Copyright New York Times, 1915.

Page 1 Young women picketing outside the White House gates with an "amnesty for war protesters" sign, with portrait of Harding, which reads: "This is the President who pleaded to set the law aside for a dog. Long after the law has been repealed he still keeps our fathers in prison for expressing their opinions in time of war." National Photo Company Collection (Library of Congress), 1922.

Page 17 The last of the Horses Engine Co. 205, New York Fire Department. National Photo Company Collection, 1922.

Page 29 View of building at corner of Broadway and Park Place, New York City, with pedestrians walking along street. Sign on top of building reads "Irving Underhill General Photographer." Copyright Irving Underhill, New York, 1922.

Page 41 New York, Ellis Island. Immigrants walking across pier from bridge. National Photo Company Collection.

Page 55 City experiment in gardening, New York City. Three men, in foreground, in garden project in New York City park. Frances Benjamin Johnston Collection, 1922.

Page 69 Women out in force: men and women at voting poll, Oliver and Henry Streets, New York City. National Photo Company Collection, 1922.

Page 83   Board room, New York City Stock Exchange. Copyright New York Stock Exchange.

Page 103   Warren G. Harding, three-quarter length portrait, seated at desk, facing left. Copyright Lucia A. Weeks, 1920.

Page 123   Woman putting flask in her Russian boot (Washington, D.C.). National Photo Company Collection, 1922.

Page 137   Large group, mostly women, raising a "No More War" banner over the headquarters of the National Council for Reduction of Armaments—the same building as headquarters for National League of Women Voters on 17th St., Washington, D.C. Herbert E. French, National Photo Company, 1922.

Page 153   Elephant caddie on Miami golf course. Herbert E. French, National Photo Company, 1922.

Page 163   Statue of Liberty, New York City. Copyright George P. Hall & Son, 1898.

Page 175   In the Surf, Atlantic City, N.J. Copyright by Standard Scenic Co., 1906.

Page 187   Lincoln Statue, Lincoln Park (Washington, D.C.). National Photo Company, 1919.

Page 197   A day on a debutante's calendar. National Photo Company Collection, 1922.

Page 211   Two panel illustrations showing a distraught Charles Dickens standing with another man behind the door to his hotel room, on the other side of which is a group of people portraying characters from Dickens' novel, "Martin Chuzzlewit." The man behind the door responds to the "acquaintances'" entreaties by stating that Mr. Dickens is "not at home." Illus. in: Harper's weekly, v. 11, no. 573 (21 December 1867), p. 812.

Page 223   Fashion show at the Wells Shop, a store specializing in corsets, brassieres, hats, and bonnets, at 1331 G Street, N.W. (Washington, D.C.). National Photo Company Collection, 1921.

Page 235   G.K. Chesterton in his study. George Grantham Bain Collection (Library of Congress).

Page 247   The biggest gun in the war for democracy. Detail from poster showing Uncle Sam firing a cannon "American industry," which is shooting supplies and munitions to "The Allies" on a distant shore. "Wage earner" and "Wage payer" look on. Library of Congress, 1917.

Introduction

One of twentieth-century England's most prolific novelists, poets, travel writers, literary critics and essayists, Gilbert Keith Chesterton was born in London on 29 May 1874. He was brought up in comfortable upper middle class surroundings, and attended the Slade School of Art, but it was in writing that Chesterton found his greatest pleasure. In 1900 he published his first volumes of poetry, and throughout the rest of his life Chesterton wrote on a vast array of topics, including editorials and essays on politics, imperialism, literature, religion and many other subjects; poetry; biography; literary criticism; fiction, especially detective novels; travel writing; and theology and religion. In his own words Chesterton was first and foremost "a roaring journalist" who wrote hard and fast, eschewing long research and slow, measured prose in his enthusiasm for whatever topic he was writing about. He died in 1936, having published over one hundred books and thousands of essays, editorials and poems. The London *Times* recorded that Chesterton's "energy and his versatility were amazing: his exuberant intellect ran riot over letters, art, religion, philosophy, and current affairs." This glowing tribute hailed Chesterton as "one of the chief figures in contemporary literature, in almost every species of which he had shown himself an adept."[1]

In detailing his many literary expressions the *Times* recalled "Chesterton the traveller," a thoughtful and perceptive observer who wrote about such foreign ventures as his first lengthy tour of the United States in 1921. Chesterton's interest in the United States had been heightened by the publication of his brother Cecil's *A History of the United States*, which was published in 1919 and for which Chesterton had provided an introduction. Cecil had died in the final year of the First World War, and his loss greatly affected Chesterton, who believed that Cecil was justifiably proud of writing "the history, so necessary and so strangely neglected, of the great democracy, which he had not only loved but honoured."[2] Somewhat restless in the years following the War, Chesterton travelled to Ireland, Poland, Jerusalem, and Rome, writing about his experiences in these varied environments in a succession of essays and books. In 1921, accompanied by his wife Frances, Chesterton embarked on a lecture tour of the United States, and he thoroughly enjoyed his first visit to America and the warm welcome that he received. Published a year later, *What I Saw in America* represented his impressions of the United States, its people, and its culture.

Chesterton's visit came at the start of a fascinating decade, and from that time all the way through to the present day the 1920s has conjured up images of Prohibition and gangsters; flappers, the Charleston dance, and the riotous excesses of the "roaring twenties" described by F. Scott Fitzgerald; women's franchise, nativism, and political

---

[1] "Obituary—Mr. G.K. Chesterton," *Times* (London), 15 June 1936, 17.
[2] G.K. Chesterton, "Introduction," Cecil Chesterton, *A History of the United States* (London: Chatto & Windus, 1919), vii.

"normalcy"; the dramatic expansion of the domestic economy and consumerism, and the rude awakening of the Wall Street Crash. The observations and musings of an observer and writer as talented as Chesterton make *What I Saw in America* a fascinating assessment of American society, politics, and culture at the beginning of one of its most perplexing decades.[3]

Chesterton began his small volume of observations with a brief chapter entitled "What is America?" in which he appeared to undermine his own endeavour by suggesting that "travel narrows the mind" (p.1). The introduction includes amusing anecdotes about an American government immigration form that had asked Chesterton whether he was an anarchist ("What the devil has that to do with you?"), (p.3) and whether he was in favour of subverting the United States government by force ("I prefer to answer that question at the end of my tour and not the beginning") (p.4). While gently lampooning such unfamiliar forms of question, Chesterton made the important point that travellers must see and acknowledge the differences between themselves and the inhabitants of the countries they visit, not looking vainly for things in common but rather finding vastly different incarnations of humanity. In the United States, however, such an approach was complicated by the lack of a standard national "type", given the "great American experiment ... of a democracy of diverse races" (p.7). Chesterton forgave America for its impertinent immigration form questions, for not only was this a nation without a shared past, shared values and shared sensibilities, it was "the only nation in the world that is founded on a creed" (p.6) of inclusion. For Chesterton what was unique was "not America but what is called Americanization," (p.11) the process of taking people of different races, ethnicities and creeds, and making them American.

What I Saw in America comprises nineteen chapters, some on specific and quite focused topics including "The American Business Man" and

---

[3] For America during the 1920s, see David J. Goldberg, *Discontented America: The United States in the 1920s* (Baltimore: Johns Hopkins University Press, 1999).

"Prohibition in Fact and Fancy," others dealing with more abstract subjects such as "The Spirit of America." While bringing a uniquely English sensibility to his musings, Chesterton nonetheless reflected upon the historical and contemporary forces shaping America during the 1920s, at times echoing contemporary Americans such as Sinclair Lewis. He was fascinated by the United States, proposing that he had not only visited but in fact had "discovered America. I cannot avoid the phrase; for it would really seem that each man discovers it for himself" (p.70).

Much of Chesterton's time was spent in larger towns and cities, and he was impressed by their diversity. He compared, for example, the apparent absence of history and historical empathy in New York City with Philadelphia, suggesting that it was

> at least as possible for a Philadelphian to feel the presence of Penn and Franklin as for an Englishman to see the ghosts of Alfred and Becket. Tradition does not mean a dead town; it does not mean that the living are dead, but that the dead are alive. It means that it still matters what Penn did two hundred years ago or what Franklin did a hundred years ago; I never could feel in New York that it mattered what anybody did an hour ago. (p.61)

Such Middle American towns as Oklahoma City fascinated Chesterton, and he wrote that "What many, quite incorrectly, imagine about all America is really true of Oklahoma. It is proud of having no history. It is glowing with the sense of having a great future—and nothing else" (p.154).

In "A Meditation in a New York Hotel" Chesterton compared English inns with hotels in the United States, concluding that "there is only one hotel in America" (p.19). He described the conformity of design and presentation, suggesting that

> If the passage outside your bedroom door, or hallway as it is called, contains, let us say, a small table with a green vase and a stuffed flamingo, or some trifle of the sort, you may be perfectly certain that

there is exactly the same table, vase and flamingo on every one of the thirty-two landings of that towering habitation. (p.19)

Along similar lines Chesterton described how sprawling new suburbs were "far more curious" than the cities that they surrounded. "I saw forests upon forests of small houses stretching away to the horizon as literal forests do" (pp.70–71). The standardization of American life and material culture stood out for Chesterton, as did the rampant consumerism that he witnessed, and he recorded and described these for his British readers.

Chesterton's impression of the bright lights of Broadway reflected his ambivalence about advertising and consumerism, subjects he touched upon often in this volume. He wondered about what these lights would mean to an illiterate immigrant who had "escaped to the land of liberty upon some general rumour and romance of the story of its liberation" (p.30). What, Chesterton wondered, would this hopeful immigrant see around him as he walked along New York's great thoroughfare?

He would be shrewd enough to guess that the three festoons fringed with fiery words of somewhat similar pattern stood for "Government of the People, For the People, By the People" ... His shrewdness would perhaps be a little shaken if he knew that the triad stood for "Tang Tonic To-day; Tang Tonic To-morrow; Tang Tonic All the Time." He will soon identify a restless ribbon of red lettering, red hot and rebellious, as the saying, "Give me liberty or give me death." He will fail to identify it as the equally famous saying, "Skyoline has Gout Beaten to a Frazzle." (p.30)

Such "modern and mercantile legends," dominating the Manhattan skyline, did not stand for any great national ideals: "it is doubtful whether any man will ever, with his last breath, frame the ecstatic words, 'Try Hugby's Chewing Gum.'" Chesterton objected that standardization and rank materialism reflected "an industrial progress which is of all things on earth the most undemocratic" (p.38).

Chesterton's discomfort with aspects of modern society that he saw so vividly in the United States was expressed in terms both subtle and nuanced. British condemnation of "the American as a materialist because of his worship of success" struck him as problematic, for to Chesterton such worship proved the American "rather a mystic than a materialist" (p.93). He believed that Americans "worship success in the abstract, as a sort of ideal vision. They follow success rather than money." It is a telling observation, and he concluded that "The dollar is an idol because it is an image; but it is an image of success and not of enjoyment" (p.93).

Alive to the larger political problems and social conflicts of early twentieth-century America, Chesterton addressed several head on while avoiding others. A man who enjoyed alcohol, he was appalled by Prohibition, and he attacked it with his customary wit. His chapter on the topic began with the observation that he had travelled to the United States with no expectation of discussing the subject, "But I soon found that well-to-do Americans were only too delighted to discuss it over nuts and wine. They were even willing, if necessary, to dispense with the nuts." While acknowledging that Prohibition "does not exist" for many Americans, he was appalled by what struck him as unequal application of a misguided law (p.123). Developing an argument that would have been unthinkable for contemporary American writers, Chesterton began discussing the enslavement of African Americans – "the crime and catastrophe of American history" (p.134)—and then equating it to aspects of Prohibition. To Chesterton, Prohibition represented the enforced application of a moral code on the poor (most particularly African Americans), a code that was wilfully ignored by those with wealth and power. He was quick, however, to point out that similar inequities had long existed in Britain, yet he was clearly disappointed by this aspect of American society. While acknowledging that black slavery had ended, he found any resulting equality disappointing, for through Prohibition "White labour is every bit as much enslaved as black labour" (p.136).

While he did not visit the Deep South, Chesterton was fascinated by the history and heritage of American race relations. He astutely observed that "the eighteenth century was *more* liberal than the nineteenth century. There was *more* sympathy for the negro in the school of Jefferson than in the school of Jefferson Davis." (p.249) While the former acknowledged the iniquity of slavery, the latter had defended it as a positive good: "that the slave was human and the servitude inhuman— that was, if anything, clearer to Jefferson than to Lincoln" (p.250). Yet again Chesterton's judgements were fair and balanced, and he highlighted the role played by British manufacturing and industry in the strengthening of nineteenth-century American slavery. He lauded Jefferson's ideals, suggesting that it was eighteenth-century principles that made nineteenth-century abolition and emancipation possible. Chesterton suggested that Lincoln was "invoking a primitive first principle of the age of innocence, and holding up the tables of an ancient law, *against* the trend of the nineteenth century; repeating, 'We hold these truths to be self-evident; that all men are created equal ...'" (p.252). To Chesterton's eyes, the traditional fault-line of colour was losing its significance in America, and as he drew his volume to a close he observed that "it is more and more obvious that the line is no longer running between black and white but between rich and poor" (p.255). It was a striking observation, and one that the Wall Street Crash and the subsequent Great Depression would render quite prophetic.

What I Saw in America was not intended to provide a comprehensive assessment of the United States and its people and society, but rather a series of impressions that he hoped might challenge a few of the misconceptions common amongst his fellow Britons, while at the same time challenging them to look at their own nation and society in a new light. He sought to free his readers "from the talismanic tyranny" of such truisms as the common description of America as "a young nation," which he pointed out should be regarded as the metaphor that it was rather than as the statement of fact that it was not (pp.164–165). While Britons were quite familiar with American literature, American history and politics were far less well known and understood: with American advertising making inroads into British society, to many of Chesterton's countrymen and women Henry Clay "is a cigar," "the State of Virginia is a cigarette," and "Plymouth Rock is a chicken" (pp.187–188).

If *What I Saw in America* informed Chesterton's contemporaries, today's reader can enjoy an insightful, well-written and often very amusing perspective on 1920s America, encompassing politics, race, consumerism, Prohibition and a host of the main themes of not just that decade but of American society in general. While at times reflecting Chesterton's particular interests and preoccupations, the volume nonetheless represents a valuable outside perspective on the United States at the beginning of a period of national introversion and isolationism. Chesterton may have criticized aspects of American society such as crass commercialism and advertising, yet he recognized that such ephemera was "the shadow of America, but it is not the light of America. The light lies far beyond, a level light upon the lands of sunset, where it shines upon wide places full of a very simple and a very happy people; and those who would see it must seek for it" (p.185).

Simon P. Newman
Sir Denis Brogan Professor of American History,
University of Glasgow

1 *Relativization*

What is America?

I have never managed to lose my old conviction that travel narrows the mind. At least a man must make a double effort of moral humility and imaginative energy to prevent it from narrowing his mind. Indeed there is something touching and even tragic about the thought of the thoughtless tourist, who might have stayed at home loving Laplanders, embracing Chinamen, and clasping Patagonians to his heart in Hampstead or Surbiton, but for his blind and suicidal impulse to go and see what they looked like. This is not meant for nonsense; still less is it meant for the silliest sort of nonsense, which is cynicism. The human bond that he feels at home is not an illusion. On the contrary, it is rather an inner reality. Man is inside all men. In a real sense any man may be inside any men. But to travel is to leave the inside and draw dangerously near the outside. So long as he thought of men in the abstract, like naked toiling figures in some classic frieze, merely as those who labour and love their children and die, he was thinking the fundamental truth about them. By going to look at their unfamiliar manners and customs he is inviting them to disguise themselves in fantastic masks and costumes. Many modern internationalists talk as if men of different nationalities had only to meet and mix and understand each other. In reality that is the moment of supreme danger—the moment when they meet. We might shiver, as at the old euphemism by which a meeting meant a duel.

Travel ought to combine amusement with instruction; but most travellers are so much amused that they refuse to be instructed. I do not blame them for being amused, it is perfectly natural to be amused at a Dutchman for being Dutch or a Chinaman for being Chinese. Where they are wrong is that they take their own amusement seriously. They base on it their serious ideas of international instruction. It was said that the Englishman takes his pleasures sadly; and the pleasure of despising foreigners is one which he takes most sadly of all. He comes to scoff and does not remain to pray, but rather to excommunicate. Hence in international relations there is far too little laughing, and far too much sneering. But I believe that there is a better way which largely consists of laughter; a form of friendship between nations which is actually founded on differences. To hint at some such better way is the only excuse of this book.

Let me begin my American impressions with two impressions I had before I went to America. One was an incident and the other an idea; and when taken together they illustrate the attitude I mean. The first principle is that nobody should be ashamed of thinking a thing funny because it is foreign; the second is that he should be ashamed of thinking it wrong because it is funny. The reaction of his senses and superficial habits of mind against something new, and to him abnormal, is a perfectly healthy reaction. But the mind which imagines that mere unfamiliarity can possibly prove anything about inferiority is a very inadequate mind. It is inadequate even in criticizing things that may really be inferior to the things involved here. It is far better to laugh at a negro for having a black face than to sneer at him for having a sloping skull. It is proportionally even more preferable to laugh rather than judge in dealing with highly civilized peoples. Therefore I put at the beginning two working examples of what I felt about America before I saw it; the sort of thing that a man has a right to enjoy as a joke, and the sort of thing he has a duty to understand and respect, because it is the explanation of the joke.

When I went to the American consulate to regularize my passports, I was capable of expecting the American consulate to be American. Embassies and consulates are by tradition like islands of the soil for which they stand; and I have often found the tradition corresponding to a truth. I have seen the unmistakable French official living on omelettes and a little wine and serving his sacred abstractions under the last palm-trees fringing a desert. In the heat and noise of quarrelling Turks and Egyptians, I have come suddenly, as with the cool shock of his own shower-bath, on the listless amiability of the English gentleman. The officials I interviewed were very American, especially in being very polite; for whatever may have been the mood or meaning of Martin Chuzzlewit, I have always found Americans by far the politest people in the world. They put in my hands a form to be filled up, to all appearances like other forms I had filled up in other passport offices. But in reality it was very different from any form I had ever filled up in my life. At least it was a little like a freer form of the game called "Confessions" which my friends and I invented in our youth; an examination paper containing questions like, "If you saw a rhinoceros in the front garden, what would you do?" One of my friends, I remember, wrote, "Take the pledge." But that is another story, and might bring Mr. Pussyfoot Johnson on the scene before his time.

One of the questions on the paper was, "Are you an anarchist?" To which a detached philosopher would naturally feel inclined to answer, "What the devil has that to do with you? Are you an atheist?" along with some playful efforts to cross-examine the official about what constitutes an ἀρχή? Then there was the question, "Are you in favour of subverting

3

the government of the United States by force?" Against this I should write, "I prefer to answer that question at the end of my tour and not the beginning." The inquisitor, in his more than morbid curiosity, had then written down, "Are you a polygamist?" The answer to this is, "No such luck" or "Not such a fool", according to our experience of the other sex. But perhaps a better answer would be that given to W. T. Stead when he circulated the rhetorical question, "Shall I slay my brother Boer?"—the answer that ran, "Never interfere in family matters." But among many things that amused me almost to the point of treating the form thus disrespectfully, the most amusing was the thought of the ruthless outlaw who should feel compelled to treat it respectfully. I like to think of the foreign desperado, seeking to slip into America with official papers under official protection, and sitting down to write with a beautiful gravity, "I am an anarchist. I hate you all and wish to destroy you." Or, "I intend to subvert by force the government of the United States as soon as possible, sticking the long sheath-knife in my left trouser-pocket into Mr. Harding at the earliest opportunity." Or again, "Yes, I am a polygamist all right, and my forty-seven wives are accompanying me on the voyage disguised as secretaries." There seems to be a certain simplicity of mind about these answers; and it is reassuring to know that anarchists and polygamists are so pure and good that the police have only to ask them questions and they are certain to tell no lies.

Now that is a model of the sort of foreign practice, founded on foreign problems, at which a man's first impulse is naturally to laugh. Nor have I any intention of apologizing for my laughter. A man is perfectly entitled to laugh at a thing because he happens to find it incomprehensible. What he has no right to do is to laugh at it as incomprehensible, and then criticize it as if he comprehended it. The very fact of its unfamiliarity and mystery ought to set him thinking about the deeper causes that make people so different from himself, and that without merely assuming that they must be inferior to himself.

Superficially this is rather a queer business. It would be easy enough to suggest that in this America has introduced a quite abnormal spirit of inquisition; an interference with liberty unknown among all the ancient despotisms and aristocracies. About that there will be something to be said later; but superficially it is true that this degree of officialism is comparatively unique. In a journey which I took only the year before I had occasion to have my papers passed by governments which many worthy people in the West would vaguely identify with corsairs and assassins; I have stood on the other side of Jordan, in the land ruled by a rude Arab chief, where the police looked so like brigands that one wondered what the brigands looked like. But they did not ask me whether I had come to subvert the power of the Shereef; and they did not exhibit the faintest curiosity about my personal views on the ethical basis of civil authority. These ministers of ancient Moslem despotism did not care about whether I was an anarchist; and naturally would not have minded if I had been a polygamist. The Arab chief was probably a polygamist himself. These slaves of Asiatic autocracy were content, in the old liberal fashion, to judge me by my actions; they did not inquire into my thoughts. They held their power as limited to the limitation of practice; they did not forbid me to hold a theory. It would be easy to argue here that Western democracy persecutes where even Eastern despotism tolerates or emancipates. It would be easy to develop the fancy that, as compared with the sultans of Turkey or Egypt, the American Constitution is a thing like the Spanish Inquisition.

Only the traveller who stops at that point is totally wrong; and the traveller only too often does stop at that point. He has found something to make him laugh, and he will not suffer it to make him think. And the remedy is not to unsay what he has said, not even, so to speak, to unlaugh what he has laughed, not to deny that there is something unique and curious about this American inquisition into our abstract opinions, but rather to continue the train of thought, and follow the admirable advice of Mr. H. G. Wells, who said, "It is not much good thinking of a thing unless you think it out." It is not to deny that American officialism is rather peculiar on this point, but to inquire what it really is which makes America peculiar, or which is peculiar to America. In short, it is to get some ultimate idea of what America *is*; and the answer to that question will reveal something much deeper and grander and more worthy of our intelligent interest.

It may have seemed something less than a compliment to compare the American Constitution to the Spanish Inquisition. But oddly enough, it does involve a truth; and still more oddly perhaps, it does involve a compliment. The American Constitution does resemble the Spanish Inquisition in this: that it is founded on a creed. America is the only nation in the world that is founded on a creed. That creed is set forth with dogmatic and even theological lucidity in the Declaration of Independence; perhaps the only piece of practical politics that is also theoretical politics and also great literature. It enunciates that all men are equal in their claim to justice, that governments exist to give them that justice, and that their authority is for that reason just. It certainly does condemn anarchism, and it does also by inference condemn atheism, since it clearly names the Creator as the ultimate authority from whom these equal rights are derived. Nobody expects a modern political system to proceed logically in the application of such dogmas, and in the matter of God and Government it is naturally God whose claim is taken more lightly. The point is that there is a creed, if not about divine, at least about human things.

Now a creed is at once the broadest and the narrowest thing in the world. In its nature it is as broad as its scheme for a brotherhood of all men. In its nature it is limited by its definition of the nature of all men. This was true of the Christian Church, which was truly said to exclude neither Jew nor Greek, but which did definitely substitute something else for Jewish religion or Greek philosophy. It was truly said to be a net drawing in of all kinds; but a net of a certain pattern, the pattern of Peter the Fisherman. And this is true even of the most disastrous distortions or degradations of that creed; and true among others of the Spanish Inquisition. It may have been narrow touching theology, it could not confess to being narrow about nationality or ethnology.

6

The Spanish Inquisition might be admittedly Inquisitorial; but the Spanish Inquisition could not be merely Spanish. Such a Spaniard, even when he was narrower than his own creed, had to be broader than his own empire. He might burn a philosopher because he was heterodox; but he must accept a barbarian because he was orthodox. And we see, even in modern times, that the same Church which is blamed for making sages heretics is also blamed for making savages priests. Now in a much vaguer and more evolutionary fashion, there is something of the same idea at the back of the great American experiment; the experiment of a democracy of diverse races which has been compared to a melting-pot. But even that metaphor implies that the pot itself is of a certain shape and a certain substance; a pretty solid substance. The melting-pot must not melt. The original shape was traced on the lines of Jeffersonian democracy; and it will remain in that shape until it becomes shapeless. America invites all men to become citizens; but it implies the dogma that there is such a thing as citizenship. Only, so far as its primary ideal is concerned, its exclusiveness is religious because it is not racial. *really?* The missionary can condemn a cannibal, precisely because he cannot condemn a Sandwich Islander. And in something of the same spirit the American may exclude a polygamist, precisely because he cannot exclude a Turk.

Now for America this is no idle theory. It may have been theoretical, though it was thoroughly sincere, when that great Virginian gentleman declared it in surroundings that still had something of the character of an English countryside. It is not merely theoretical now. There is nothing to prevent America being literally invaded by Turks, as she is invaded by Jews or Bulgars. In the most exquisitely inconsequent of the *Bab Ballads*, we are told concerning Pasha Bailey Ben:

> One morning knocked at half-past eight
> A tall Red Indian at his gate.
> In Turkey, as you 'r' p'haps aware,
> Red Indians are extremely rare.

But the converse need by no means be true. There is nothing in the nature of things to prevent an emigration of Turks increasing and multiplying on the plains where the Red Indians wandered; there is nothing to necessitate the Turks being extremely rare. The Red Indians, alas, are likely to be rarer. And as I much prefer Red Indians to Turks, not to mention Jews, I speak without prejudice; but the point here is that America, partly by original theory and partly by historical accident, does lie open to racial admixtures which most countries would think incongruous or comic. That is why it is only fair to read any American definitions or rules in a certain light, and relatively to a rather unique position. It is not fair to compare the position of those who may meet Turks in the back street with that of those who have never met Turks except in the *Bab Ballads*. It is not fair simply to compare America with England in its regulations about the Turk. In short, it is not fair to do what almost every Englishman probably does; to look at the American international examination paper, and laugh and be satisfied with saying: "We don't have any of that nonsense in England."

We do not have any of that nonsense in England because we have never attempted to have any of that philosophy in England. And, above all, because we have the enormous advantage of feeling it natural to be national, because there is nothing else to be. England in these days is not well governed; England is not well educated; England suffers from wealth and poverty that are not well distributed. But England is English; *esto perpetua*. England is English as France is French or Ireland Irish; the great mass of men taking certain national traditions for granted. Now this gives us a totally different and a very much easier task. We have not got an inquisition, because we have not got a creed; but it is arguable that we do not need a creed, because we have got a character. In any of the old nations the national unity is preserved by the national type. Because we have a type we do not need to have a test.

Take that innocent question: "Are you an anarchist?" which is intrinsically quite as impudent as "Are you an optimist?" or "Are you a philanthropist?" I am not discussing here whether these things are right, but whether most of us are in a position to know them rightly. Now it is quite true that most Englishmen do not find it necessary to go about all day asking each other whether they are anarchists. It is quite true that the phrase occurs on no British forms that I have seen. But this is not only because most of the Englishmen are not anarchists. It is even more because even the anarchists are Englishmen. For instance, it would be easy to make fun of the American formula by noting that the cap would fit all sorts of bald academic heads. It might well be maintained that Herbert Spencer was an anarchist. It is practically certain that Auberon Herbert was an anarchist. But Herbert Spencer was an extraordinarily typical Englishman of the Nonconformist middle class. And Auberon Herbert was an extraordinarily typical English aristocrat of the old and genuine aristocracy. Every one knew in his heart that the squire would not throw a bomb at the Queen, and the Nonconformist would not throw a bomb at anybody. Every one knew that there was something subconscious in a man like Auberon Herbert, which would have come out only in throwing bombs at the enemies of England; as it did come out in his son and namesake, the generous and unforgotten, who fell flinging bombs from the sky far beyond the German line. Every one knows that normally, in the last resort, the English gentleman is patriotic. Every one knows that the English Nonconformist is national even when he denies that he is patriotic. Nothing is more notable indeed than the fact that nobody is more stamped with the mark of his own nation than the man who says that there ought to be no nations. Somebody called Cobden the International Man; but no man could be more English than Cobden. Everybody recognizes Tolstoy as the iconoclast of all patriotism; but nobody could be more Russian than Tolstoy. In the old countries where there are these national types, the types may be allowed to hold any theories. Even if they hold certain theories, they are unlikely to do certain things. So the conscientious objector, in the English sense, may be and is one of the peculiar

9

by-products of England. But the conscientious objector will probably have a conscientious objection to throwing bombs.

Now I am very far from intending to imply that these American tests are good tests, or that there is no danger of tyranny becoming the temptation of America. I shall have something to say later on about that temptation or tendency. Nor do I say that they apply consistently this conception of a nation with the soul of a church, protected by religious and not racial selection. If they did apply that principle consistently, they would have to exclude pessimists and rich cynics who deny the democratic ideal; an excellent thing but a rather improbable one. What I say is that when we realize that this principle exists at all, we see the whole position in a totally different perspective. We say that the Americans are doing something heroic or doing something insane, or doing it in an unworkable or unworthy fashion, instead of simply wondering what the devil they are doing.

When we realize the democratic design of such a cosmopolitan commonwealth, and compare it with our insular reliance or instincts, we see at once why such a thing has to be not only democratic but dogmatic. We see why in some points it tends to be inquisitive or intolerant. Any one can see the practical point by merely transferring into private life a problem like that of the two academic anarchists, who might by a coincidence be called the two Herberts. Suppose a man said: "Buffle, my old Oxford tutor, wants to meet you; I wish you'd ask him down for a day or two. He has the oddest opinions, but he's very stimulating." It would not occur to us that the oddity of the Oxford don's opinions would lead him to blow up the house; because the Oxford don is an English type. Suppose somebody said, "Do let me bring old Colonel Robinson down for the week-end; he's a bit of crank but quite interesting." We should not anticipate the colonel running amuck with a carving-knife and offering up human sacrifice in the garden; for these are not among the daily habits of an old English colonel; and because we know his habits, we do not care about his opinions. But suppose somebody offered to bring a person from the interior of Kamskatka to stay with us for a week or two, and added that his religion was a very extraordinary religion, we should feel a little more inquisitive about what kind of a religion it was. If somebody wished to add a Hairy Ainu to the family party at Christmas, explaining that his point of view was so individual and interesting, we should want to know a little more about it and him. We should be tempted to draw up as fantastic an examination paper as that presented to the emigrant going to America. We should ask what a Hairy Ainu was, and how hairy he was, and above all what sort of Ainu he was. Would etiquette require us to ask him to bring his wife? And if we did ask him to bring his wife, how many wives would he bring? In short, as in the American formula, is he a polygamist? Merely as a point of housekeeping and accommodation the question is not irrelevant. Is the Hairy Ainu content with hair, or does he wear any clothes? If the police insist on his wearing clothes, will he recognize the authority of the police? In short, as in the American formula, is he an anarchist?

Of course this generalization about America, like other historical things, is subject to all sorts of cross divisions and exceptions, to be considered in their place. The negroes are a special problem, because of what white men in the past did to them. The Japanese are a special problem, because of what men fear that they in the future may do to white men. The Jews are a special problem, because of what they and the Gentiles, in the past, present, and future, seem to have the habit of doing to each other. But the point is not that nothing exists in America except this idea; it is that nothing like this idea exists anywhere except in America. This idea is not internationalism; on the contrary it is decidedly nationalism. The Americans are very patriotic, and wish to make their new citizens patriotic Americans. But it is the idea of making a new nation literally out of any old nation that comes along. In a word, what is unique is not America, but what is called Americanization. We understand nothing till we understand the amazing ambition to Americanize the Kamskatkan and the Hairy Ainu. We are not trying to Anglicize thousands of French cooks or

Italian organ-grinders. France is not trying to Gallicize thousands of English trippers or German prisoners of war. America is the one place in the world where this process, healthy or unhealthy, possible or impossible, is going on. And the process, as I have pointed out, is *not* internationalization. It would be truer to say it is the nationalization of the internationalized. It is making a home out of vagabonds and a nation out of exiles. This is what at once illuminates and softens the moral regulations which we may really think faddist or fanatical. They are abnormal; but in one sense this experiment of a home for the homeless is abnormal. In short, it has long been recognized that America was an asylum. It is only since Prohibition that it has looked a little like a lunatic asylum.

It was before sailing for America, as I have said, that I stood with the official paper in my hand and these thoughts in my head. It was while I stood on English soil that I passed through the two stages of smiling and then sympathizing; of realizing that my momentary amusement, at being asked if I were not an Anarchist, was partly due to the fact that I was not an American. And in truth I think there are some things a man ought to know about America before he sees it. What we know of a country beforehand may not affect what we see that it is; but it will vitally affect what we appreciate it for being, because it will vitally affect what we expected it to be. I can honestly say that I had never expected America to be what nine-tenths of the newspaper critics invariably assume it to be. I never thought it was a sort of Anglo-Saxon colony, knowing that it was more and more thronged with crowds of very different colonists. During the war I felt that the very worst propaganda for the Allies was the propaganda for the Anglo-Saxons. I tried to point out that in one way America is nearer to Europe than England is. If she is not nearer to Bulgaria, she is nearer to Bulgars; if she is not nearer to Bohemia, she is nearer to Bohemians. In my New York hotel the head waiter in the dining-room was a Bohemian; the head waiter in the grill-room was a Bulgar. Americans have nationalities at the end of the street which for us are at the ends of the earth. I did my best to persuade my countrymen not to appeal to the American as if he were a rather dowdy Englishman, who had been rusticating in the provinces and had not heard the latest news about the town. I shall record later some of those arresting realities which the traveller does not expect, and which, in some cases I fear, he actually does not see because he does not expect. I shall try to do justice to the psychology of what Mr. Belloc has called "Eye-Openers in Travel." But there are some things about America that a man ought to see even with his eyes shut. One is that a state that came into existence solely through its repudiation and abhorrence of the British Crown is not likely to be a respectful copy of the British Constitution. Another is that the chief mark of the Declaration of Independence is something that is not only absent from the British Constitution, but something which all our constitutionalists have invariably thanked God, with the jolliest boasting and bragging, that they had kept out of the British Constitution. It is the thing called abstraction or academic logic. It is the thing which such jolly people call theory; and which those who can practice it call thought. And the theory or thought is the very last to which English people are accustomed, either by their social structure or their traditional teaching. It is the theory of equality. It is the pure classic conception that no man must aspire to be anything more than a citizen, and that no man should endure to be anything less. It is by no means especially intelligible to an Englishman, who tends at his best to the virtues of the gentleman and at his worst to the vices of the snob. The idealism of England, or if you will, the romance of England, has not been primarily the romance of the citizen. But the idealism of America, we may safely say, still revolves entirely round the citizen and his romance. The realities are quite another matter, and we shall consider in its place the question of whether the ideal will be able to shape the realities or will merely be beaten shapeless by them. The ideal is besieged by inequalities of the most towering and insane description in the industrial and economic field. It may be devoured by modern capitalism,

13

perhaps the worst inequality that ever existed among men. Of all that we shall speak later. But citizenship is still the American ideal; there is an army of actualities opposed to that ideal; but there is no ideal opposed to that ideal. American plutocracy has never got itself respected like English aristocracy. Citizenship is the American ideal; and it has never been the English ideal. But it is surely an ideal that may stir some imaginative generosity and respect in an Englishman, if he will condescend to be also a man. In this vision of moulding many peoples into the visible image of the citizen, he may see a spiritual adventure which he can admire from the outside, at least as much as he admires the valour of the Moslems and much more than he admires the virtue of the Middle Ages. He need not set himself to develop equality, but he need not set himself to misunderstand it. He may at least understand what Jefferson and Lincoln meant, and he may possibly find some assistance in this task by reading what they said. He may realize that equality is not some crude fairy tale about all men being equally tall or equally tricky; which we not only cannot believe but cannot believe in anybody believing. It is an absolute of morals by which all men have a value invariable and indestructible and a dignity as intangible as death. He may at least be a philosopher and see that equality is an idea; and not merely one of these soft-headed sceptics who, having risen by low tricks to high places, drink bad champagne in tawdry hotel lounges, and tell each other twenty times over, with unwearied iteration, that equality is an illusion.

In truth it is inequality that is the illusion. The extreme disproportion between men, that we seem to see in life, is a thing of changing lights and lengthening shadows, a twilight full of fancies and distortions. We find a man famous and cannot live long enough to find him forgotten; we see a race dominant and cannot linger to see it decay. It is the experience of men that always returns to the equality of men; it is the average that ultimately justifies the average man. It is when men have seen and suffered much and come at the end of more elaborate experiments, that they see men as men under an equal light of death and daily laughter; and none the less mysterious for being many. Nor is it in vain that these Western democrats have sought the blazonry of their flag in that great multitude of immortal lights that endure behind the fires we see, and gathered them into the corner of Old Glory whose ground is like the glittering night. For veritably, in the spirit as well as in the symbol, suns and moons and meteors pass and fill our skies with a fleeting and almost theatrical conflagration; and wherever the old shadow stoops upon the earth, the stars return.

2

A Meditation in
a New York Hotel

All this must begin with an apology and not an apologia. When I went wandering about the States disguised as a lecturer, I was well aware that I was not sufficiently well disguised to be a spy. I was even in the worst possible position to be a sight-seer. A lecturer to American audiences can hardly be in the holiday mood of a sight-seer. It is rather the audience that is sight-seeing; even if it is seeing a rather melancholy sight. Some say that people come to see the lecturer and not to hear him; in which case it seems rather a pity that he should disturb and distress their minds with a lecture. He might merely display himself on a stand or platform for a stipulated sum; or be exhibited like a monster in a menagerie. The circus elephant is not expected to make a speech. But it is equally true that the circus elephant is not allowed to write a book. His impressions of travel would be somewhat sketchy and perhaps a little over-specialized. In merely travelling from circus to circus he would, so to speak, move in rather narrow circles. Jumbo, the great elephant (with whom I am hardly so ambitious as to compare myself), before he eventually went to the Barnum show, passed a considerable and I trust happy part of his life in the Regent's Park. But if he had written a book on England, founded on his impressions of the Zoo, it might have been a little disproportionate and even misleading in its version of the flora and fauna of that country. He might imagine that lions and leopards were commoner than they are in our hedgerows and country lanes, or that the head and neck of a giraffe was as native to our landscapes as a village spire. And that is why I apologize in anticipation for a probable lack of proportion in this work. Like the elephant, I may have seen too much of a special enclosure where a special sort of lions are gathered together. I may exaggerate the territorial, as distinct from the vertical space occupied by the spiritual giraffe; for the giraffe may surely be regarded as an example of Uplift, and is even, in a manner of speaking, a high-brow. Above all, I shall probably make generalizations that are much too general; and are insufficient through being exaggerative. To this sort of doubt all my impressions are subject; and among them the negative generalization with which I shall begin this rambling meditation on American hotels.

In all my American wanderings I never saw such a thing as an inn. They may exist; but they do not arrest the traveller upon every road as they do in England and in Europe. The saloons no longer existed when I was there, owing to the recent reform which restricted intoxicants to the wealthier classes. But we feel that the saloons have been there; if one may so express it, their absence is still present. They remain in the structure of the street and the idiom of the language. But the saloons were not inns. If they had been inns, it would have been far harder even for the power of modern plutocracy to root them out. There will be a very different chase when the White Hart is hunted to the forests or when the Red Lion turns to bay. But people could not feel about the

American saloon as they will feel about the English inns. They could not feel that the Prohibitionist, that vulgar chucker-out, was chucking Chaucer out of the Tabard and Shakespeare out of the Mermaid. In justice to the American Prohibitionists it must be realized that they were not doing quite such a desecration; and that many of them felt the saloon a specially poisonous sort of place. They did feel that drinking-places were used only as drug-shops. So they have effected the great reconstruction, by which it will be necessary to use only drug-shops as drinking-places. But I am not dealing here with the problem of Prohibition except in so far as it is involved in the statement that the saloons were in no sense inns. Secondly, of course, there are the hotels. There are, indeed. There are hotels toppling to the stars, hotels covering the acreage of villages, hotels in multitudinous number like a mob of Babylonian or Assyrian monuments; but the hotels also are not inns.

Broadly speaking, there is only one hotel in America. The pattern of it, which is a very rational pattern, is repeated in cities as remote from each other as the capitals of European empires. You may find that hotel rising among the red blooms of the warm spring woods of Nebraska, or whitened with Canadian snows near the eternal noise of Niagara. And before touching on this solid and simple pattern itself, I may remark that the same system of symmetry runs through all the details of the interior. As one hotel is like another hotel, so one hotel floor is like another hotel floor. If the passage outside your bedroom door, or hallway as it is called, contains, let us say, a small table with a green vase and a stuffed flamingo, or some trifle of the sort, you may be perfectly certain that there is exactly the same table, vase and flamingo on every one of the thirty-two landings of that towering habitation. This is where it differs most, perhaps, from the crooked landings and unexpected levels of the old English inns, even when they call themselves hotels. To me there was something weird, like a magic multiplication, in the exquisite sameness of these suites. It seemed to suggest the still atmosphere of some eerie psychological story. I once myself entertained the notion of a story, in which a man was to be prevented from entering his house

19

(the scene of some crime or calamity) by people who painted and furnished the next house to look exactly like it; the assimilation going to the most fantastic lengths, such as altering the numbering of houses in the street. I came to America and found an hotel fitted and upholstered throughout for the enactment of my phantasmal fraud. I offer the skeleton of my story with all humility to some of the admirable lady writers of detective stories in America, to Miss Carolyn Wells, or Miss Mary Roberts Rinehart, or Mrs. A. K. Green of the unforgotten Leavenworth Case. Surely it might be possible for the unsophisticated Nimrod K. Moose, of Yellow Dog Flat, to come to New York and be entangled somehow in this net of repetitions or recurrences. Surely something tells me that his beautiful daughter, the Rose of Red Murder Gulch, might seek for him in vain amid the apparently unmistakable surroundings of the thirty-second floor, while he was being quietly butchered by the floor-clerk on the thirty-third floor, an agent of the Green Claw (that formidable organization); and all because the two floors looked exactly alike to the virginal Western eye. The original point of my own story was that the man to be entrapped walked into his own house after all, in spite of it being differently painted and numbered, simply because he was absent-minded and used to taking a certain number of mechanical steps. This would not work in the hotel; because a lift has no habits. It is typical of the real tameness of machinery, that even when we talk of a man turning mechanically we only talk metaphorically; for it is something that a mechanism cannot do. But I think there is only one real objection to my story of Mr. Moose in a New York hotel. And that is, unfortunately, a rather fatal one. It is that far away in the remote desolation of Yellow Dog, among those outlying and outlandish rocks that almost seem to rise beyond the sunset, there is, undoubtedly, an hotel of exactly the same sort, with all its floors exactly the same.

Anyhow, the general plan of the American hotel is commonly the same, and, as I have said, it is a very sound one so far as it goes. When I first went into one of the big New York hotels, the first impression was certainly its bigness. It was called the Biltmore; and I wondered how many national humorists had made the obvious comment of wishing they had built less. But it was not merely the Babylonian size and scale of such things, it was the way in which they are used. They are used almost as public streets, or rather as public squares. My first impression was that I was in some sort of high street or market-place during a carnival or a revolution. True, the people looked rather rich for a revolution, and rather grave for a carnival; but they were congested in great crowds that moved slowly like people passing through an overcrowded railway station. Even in the dizzy heights of such a sky-scraper there could not possibly be room for all those people to sleep in the hotel, or even to dine in it. And, as a matter of fact, they did nothing whatever except drift into it and drift out again. Most of them had no more to do with the hotel than I have with Buckingham Palace. I have never been in Buckingham Palace, and I have very seldom, thank God; been in the big hotels of this type that exist in London or Paris. But I cannot believe that mobs are perpetually pouring through the Hotel Cecil or the Savoy in this fashion, calmly coming in at one door and going out of the other. But this fact is part of the fundamental structure of the American hotel; it is built upon a compromise that makes it possible. The whole of the lower floor is thrown open to the public streets and treated as a public square. But above it and all round it runs another floor in the form of a sort of deep gallery, furnished more luxuriously and looking down on the moving mobs beneath. No one is allowed on this floor except the guests or clients of the hotel. As I have been one of them myself, I trust it is not unsympathetic to compare them to active anthropoids who can climb trees, and so look down in safety on the herds or packs of wilder animals wandering and prowling below. Of course there are modifications of this architectural plan, but they are generally approximations to it; it is the plan that seems to suit the social life of the American cities. There is generally something like a ground floor that is more public, a half-floor or gallery above that is more private, and above that the bulk of the block of bedrooms, the huge hive with its innumerable and identical cells.

The ladder of ascent in this tower is, of course, the lift, or, as it is called, the elevator. With all that we hear of American hustle and hurry it is rather strange that Americans seem to like more than we do to linger upon long words. And indeed there is an element of delay in their diction and spirit; very little understood, which I may discuss elsewhere. Anyhow, they say elevator when we say lift, just as they say automobile when we say motor, and stenographer when we say typist, or sometimes (by a slight confusion) typewriter. Which reminds me of another story that never existed, about a man who was accused of having murdered and dismembered his secretary when he had only taken his typing machine to pieces; but we must not dwell on these digressions. The Americans may have another reason for giving long and ceremonious titles to the lift. When first I came among them I had a suspicion that they possessed and practised a new and secret religion, which was the cult of the elevator. I fancied they worshipped the lift, or at any rate worshipped in the lift. The details or data of this suspicion it were now vain to collect, as I have regretfully abandoned it, except in so far as they illustrate the social principles underlying the structural plan of the building. Now an American gentleman invariably takes off his hat in the lift. He does not take off his hat in the hotel, even if it is crowded with ladies. But he always so salutes a lady in the elevator; and this marks the difference of atmosphere. The lift is a room, but the hotel is a street. But during my first delusion, of course, I assumed that he uncovered in this tiny temple merely because he was in church. There is something about the very word elevator that expresses a great deal of his vague but idealistic religion. Perhaps that flying chapel will eventually be ritualistically decorated like a chapel; possibly with a symbolic scheme of wings. Perhaps a brief religious service will be held in the elevator as it ascends; in a few well-chosen words touching the Utmost for the Highest. Possibly he would consent even to call the elevator a lift, if he could call it an uplift. There would be no difficulty, except what I cannot

22

but regard as the chief moral problem of all optimistic modernism. I mean the difficulty of imagining a lift which is free to go up, if it is not also free to go down.

I think I know my American friends and acquaintances too well to apologize for any levity in these illustrations. Americans make fun of their own institutions; and their own journalism is full of such fanciful conjectures. The tall building is itself artistically akin to the tall story. The very word sky-scraper is an admirable example of an American lie. But I can testify quite as eagerly to the solid and sensible advantages of the symmetrical hotel. It is not only a pattern of vases and stuffed flamingoes; it is also an equally accurate pattern of cupboards and baths. It is a dignified and humane custom to have a bathroom attached to every bedroom; and my impulse to sing the praises of it brought me once, at least, into a rather quaint complication. I think it was in the city of Dayton; anyhow, I remember there was a Laundry Convention going on in the same hotel, in a room very patriotically and properly festooned with the stars and stripes, and doubtless full of promise for the future of laundering. I was interviewed on the roof, within earshot of this debate, and may have been the victim of some association or confusion; anyhow, after answering the usual questions about Labour, the League of Nations, the length of ladies' dresses, and other great matters, I took refuge in a rhapsody of warm and well-deserved praise of American bathrooms. The editor, I understand, running a gloomy eye down the column of his contributor's "story", and seeing nothing but metaphysical terms such as justice, freedom, the abstract disapproval of sweating, swindling, and the like, paused at last upon the ablutionary allusion and his eye brightened. "That's the only copy in the whole thing," he said, "A Bath-Tub in Every Home." So these words appeared in enormous letters above my portrait in the paper. It will be noted that, like many things that practical men make a great point of, they miss the point. What I had commended as new and national was a bathroom in every bedroom. Even feudal and moss-grown England is not entirely ignorant of an occasional bath-tub in the home. But what gave me great joy was what followed. I discovered with delight that many people, glancing rapidly at my portrait with its prodigious legend, imagined that it was a commercial advertisement, and that I was a very self-advertising commercial traveller. When I walked about the streets, I was supposed to be travelling in bath-tubs. Consider the caption of the portrait, and you will see how similar it is to the true commercial slogan: "We offer a Bath-Tub in Every Home." And this charming error was doubtless clinched by the fact that I had been found haunting the outer courts of the temple of the ancient Guild of Lavenders. I never knew how many shared the impression; I regret to say that I only traced it with certainty in two individuals. But I understand that it included the idea that I had come to the town to attend the Laundry Convention, and had made an eloquent speech to that senate, no doubt exhibiting my tubs.

Such was the penalty of too passionate and unrestrained an admiration for American bathrooms; yet the connection of ideas, however inconsequent, does cover the part of social practice for which these American institutions can really be praised. About everything like laundry or hot and cold water there is not only organization, but what does not always or perhaps often go with it, efficiency. Americans are particular about these things of dress and decorum; and it is a virtue which I very seriously recognize, though I find it very hard to emulate. But with them it is a virtue; it is not a mere convention, still less a mere fashion. It is really related to human dignity rather than to social superiority. The really glorious thing about the American is that he does not dress like a gentleman; he dresses like a citizen or a civilized man. His Puritanic particularity on certain points is really detachable from any definite social ambitions; these things are not a part of getting into society but merely of keeping out of savagery. Those millions and millions of middling people, that huge middle class especially of the Middle West, are not near enough to any aristocracy even to be sham aristocrats, or to be real snobs. But their standards are secure; and though I do not really travel in a bath-tub, or believe in the bath-tub philosophy and religion, I will not on this matter recoil misanthropically from them: I prefer the tub of Dayton to the tub of Diogenes. On these points there is really something a million times better than efficiency, and that is something like equality.

In short, the American hotel is not America; but it is American. In some respects it is as American as the English inn is English. And it is symbolic of that society in this among other things: that it does tend too much to uniformity; but that that very uniformity disguises not a disguises not a little natural dignity. The old Romans boasted that their republic was a nation of kings. If we really walked abroad in such a kingdom, we might very well grow tired of the sight of a crowd of kings, of every man with a gold crown on his head or an ivory sceptre in his hand. But it is arguable that we ought not to grow tired of the repetition of crowns and sceptres, any more than of the repetition of flowers and stars. The whole imaginative effort of Walt Whitman was really an effort to absorb and animate these multitudinous modern repetitions; and Walt Whitman would be quite capable of including in his lyric litany of optimism a list of the nine hundred and ninety-nine identical bathrooms. I do not sneer at the generous effort of the giant; though I think when all is said, that it is a criticism of modern machinery that the effort should be gigantic as well as generous.

While there is so much repetition, there is little repose. It is the pattern of a kaleidoscope rather than a wall-paper; a pattern of figures running and even leaping like the figures in a zoetrope. But even in the groups where there was no hustle there was often something of homelessness. I do not mean merely that they were not dining at home; but rather that they were not at home even when dining, and dining at their favourite hotel. They would frequently start up and dart from the room at a summons from the telephone. It may have been fanciful, but I could not help feeling a breath of home, as from a flap or flutter of St. George's Cross, when I first sat down in a Canadian hostelry, and read the announcement that no such telephonic or other summonses were allowed in the dining-room. It may have been a coincidence, and there may be American hotels with this merciful proviso and Canadian hotels without it; but the thing was symbolic even if it was not evidential. I felt as if I stood indeed upon English soil, in a place where people liked to have their meals in peace.

The process of the summons is called "paging," and consists of sending a little boy with a large voice through all the halls and corridors of the building, making them resound with a name. The custom is common, of course, in clubs and hotels even in England; but in England it is a mere whisper compared with the wail with which the American page repeats the formula of calling "Mr. So and So," I remember a particularly crowded *parterre* in the somewhat smoky and oppressive atmosphere of Pittsburgh, through which wandered a youth with a voice the like of which I have never heard in the land of the living, a voice like the cry of a lost spirit, saying again and again for ever, "Calling Mr. Anderson." One felt that he never would find Mr. Anderson. Perhaps there never had been any Mr. Anderson to be found. Perhaps he and every one else wandered in an abyss of bottomless scepticism; and he was but the victim of one out of numberless nightmares of eternity, as he wandered a shadow with shadows and wailed by impassable streams. This is not exactly my philosophy, but I feel sure it was his. And it is a mood that may frequently visit the mind in the centres of highly active and successful industrial civilization.

Such are the first idle impressions of the great American hotel, gained by sitting for the first time in its gallery and gazing on its drifting crowds with thoughts equally drifting. The first impression is of something enormous and rather unnatural, an impression that is gradually tempered by experience of the kindliness and even the tameness of so much of that social order. But I should not be recording the sensations with sincerity, if I did not touch, in passing, the note of something unearthly about the vast system to an insular traveller who sees it for the first time. It is as if he were wandering in another world among the fixed stars; or worse still, in an ideal Utopia of the future.

Yet I am not certain; and perhaps the best of all news is that nothing is really new. I sometimes have a fancy that many of these new things in new countries are but the resurrections of old things which have been wickedly killed or stupidly stunted in old countries. I have looked over the sea of little tables in some light and airy open-air café; and my thoughts have gone back to the plain wooden bench and wooden table that stands solitary and weather-stained outside so many neglected English inns. We talk of experimenting in the French café, as of some fresh and almost impudent innovation. But our fathers had the French café, in the sense of the free-and-easy table in the sun and air. The only difference was that French democracy was allowed to develop its café, or multiply its tables, while English plutocracy prevented any such popular growth. Perhaps there are other examples of old types and patterns, lost in the old oligarchy and saved in the new democracies. I am haunted with a hint that the new structures are not so very new; and that they remind me of something very old. As I look from the balcony floors the crowds seem to float away and the colours to soften and grow pale, and I know I am in one of the simplest and most ancestral of human habitations. I am looking down from the old wooden gallery upon the courtyard of an inn. This new architectural model, which I have described, is after all, one of the oldest European models, now neglected in Europe, and especially in England. It was the theatre in which were enacted innumerable picaresque comedies and romantic plays, with figures ranging from Sancho Panza to Sam Weller. It served as the apparatus, like some gigantic toy set up in bricks and timber, for the ancient and perhaps eternal game of tennis. The very terms of the original game were taken from the inn courtyard, and the players scored accordingly as they hit the buttery-hatch or the roof. Singular speculations hover in my mind as the scene darkens and the quadrangle below begins to empty in the last hours of night. Some day, perhaps, this huge structure will be found standing in solitude like a skeleton; and it will be the skeleton of the Spotted Dog or the Blue Boar. It will wither and decay until it is worthy at last to be a tavern.

27

I do not know whether men will play tennis on its ground floor, with various scores and prizes for hitting the electric fan, or the lift, or the head waiter. Perhaps the very words will only remain as part of some such rustic game. Perhaps the electric fan will no longer be electric, and the elevator will no longer elevate, and the waiter will only wait to be hit. But at least it is only by the decay of modern plutocracy, which seems already to have begun, that the secret of the structure even of this plutocratic palace can stand revealed. And after long years, when its lights are extinguished and only the long shadows inhabit its halls and vestibules, there may come a new noise like thunder; of D' Artagnan knocking at the door.

3

A Meditation in Broadway

When I had looked at the lights of Broadway by night, I made to my American friends an innocent remark that seemed for some reason to amuse them. I had looked, not without joy, at that long kaleidoscope of coloured lights arranged in large letters and sprawling trade-marks, advertising everything, from pork to pianos, through the agency of the two most vivid and most mystical of the gifts of God; colour and fire. I said to them, in my simplicity, "What a glorious garden of wonders this would be, to any one who was lucky enough to be unable to read."

Here it is but a text for a further suggestion. But let us suppose that there does walk down this flaming avenue a peasant, of the sort called scornfully an illiterate peasant; by those who think that insisting on people reading and writing is the best way to keep out the spies who read in all languages and the forgers who write in all hands. On this principle indeed, a peasant merely acquainted with things of little practical use to mankind, such as ploughing, cutting wood, or growing vegetables, would very probably be excluded; and it is not for us to criticize from the outside the philosophy of those who would keep out the farmer and let in the forger. But let us suppose, if only for the sake of argument, that the peasant is walking under the artificial suns and stars of this tremendous thoroughfare; that he has escaped to the land of liberty upon some general rumour and romance of the story of its liberation, but without being yet able to understand the arbitrary signs of its alphabet. The soul of such a man would surely soar higher than the sky-scrapers, and embrace a brotherhood broader than Broadway. Realizing that he had arrived on an evening of exceptional festivity, worthy to be blazoned with all this burning heraldry, he would please himself by guessing what great proclamation or principle of the Republic hung in the sky like a constellation or rippled across the street like a comet. He would be shrewd enough to guess that the three festoons fringed with fiery words of somewhat similar pattern stood for "Government of the People, For the People, By the People"; for it must obviously be that, unless it were "Liberty, Equality, Fraternity." His shrewdness would perhaps be a little shaken if he knew that the triad stood for "Tang Tonic To-day; Tang Tonic To-morrow; Tang Tonic All the Time". He will soon identify a restless ribbon of red lettering, red hot and rebellious, as the saying, "Give me liberty or give me death." He will fail to identify it as the equally famous saying, "Skyoline Has Gout Beaten to a Frazzle." Therefore it was that I desired the peasant to walk down that grove of fiery trees, under all that golden foliage, and fruits like monstrous jewels, as innocent as Adam before the fall. He would see sights almost as fine as the flaming sword or the purple and peacock plumage of the seraphim; so long as he did not go near the Tree of Knowledge.

In other words, if once he went to school it would be all up; and indeed I fear in any case he would soon discover his error. If he stood wildly waving his hat for liberty in the middle of the road as Chunk Chutney picked itself out in ruby stars upon the sky, he would impede the excellent but extremely rigid traffic system of New York. If he fell on his knees before a sapphire splendour, and began saying an Ave Maria under a mistaken association, he would be conducted kindly but firmly by an Irish policeman to a more authentic shrine. But though the foreign simplicity might not long survive in New York, it is quite a mistake to suppose that such foreign simplicity cannot enter New York. He may be excluded for being illiterate, but he cannot be excluded for being ignorant, nor for being innocent. Least of all can he be excluded for being wiser in his innocence than the world in its knowledge. There is here indeed more than one distinction to be made. New York is a cosmopolitan city; but it is not a city of cosmopolitans. Most of the masses in New York have a nation, whether or no it be the nation to which New York belongs. Those who are Americanized are American, and very patriotically American. Those who are not thus nationalized are not in the least internationalized. They simply continue to be themselves; the Irish are Irish; the Jews are Jewish; and all sorts of other tribes carry on the traditions of remote European valleys almost untouched. In short, there is a sort of slender bridge between their old country and their new, which they either cross or do not cross, but which they seldom simply occupy. They are exiles or they are citizens; there is no moment when they are cosmopolitans. But very often the exiles bring with them not only rooted traditions, but rooted truths.

Indeed it is to a great extent the thought of these strange souls in crude American garb that gives a meaning to the masquerade of New York. In the hotel where I stayed the head waiter in one room was a Bohemian; and I am glad to say that he called himself a Bohemian. I have already protested sufficiently, before American audiences, against the pedantry of perpetually talking about Czecho-Slovakia. I suggested to my American friends that the abandonment of the word Bohemian in its historical sense might well extend to its literary and figurative sense. We might be expected to say, "I' m afraid Henry has got into very Czecho-Slovakian habits lately," or "Don't bother to dress; it's quite a Czecho-Slovakian affair." Anyhow my Bohemian would have nothing to do with such nonsense; he called himself a son of Bohemia, and spoke as such in his criticisms of America, which were both favourable and unfavourable. He was a squat man, with a sturdy figure and a steady smile; and his eyes were like dark pools in the depth of a darker forest, but I do not think he had ever been deceived by the lights of Broadway.

But I found something like my real innocent abroad, my real peasant among the sky-signs, in another part of the same establishment. He was a much leaner man, equally dark, with a hook nose, hungry face, and fierce black moustaches. He also was a waiter, and was in the costume of a waiter, which is a smarter edition of the costume of a lecturer. As he was serving me with clam chowder or some such thing, I fell into speech with him and he told me he was a Bulgar. I said something like, "I'm afraid I don't know as much as I ought to about Bulgaria. I suppose most of your people are agricultural, aren't they?" He did not stir an inch from his regular attitude, but he slightly lowered his low voice and said, "Yes. From the earth we come and to the earth we return; when people get away from that they are lost."

To hear such a thing said by the waiter was alone an epoch in the life of an unfortunate writer of fantastic novels. To see him clear away the clam chowder like an automaton, and bring me more iced water like an automaton or like nothing on earth except an American waiter (for piling up ice is the cold passion of their lives), and all this after having uttered something so dark and deep, so starkly incongruous and so startlingly true, was an indescribable thing, but very like the picture of the peasant admiring Broadway. So he passed, with his artificial clothes and manners, lit up with all the ghastly artificial light of the hotel, and all the ghastly artificial life of the city; and his heart was like his own remote and rocky valley, where those unchanging words were carved as on a rock.

I do not profess to discuss here at all adequately the question this raises about the Americanization of the Bulgar. It has many aspects, of some of which most Englishmen and even some Americans are rather unconscious. For one thing, a man with so rugged a loyalty to land could not be Americanized in New York; but it is not so certain that he could not be Americanized in America. We might almost say that a peasantry is hidden in the heart of America. So far as our impressions go, it is a secret. It is rather an open secret; covering only some thousand square miles of open prairie. But for most of our countrymen it is something invisible, unimagined, and unvisited; the simple truth that where all those acres are there is agriculture, and where all that agriculture is there is considerable tendency towards distributive or decently equalized property, as in a peasantry. On the other hand, there are those who say that the Bulgar will never be Americanized, that he only comes to be a waiter in America that he may afford to return to be a peasant in Bulgaria. I cannot decide this issue, and indeed I did not introduce it to this end. I was led to it by a certain line of reflection that runs along the Great White Way, and I will continue to follow it. The criticism, if we could put it rightly, not only covers more than New York but more than the whole New World. Any argument against it is quite as valid against the largest and richest cities of the Old World, against London or Liverpool or Frankfort or Belfast. But it is in New York that we see the argument most clearly, because we see the thing thus towering into its own turrets and breaking into its own fireworks.

I disagree with the aesthetic condemnation of the modern city with its sky-scrapers and sky-signs. I mean that which laments the loss of beauty and its sacrifice to utility. It seems to me the very reverse of the truth. Years ago, when people used to say the Salvation Army doubtless had good intentions but we must all deplore its methods, I pointed out that the very contrary is the case. Its method, the method of drums and democratic appeal, is that of the Franciscans or any other march of the Church Militant. It was precisely its aims that were dubious, with their dissenting morality and despotic finance. It is somewhat the same with things like the sky-signs in Broadway. The aesthete must not ask me to mingle my tears with his, because these things are merely useful and ugly. For I am not specially inclined to think them ugly; but I am strongly inclined to think them useless. As a matter of art for art's sake, they seem to me rather artistic. As a form of practical social work they seem to me stark stupid waste. If Mr. Bilge is rich enough to build a tower four hundred feet high and give it a crown of golden crescents and crimson stars, in order to draw attention to his manufacture of the Paradise Tooth Paste or the Seventh Heaven Cigar, I do not feel the least disposition to thank him for any serious form of social service. I have never tried the Seventh Heaven Cigar; indeed a premonition moves me towards the belief that I shall go down to the dust without trying it. I have every reason to doubt whether it does any particular good to those who smoke it, or any good to anybody except those who sell it. In short Mr. Bilge's usefulness consists in being useful to Mr. Bilge, and all the rest is illusion and sentimentalism. But because I know that Bilge is only Bilge, shall I stoop to the profanity of saying that fire is only fire? Shall I blaspheme crimson stars any more than crimson sunsets, or deny that those moons are golden any more than that this grass is green? If a child saw these coloured lights, he would dance with as much delight as at any other coloured toys; and it is the duty of every poet, and even of every critic, to dance in respectful imitation of the child. Indeed I am in a mood of so much sympathy with the fairy lights of this pantomime city, that I should be almost sorry to see social sanity and a sense of proportion return to extinguish them. I fear the day is breaking, and the broad daylight of tradition and ancient truth is coming to end all this delightful nightmare of New York at night. Peasants and priests and all sorts of practical and sensible people are coming back into power, and their stern realism may wither all these beautiful, unsubstantial, useless things. They will not believe in the Seventh Heaven Cigar, even when they see it shining as with stars in the seventh heaven. They will not be affected by advertisements, any more than the priests and peasants of the Middle Ages would have been affected by advertisements. Only a very soft-headed, sentimental, and rather servile generation of men could possibly be affected by advertisements at all. People who are a little more hard-headed, humorous, and intellectually independent, see the rather simple joke; and are not impressed by this or any other form of self-praise. Almost any other men in almost any other age would have seen the joke. If you had said to a man in the Stone Age, "Ugg says Ugg makes the best stone hatchets," he would have perceived a lack of detachment and disinterestedness about the testimonial. If you had said to a medieval peasant, "Robert the Bowyer proclaims, with three blasts of a horn, that he makes good bows," the peasant would have said, "Well, of course he does," and thought about something more important. It is only among people whose minds have been weakened by a sort of mesmerism that so transparent a trick as that of advertisement could ever have been tried at all. And if ever we have again, as for other reasons I cannot but hope we shall, a more democratic distribution of property and a more agricultural basis of national life, it would seem at first sight only too likely that all this beautiful superstition will perish, and the fairyland of Broadway with all its varied rainbows fade away. For such people the Seventh Heaven Cigar, like the nineteenth-century city, will have ended in smoke. And even the smoke of it will have vanished.

distributism

But the next stage of reflection brings us back to the peasant looking at the lights of Broadway. It is not true to say in the strict sense that the peasant has never seen such things before. The truth is that he has seen them on a much smaller scale, but for a much larger purpose. Peasants also have their ritual and ornament, but it is to adorn more real things. Apart from our first fancy about the peasant who could not read, there is no doubt about what would be apparent to a peasant who could read, and who could understand. For him also fire is sacred, for him also colour is symbolic. But where he sets up a candle to light the little shrine of St. Joseph, he finds it takes twelve hundred candles to light the Seventh Heaven Cigar. He is used to the colours in church windows showing red for martyrs or blue for madonnas; but here he can only conclude that all the colours of the rainbow belong to Mr. Bilge. Now upon the aesthetic side he might well be impressed; but it is exactly on the social and even scientific side that he has a right to criticize. If he were a Chinese peasant, for instance, and came from a land of fireworks, he would naturally suppose that he had happened to arrive at a great fireworks display in celebration of something; perhaps the Sacred Emperor's birthday, or rather birth night. It would gradually dawn on the Chinese philosopher that the Emperor could hardly be born every night. And when he learnt the truth the philosopher, if he was a philosopher, would be a little disappointed ... possibly a little disdainful.

Compare, for instance, these everlasting fireworks with the damp squibs and dying bonfires of Guy Fawkes Day. That quaint and even queer national festival has been fading for some time out of English life. Still, it was a national festival, in the double sense that it represented some sort of public spirit pursued by some sort of popular impulse. People spent money on the display of fireworks; they did not get money by it. And the people who spent money were often those who had very little money to spend. It had something of the glorious and fanatical character of making the poor poorer. It did not, like the advertisements, have only the mean and materialistic character of making the rich richer. In short, it came from the people and it appealed to the nation. The historical and religious cause in which it originated is not mine; and I think it has perished partly through being tied to a historical theory for which there is no future. I think this is illustrated in the very fact that the ceremonial is merely negative and destructive. Negation and destruction are very noble things as far as they go, and when they go in the right direction; and the popular expression of them has always something hearty and human about it. I shall not therefore bring any fine or fastidious criticism, whether literary or musical, to bear upon the little boys who drag about a bolster and a paper mask, calling out

Guy Fawkes Guy
Hit him in the eye.

But I admit it is a disadvantage that they have not a saint or hero to crown in effigy as well as a traitor to burn in effigy. I admit that popular Protestantism has become too purely negative for people to wreathe in flowers the statue of Mr. Kensit or even of Dr. Clifford. I do not disguise my preference for popular Catholicism; which still has statues that can be wreathed in flowers. I wish our national feast of fireworks revolved round something positive and popular. I wish the beauty of a Catherine Wheel were displayed to the glory of St. Catherine. I should not especially complain if Roman candles were really Roman candles. But this negative character does not destroy the national character; which began at least in disinterested faith and has ended at last in disinterested fun. There is nothing disinterested at all about the new commercial fireworks. There is nothing so dignified as a dingy guy among the lights of Broadway. In that thoroughfare, indeed, the very word guy has another and milder significance. An American friend congratulated me on the impression I produced on a lady interviewer, observing, "She says you're a regular guy." This puzzled me a little at the time. "Her description is no doubt correct," I said, "but I confess that it would never have struck me as specially complimentary." But it appears that it is one of the most graceful of compliments, in the original American. A guy in America is a colourless term for a human being. All men are guys, being endowed by their Creator with certain ... but I am misled by another association. And a regular guy means, I presume, a reliable or respectable guy. The point here, however, is that the guy in the grotesque English sense does represent the dilapidated remnant of a real human tradition of symbolizing real historic ideals by the sacramental mystery of fire. It is a great fall from the lowest of these lowly bonfires to the highest of the modern sky-signs. The new illumination does not stand for any national ideal at all; and what is yet more to the point, it does not come from any popular enthusiasm at all. That is where it differs from the narrowest national Protestantism of the English institution. Mobs have risen in support of No Popery; no mobs are likely to rise in defence of the New Puffery. Many a poor crazy

Orangeman has died saying, "To Hell with the Pope"; it is doubtful whether any man will ever, with his last breath, frame the ecstatic words, "Try Hugby's Chewing Gum." These modern and mercantile legends are imposed upon us by a mercantile minority, and we are merely passive to the suggestion. The hypnotist of high finance or big business merely writes his commands in heaven with a finger of fire. All men really are guys, in the sense of dummies. We are only the victims of his pyrotechnic violence; and it is he who hits us in the eye.

This is the real case against that modern society that is symbolized by such art and architecture. It is not that it is toppling, but that it is top-heavy. It is not that it is vulgar, but rather that it is not popular. In other words, the democratic ideal of countries like America, while it is still generally sincere and sometimes intense, is at issue with another tendency, an industrial progress which is of all things on earth the most undemocratic. America is not alone in possessing the industrialism, but she is alone in emphasizing the ideal that strives with industrialism. Industrial capitalism and ideal democracy are everywhere in controversy; but perhaps only here are they in conflict. France has a democratic ideal; but France is not industrial. England and Germany are industrial; but England and Germany are not really democratic. Of course when I speak here of industrialism I speak of great industrial areas; there is, as will be noted later, another side to all these countries; there is in America itself not only a great deal of agricultural society, but a great deal of agricultural equality; just as there are still peasants in Germany and may some day again be peasants in England. But the point is that the ideal and its enemy the reality are here crushed very close to each other in the high, narrow city; and that the sky-scraper is truly named because its top, towering in such insolence, is scraping the stars off the American sky, the very heaven of the American spirit.

That seems to me the main outline of the whole problem. In the first chapter of this book, I have emphasized the fact that equality is still the ideal though no longer the reality of America. I should like to conclude this one by emphasizing the fact that the reality of modern capitalism is menacing that ideal with terrors and even splendours that might well stagger the wavering and impressionable modern spirit. Upon the issue of that struggle depends the question of whether this new great civilization continues to exist, and even whether any one cares if it exists or not. I have already used the parable of the American flag, and the stars that stand for a multitudinous equality; I might here take the opposite symbol of these artificial and terrestrial stars flaming on the forehead of the commercial city; and note the peril of the last illusion, which is that the artificial stars may seem to fill the heavens, and the real stars to have faded from sight. But I am content for the moment to reaffirm the merely imaginative pleasure of those dizzy turrets and dancing fires. If those nightmare buildings were really all built for nothing, how noble they would be! The fact that they were really built for something need not unduly depress us for a moment, or drag down our soaring fancies. There is something about these vertical lines that suggests a sort of rush upwards, as of great cataracts topsy-turvy. I have spoken of fireworks, but here I should rather speak of rockets. There is only something underneath the mind murmuring that nothing remains at last of a flaming rocket except a falling stick. I have spoken of Babylonian perspectives, and of words written with a fiery finger, like that huge unhuman finger that wrote on Belshazzar's wall ... But what did it write on Belshazzar's wall ? ... I am content once more to end on a note of doubt and a rather dark sympathy with those many-coloured solar systems turning so dizzily, far up in the divine vacuum of the night.

"From the earth we come and to the earth we return; when people get away from that they are lost."

4

Irish and Other Interviewers

It is often asked what should be the first thing that a man sees when he lands in a foreign country; but I think it should be the vision of his own country. At least when I came into New York Harbour, a sort of grey and green cloud came between me and the towers with multitudinous windows, white in the winter sun light; and I saw an old brown house standing back among the beech trees at home, the house of only one among many friends and neighbours, but one somehow so sunken in the very heart of England as to be unconscious of her imperial or international position, and out of the sound of her perilous seas. But what made most clear the vision that revisited me was something else. Before we touched land the men of my own guild, the journalists and reporters, had already boarded the ship like pirates. And one of them spoke to me in an accent that I knew; and thanked me for all I had done for Ireland. And it was at that moment that I knew most vividly that what I wanted was to do something for England.

Then, as it chanced, I looked across at the statue of Liberty, and saw that the great bronze was gleaming green in the morning light. I had made all the obvious jokes about the statue of Liberty. I found it had a soothing effect on earnest Prohibitionists on the boat to urge, as a point of dignity and delicacy, that it ought to be given back to the French, a vicious race abandoned to the culture of the vine. I proposed that the last liquors on board should be poured out in a pagan libation before it. And then I suddenly remembered that this Liberty was still in some sense enlightening the world, or one part of the world; was a lamp for one sort of wanderer, a star of one sort of seafarer. To one persecuted people at least this land had really been an asylum; even if recent legislation (as I have said) had made them think it a lunatic asylum. They had made it so much their home that the very colour of the country seemed to change with the infusion; as the bronze of the great statue took on a semblance of the wearing of the green.

It is a commonplace that the Englishman has been stupid in his relations with the Irish; but he has been far more stupid in his relations with the Americans on the subject of the Irish. His propaganda has been worse than his practice; and his defence more ill-considered than the most indefensible things that it was intended to defend. There is in this matter a curious tangle of cross-purposes, which only a parallel example can make at all clear. And I will note the point here, because it is some testimony to its vivid importance that it was really the first I had to discuss on American soil with an American citizen. In a double sense I touched Ireland before I came to America. I will take an imaginary instance from another controversy; in order to show how the apology can be worse than the action. The best we can say for ourselves is worse than the worst that we can do.

There was a time when English poets and other publicists could always be inspired with instantaneous indignation about the persecuted Jews in Russia. We have heard less about them since we heard more about the persecuting Jews in Russia. I fear there are a great many middle-class Englishmen already who wish that Trotsky had been persecuted a little more. But even in those days Englishmen divided their minds in a curious fashion; and unconsciously distinguished between the Jews whom they had never seen, in Warsaw, and the Jews whom they had often seen in Whitechapel. It seemed to be assumed that, by a curious coincidence, Russia possessed not only the very worst Anti-Semites but the very best Semites. A moneylender in London might be like Judas Iscariot; but a moneylender in Moscow must be like Judas Maccabaeus.

Nevertheless there remained in our common sense an unconscious but fundamental comprehension of the unity of Israel; a sense that somethings could be said, and some could not be said, about the Jews as a whole. Suppose that even in those days, to say nothing of these, an English protest against Russian Anti-Semitism had been answered by the Russian Anti-Semites, and suppose the answer had been somewhat as follows:

"It is all very well for foreigners to complain of our denying civic rights to our Jewish subjects; but we know the Jews better than they do. They are a barbarous people, entirely primitive, and very like the simple savages who cannot count beyond five on their fingers. It is quite impossible to make them understand ordinary numbers, to say nothing of simple economics. They do not realize the meaning or the value of money. No Jew anywhere in the world can get into his stupid head the notion of a bargain, or of exchanging one thing for another. Their hopeless incapacity for commerce or finance would retard the progress of our people, would prevent the spread of any sort of economic education, would keep the whole country on a level lower than that of the most prehistoric methods of barter. What Russia needs most is a mercantile middle class; and it is unjust to ask us to swamp its small beginnings in thousands of these rude tribesmen, who cannot do a sum of simple addition, or understand the symbolic character of a threepenny bit. We might as well be asked to give civic rights to cows

43

and pigs as to this unhappy, half-witted race who can no more count than the beasts of the field. In every intellectual exercise they are hopelessly incompetent; no Jew can play chess; no Jew can learn languages; no Jew has ever appeared in the smallest part in any theatrical performance; no Jew can give or take any pleasure connected with any musical instrument. These people are our subjects; and we understand them. We accept full responsibility for treating such troglodytes on our own terms."

It would not be entirely convincing. It would sound a little far-fetched and unreal. But it would sound exactly like our utterances about the Irish, as they sound to all Americans, and rather especially to Anti-Irish Americans. That is exactly the impression we produce on the people of the United States when we say, as we do say in substance, something like this: "We mean no harm to the poor dear Irish, so dreamy, so irresponsible, so incapable of order or organization. If we were to withdraw from their country they would only fight among themselves; they have no notion of how to rule themselves. There is something charming about their unpracticability, about their very incapacity for the coarse business of politics. But for their own sakes it is impossible to leave these emotional visionaries to ruin themselves in the attempt to rule themselves. They are like children; but they are our own children, and we understand them. We accept full responsibility for acting as their parents and guardians."

Now the point is not only that this view of the Irish is false, but that it is the particular view that the Americans know to be false. While we are saying that the Irish could not organize, the Americans are complaining, often very bitterly, of the power of Irish organization. While we say that the Irishman could not rule himself, the Americans are saying, more or less humorously, that the Irishman rules them. A highly intelligent professor said to me in Boston, "We have solved the Irish problem here; we have an entirely independent Irish Government." While we are complaining, in an almost passionate manner, of the impotence of mere cliques of idealists and dreamers, they are complaining, often in a very indignant manner, of the power of great gangs of bosses and bullies. There are a great many Americans who pity the Irish, very naturally and very rightly, for the historic martyrdom which their patriotism has endured. But there are a great many Americans who do not pity the Irish in the least. They would be much more likely to pity the English; only this particular way of talking tends rather to make them despise the English. Thus both the friends of Ireland and the foes of Ireland tend to be the foes of England. We make one set of enemies by our action, and another by our apology.

It is a thing that can from time to time be found in history; a misunderstanding that really has a moral. The English excuse would carry much more weight if it had more sincerity and more humility. There are a considerable number of people in the United States who could sympathize with us, if we would say frankly that we fear the Irish. Those who thus despise our pity might possibly even respect our fear. The argument I have often used in other places comes back with prodigious and redoubled force, after hearing anything of American opinion; the argument that the only reasonable or reputable excuse for the English is the excuse of a patriotic sense of peril; and that the Unionist, if he must be a Unionist, should use that and no other. When the Unionist has said that he dare not let loose against himself a captive he has so cruelly wronged, he has said all that he has to say; all that he has ever had to say; all that he will ever have to say. He is like a man who has sent a virile and rather vindictive rival unjustly to penal servitude; and who connives at the continuance of the sentence, not because he himself is particularly vindictive, but because he is afraid of what the convict will do when he comes out of prison. This is not exactly a moral strength, but it is a very human weakness; and that is the most that can be said for it. All other talk, about Celtic frenzy or Catholic superstition, is cant invented to deceive himself or to deceive the world. But the vital point to realize is that it is cant that cannot possibly deceive the American world. In the matter of the Irishman the American is not to be deceived. It is not merely true to say that he knows better. It is equally true to say that he knows worse. He knows vices and evils in the Irishman that are entirely hidden in the hazy vision of the Englishman. He knows that our unreal slanders are inconsistent even with the real sins. To us Ireland is a shadowy Isle of Sunset, like Atlantis, about which we can make up legends. To him it is a positive ward or parish in the heart of his huge cities, like Whitechapel; about which even we cannot make legends but only lies. And, as I have said, there are some lies we do not tell even about Whitechapel. We do not say it is inhabited by Jews too stupid to count or know the value of a coin.

The first thing for any honest Englishman to send across the sea is this; that the English have not the shadow of a notion of what they are up against in America. They have never even heard of the batteries of almost brutal energy, of which I had thus touched a live wire even before I landed. People talk about the hypocrisy of England in dealing with a small nationality. What strikes me is the stupidity of England in supposing that she is dealing with a small nationality; when she is really dealing with a very large nationality. She is dealing with a nationality that often threatens, even numerically, to dominate all the other nationalities of the United States. The Irish are not decaying; they are not unpractical; they are scarcely even scattered; they are not even poor. They are the most powerful and practical world-combination with whom we can decide to be friends or foes; and that is why I thought first of that still and solid brown house in Buckinghamshire, standing back in the shadow of the trees.

Among my impressions of America I have deliberately put first the figure of the Irish-American interviewer, standing on the shore more symbolic than the statue of Liberty. The Irish interviewer's importance for the English lay in the fact of his being an Irishman, but there was also considerable interest in the circumstance of his being an interviewer. And as certain wild birds sometimes wing their way far out to sea and are the first signal of the shore, so the first Americans the traveller meets are often American interviewers; and they are generally birds of a feather, and they certainly flock together. In this respect, there is a slight difference in the etiquette of the craft in the two countries, which I was delighted to discuss with my fellow craftsmen. If I could at that moment have flown back to Fleet Street I am happy to reflect that nobody in the world would in the least wish to interview me. I should attract no more attention than the stone griffin opposite the Law Courts; both monsters; being grotesque but also familiar. But supposing for the sake of argument that anybody did want to interview me, it is fairly certain that the fact of one paper publishing such an interview would rather prevent the other papers from doing so. The repetition of the same views of the same individual in two places would be considered rather bad journalism; it would have an air of stolen thunder, not to say stage thunder.

But in America the fact of my landing and lecturing was evidently regarded in the same light as a murder or a great fire, or any other terrible but incurable catastrophe, a matter of interest to all pressmen concerned with practical events. One of the first questions I was asked was how I should be disposed to explain the wave of crime in New York. Naturally I replied that it might possibly be due to the number of English lecturers who had recently landed. In the mood of the moment it seemed possible that, if they had all been interviewed, regrettable incidents might possibly have taken place. But this was only the mood of the moment, and even as a mood did not last more than a moment. And since it has reference to a rather common and a rather unjust conception of American journalism, I think it well to take it first as a fallacy to be refuted, though the refutation may require a rather longer approach.

I have generally found that the traveller fails to understand a foreign country, through treating it as a tendency and not as a balance. But if a thing were always tending in one direction it would soon tend to destruction. Everything that merely progresses finally perishes. Every nation, like every family, exists upon a compromise, and commonly a rather eccentric compromise; using the word "eccentric" in the sense of something that is somehow at once crazy and healthy.

Now the foreigner commonly sees some feature that he thinks fantastic without seeing the feature that balances it. The ordinary examples are obvious enough. An Englishman dining inside a hotel on the boulevards thinks the French eccentric in refusing to open a window. But he does not think the English eccentric in refusing to carry their chairs and tables out on to the pavement in Ludgate Circus. An Englishman will go poking about in little Swiss or Italian villages, in wild mountains or in remote islands, demanding tea; and never reflects that he is like a Chinaman who should enter all the wayside public-houses in Kent or Sussex and demand opium. But the point is not merely that he demands what he cannot expect to enjoy; it is that he ignores even what he does enjoy. He does not realize the sublime and starry paradox of the phrase, *vin ordinaire*, which to him should be a glorious jest like the phrase "common gold" or "daily diamonds." These are the simple and self-evident cases; but there are many more subtle cases of the same thing; of the tendency to see that the nation fills up its own gap with its own substitute; or corrects its own extravagance with its own precaution. The national antidote generally grows wild in the woods side by side with the national poison. If it did not, all the natives would be dead. For it is so, as I have said, that nations necessarily die of the undiluted poison called progress.

It is so in this much-abused and over-abused example of the American journalist. The American interviewers really have exceedingly good manners for the purposes of their trade, granted that it is necessary to pursue their trade. And even what is called their hustling method can truly be said to cut both ways, or hustle both ways; for if they hustle in, they also hustle out. It may not at first sight seem the very warmest compliment to a gentleman to congratulate him on the fact that he soon goes away. But it really is a tribute to his perfection in a very delicate social art; and I am quite serious when I say that in this respect the interviewers are artists. It might be more difficult for an Englishman to come to the point, particularly the sort of point which American journalists are supposed, with some

48

exaggeration, to aim at. It might be more difficult for an Englishman to ask a total stranger on the spur of the moment for the exact inscription on his mother's grave; but I really think that if an Englishman once got so far as that he would go very much farther, and certainly go on very much longer. The Englishman would approach the churchyard by a rather more wandering woodland path; but if once he had got to the grave I think he would have much more disposition, so to speak, to sit down on it. Our own national temperament would find it decidedly more difficult to disconnect when connections had really been established. Possibly that is the reason why our national temperament does not establish them. I suspect that the real reason that an Englishman does not talk is that he cannot leave off talking. I suspect that my solitary countrymen, hiding in separate railway compartments, are not so much retiring as a race of Trappists as escaping from a race of talkers.

However this may be, there is obviously something of practical advantage in the ease with which the American butterfly flits from flower to flower. He may in a sense force his acquaintance on us, but he does not force himself on us. Even when, to our prejudices, he seems to insist on knowing us, at least he does not insist on our knowing him. It may be, to some sensibilities, a bad thing that a total stranger should talk as if he were a friend, but it might possibly be worse if he insisted on being a friend before he would talk like one. To a great deal of the interviewing, indeed much the greater part of it, even this criticism does not apply; there is nothing which even an Englishman of extreme sensibility could regard as particularly private; the questions involved are generally entirely public, and treated with not a little public spirit. But my only reason for saying here what can be said even for the worst exceptions is to point out this general and neglected principle; that the very thing that we complain of in a foreigner generally carries with it its own foreign cure. American interviewing is generally very reasonable, and it is always very rapid. And even those to whom talking to an intelligent fellow creature

49

is as horrible as having a tooth out may still admit that American interviewing has many of the qualities of American dentistry.

Another effect that has given rise to this fallacy, this exaggeration of the vulgarity and curiosity of the press, is the distinction between the articles and the headlines; or rather the tendency to ignore that distinction. The few really untrue and unscrupulous things I have seen in American "stories" have always been the headlines. And the headlines are written by somebody else; some solitary and savage cynic locked up in the office, hating all mankind, and raging and revenging himself at random, while the neat, polite, and rational pressman can safely be let loose to wander about the town.

For instance, I talked to two decidedly thoughtful fellow journalists immediately on my arrival at a town in which there had been some labour troubles. I told them my general view of Labour in the very largest and perhaps the vaguest historical outline; pointing out that the one great truth to be taught to the middle classes was that Capitalism was itself a crisis, and a passing crisis; that it was not so much that it was breaking down as that it had never really stood up. Slaveries could last, and peasantries could last; but wage-earning communities could hardly even live, and were already dying.

All this moral and even metaphysical generalization was most fairly and most faithfully reproduced by the interviewer, who had actually heard it casually and idly spoken. But on the top of this column of political philosophy was the extraordinary announcement in enormous letters, "Chesterton Takes Sides in Trolley Strike." This was inaccurate. When I spoke, I not only did not know that there was any trolley strike, but I did not know what a trolley strike was. I should have had an indistinct idea that a large number of citizens earned their living by carrying things about in wheel-barrows, and that they had desisted from the beneficent activities. Any one who did not happen to be a journalist, or know a little about journalism, American and English, would have Supposed that the same man who wrote the article had suddenly gone mad and written the title. But I know that we have here to deal with two different types of journalists; and the man who writes the headlines I will not dare to describe; for I have not seen him except in dreams.

Another innocent complication is that the interviewer does sometimes translate things into his native language. It would not seem odd that a French interviewer should translate them into French; and it is certain that the American interviewer sometimes translates them into American. Those who imagine the two languages to be the same are more innocent than any interviewer. To take one out of the twenty examples, some of which I have mentioned elsewhere, suppose an interviewer had said that I had the reputation of being a nut. I should be flattered but faintly surprised at such a tribute to my dress and dashing exterior. I should afterwards be sobered and enlightened by discovering that in America a nut does not mean a dandy but a defective or imbecile person. And as I have here to translate their American phrase into English, it may be very defensible that they should translate my English phrases into American. Anyhow they often do translate them into American. In answer to the usual question about Prohibition I had made the usual answer, obvious to the point of dullness to those who are in daily contact with it, that it is a law that the rich make knowing they can always break it. From the printed interview it appeared that I had said, "Prohibition! All matter of dollar sign." This is almost avowed translation, like a French translation. Nobody can suppose that it would come natural to an Englishman to talk about a dollar, still less about a dollar sign—whatever that may be. It is exactly as if he had made me talk about the Skelt and Stevenson Toy Theatre as a "cent plain, and two cents coloured" or condemned a parsimonious policy as dime-wise and dollar-foolish. Another interviewer once asked me who was the greatest American writer. I have forgotten exactly what I said, but after mentioning several names, I said that the greatest natural genius and artistic force was probably Walt Whitman. The printed interview is more precise; and students of my literary and conversational style will be interested to know that I said, "See here, Walt Whitman was your one real red-blooded man." Here again I hardly think the translation can have been quite unconscious; most of my intimates are indeed aware that I do not talk like that, but I fancy that the same fact would have dawned on the journalist to whom I had been talking. And even this trivial point carries with it the two truths which must be, I fear, the rather monotonous moral of these pages. The first is that America and England can be far better friends when sharply divided than when shapelessly amalgamated. These two journalists were false reporters, but they were true translators. They were not so much interviewers as interpreters. And the second is that in any such difference it is often wholesome to look beneath the surface for a superiority. For ability to translate does imply ability to understand; and many of these journalists really did understand. I think there are many English journalists who would be more puzzled by so simple an idea as the plutocratic foundation of Prohibition. But the American knew at once that I meant it was a matter of dollar sign; probably because he knew very well that it is.

Then again there is a curious convention by which American interviewing makes itself out much worse than it is. The reports are far more rowdy and insolent than the conversations. This is probably a part of the fact that a certain vivacity, which to some seems vitality and to some vulgarity, is not only an ambition but an ideal. It must always be grasped that this vulgarity is an ideal even more than it is a reality. It is an ideal when it is not a reality. A very quiet and intelligent young man, in a soft black hat and tortoiseshell spectacles, will ask for an interview with unimpeachable politeness, wait for his living subject with unimpeachable patience, talk to him quite sensibly for twenty minutes, and go noiselessly away. Then in the newspaper next morning you will read how he beat the bedroom door in, and pursued his victim on to the roof or dragged him from under the bed, and tore from him replies to all sorts of bald and ruthless questions printed in large black letters. I was often interviewed in the evening, and had no notion of how atrociously I had been insulted till I saw it in the paper next morning. I had no notion I had been on the rack of an inquisitor until I saw it in plain print; and then of course I believed it, with a faith and docility unknown in any previous epoch of history. An interesting essay might be written upon points upon which nations affect more vices than they possess; and it might deal more fully with the American pressman, who is a harmless clubman in private, and becomes a sort of highway-robber in print.

I have turned this chapter into something like a defence of interviewers, because I really think they are made to bear too much of the burden of the bad developments of modern journalism. But I am very far from meaning to suggest that those bad developments are not very bad. So far from wishing to minimize the evil, I would in a real sense rather magnify it. I would suggest that the evil itself is a much larger and more fundamental thing; and that to deal with it by abusing poor journalists, doing their particular and perhaps peculiar duty, is like dealing with a pestilence by rubbing at one of the spots. What is wrong with the modern world will not be righted by attributing the whole disease to each of its symptoms in turn; first to the tavern and then to the cinema and then to the reporter's room. The evil of journalism is not in the journalists. It is not in the poor men on the lower level of the profession, but in the rich men at the top of the profession; or rather in the rich men who are too much on top of the profession even to belong to it. The trouble with newspapers is the Newspaper Trust, as the trouble might be with a Wheat Trust, without involving a vilification of all the people who grow wheat. It is the American plutocracy and not the American press. What is the matter with the modern world is not modern headlines or modern films or modern machinery. What is the matter with the modern world is the modern world; and the cure will come from another.

5

Some American Cities

There is one point, almost to be called a paradox, to be noted about
New York; and that is that in one sense it is really new. The term very
seldom has any relevance to the reality. The New Forest is nearly as old
as the Conquest, and the New Theology is nearly as old as the Creed.
Things have been offered to me as the new thought that might more
properly be called the old thoughtlessness; and the thing we call the
New Poor Law is already old enough to know better. But there is a
sense in which New York is always new; in the sense that it is always
being renewed. A stranger might well say that the chief industry of the
citizens consists of destroying their city; but he soon realizes that they
always start it all over again with undiminished energy and hope.
At first I had a fancy that they never quite finished putting up a big
building without feeling that it was time to pull it down again; and

that somebody began to dig up the first foundations while somebody else was putting on the last tiles. This fills the whole of this brilliant and bewildering place with a quite unique and unparalleled air of rapid ruin. Ruins spring up so suddenly like mushrooms, which with us are the growth of age like mosses, that one half expects to see ivy climbing quickly up the broken walls as in the nightmare of the Time Machine, or in some incredibly accelerated cinema.

There is no sight in any country that raises my own spirits so much as a scaffolding. It is a tragedy that they always take the scaffolding away, and leave us nothing but a mere building. If they would only take the building away and leave us a beautiful scaffolding, it would, in most cases, be a gain to the loveliness of earth. If I could analyse what it is that lifts the heart about the lightness and clarity of such a white and wooden skeleton, I could explain what it is that is really charming about New York; in spite of its suffering from the curse of cosmopolitanism and even the provincial superstition of progress. It is partly that all this destruction and reconstruction is an unexhausted artistic energy; but it is partly also that it is an artistic energy that does not take itself too seriously. It is first because man is here a carpenter; and secondly because he is a stage carpenter. Indeed, there is about the whole scene the spirit of scene-shifting. It therefore touches whatever nerve in us has since childhood thrilled at all theatrical things. But the picture will be imperfect unless we realize something which gives it unity and marks its chief difference from the climate and colours of Western Europe. We may say that the back-scene remains the same. The sky remained, and in the depths of winter it seemed to be blue with summer; and so clear that I almost flattered myself that clouds were English products like primroses. An American would probably retort on my charge of scene-shifting by saying that at least he only shifted the towers and domes of the earth; and that in England it is the heavens that are shifty. And indeed we have changes from day to day that would seem to him as distinct as different magic-lantern slides; one view showing the Bay of Naples and the next the North Pole.

I do not mean, of course, that there are no changes in American weather; but as a matter of proportion it is true that the most unstable part of our scenery is the most stable part of theirs. Indeed, we might almost be pardoned the boast that Britain alone really possesses the noble thing called weather; most other countries having to be content with climate. It must be confessed, however, that they often are content with it. And the beauty of New York, which is considerable, is very largely due to the clarity that brings out the colours of varied buildings against the equal colour of the sky. Strangely enough I found myself repeating about this vista of the West two vivid lines in which Mr. W. B. Yeats has called up a vision of the East:

> And coloured like the eastern birds
> At evening in their rainless skies.

To invoke a somewhat less poetic parallel, even the untravelled Englishman has probably seen American posters and trade advertisements of a patchy and gaudy kind, in which a white house or a yellow motor-car are cut out as in cardboard against a sky like blue marble. I used to think it was only New Art, but I found that it is really New York.

It is not for nothing that the very nature of local character has gained the nickname of local colour. Colour runs through all our experience; and we all know that our childhood found talismanic gems in the very paints in the paint-box, or even in their very names. And just as the very name of "crimson lake" really suggested to me some sanguine and mysterious mere, dark yet red as blood, so the very name of burnt sienna became afterwards tangled up in my mind with the notion of something traditional and tragic; as if some such golden Italian city had really been darkened by many conflagrations in the wars of mediaeval democracy. Now, if one had the caprice of conceiving some city exactly contrary to one thus seared and seasoned by fire, its colour might be called up to a childish fancy by the mere name of "raw umber"; and such a city is New York. I used to be puzzled by the name of "raw umber" being unable to imagine the effect of fried umber or stewed umber. But the colours of New York are exactly in that key; and might be adumbrated by phrases like raw pink or raw yellow. It is really in a sense like something uncooked; or something which the satiric would call half-baked. And yet the effect is not only beautiful, it is even delicate. I had no name for this nuance; until I saw that somebody had written of "the pastel-tinted towers of New York"; and I knew that the name had been found. There are no paints dry enough to describe all that dry light; and it is not a box of colours but of crayons. If the Englishman returning to England is moved at the sight of a block of white chalk, the American sees rather a bundle of chalks. Nor can I imagine anything more moving. Fairy tales are told to children about a country where the trees are like sugar-sticks and the lakes like treacle, but most children would feel almost as greedy for a fairyland where the trees were like brushes of green paint and the hills were of coloured chalks.

But here what accentuates this arid freshness is the fragmentary look of the continual reconstruction and change. The strong daylight finds everywhere the broken edges of things, and the sort of hues we see in newly-turned earth or the white sections of trees. And it is in this respect that the local colour can literally be taken as local character. For New York considered in itself is primarily a place of unrest, and those who sincerely love it, as many do, love it for the romance of its restlessness. A man almost looks at a building as he passes to wonder whether it will be there when he comes back from his walk; and the doubt is part of an indescribable notion, as of a white nightmare of daylight, which is increased by the very numbering of the streets, with its tangle of numerals which at first makes an English head reel. The detail is merely a symbol; and when he is used to it he can see that it is, like the most humdrum human customs, both worse and better than his own. "271 West 52nd Street" is the easiest of all addresses to find, but the hardest of all addresses to remember. He who is, like myself, so constituted as necessarily to lose any piece of paper he has particular reason to preserve, will find himself wishing the place were called "Pine Crest" or "Heather Crag" like any unobtrusive villa in Streatham. But his sense of some sort of incalculable calculations, as of the vision of a mad mathematician, is rooted in a more real impression. His first feeling that his head is turning round is due to something really dizzy in the movement of a life that turns dizzily like a wheel. If there be in the modern mind something paradoxical that can find peace in change, it is here that it has indeed built its habitation or rather is still building and unbuilding it. One might fancy that it changes in everything and that nothing endures but its invisible name; and even its name, as I have said, seems to make a boast of novelty.

That is something like a sincere first impression of the atmosphere of New York. Those who think that is the atmosphere of America have never got any farther than New York. We might almost say that they have never entered America, any more than if they had been detained like undesirable aliens at Ellis Island. And, indeed, there are a good many undesirable aliens detained in Manhattan Island too. But of that I will not speak, being myself an alien with no particular pretensions to be desirable. Anyhow, such is New York; but such is not the New World. The great American Republic contains very considerable varieties, and of these varieties, I necessarily saw far too little to allow me to generalize. But from the little I did see, I should venture on the generalization that the great part of America is singularly and even strikingly unlike New York. It goes without saying that New York is very unlike the vast agricultural plains and small agricultural towns of the Middle West, which I did see. It may be conjectured with some confidence that it is very unlike what is called the Wild and sometimes the Woolly West, which I did not see. But I am here comparing New York, not with the newer states of the prairie or the mountains, but with the other older cities of the Atlantic coast. And New York, as it seems to me, is quite vitally different from the other historic cities of America. It is so different that it shows them all for the moment in a false light, as a long white searchlight will throw a light that is fantastic and theatrical upon ancient and quiet villages folded in the everlasting hills. Philadelphia and Boston and Baltimore are more like those quiet villages than they are like New York.

If I were to call this book "The Antiquities of America," I should give rise to misunderstanding, and possibly to annoyance. And yet the double sense in such words is an undeserved misfortune for them. We talk of Plato or the Parthenon or the Greek passion for beauty as parts of the antique, but hardly of the antiquated. When we call them ancient it is not because they have perished, but rather because they have survived. In the same way I hear some New Yorkers refer to Philadelphia or Baltimore as "dead towns." They mean by a dead town a town that has had the impudence not to die. Such people are astonished to find an ancient thing alive, just as they are now astonished, and will be increasingly astonished, to find Poland or the Papacy or the French nation still alive. And what I mean by Philadelphia and Baltimore being alive is precisely what these people mean by their being dead; it is continuity; it is the presence of the life first breathed into them and of the purpose of their being; it is the benediction of the founders of the colonies and the fathers of the republic. This tradition is truly to be called life; for life alone can link the past and the future. It merely means that as what was done yesterday makes some difference to-day, so what is done to-day will make some difference to-morrow. In New York it is difficult to feel that any day will make any difference. These moderns only die daily without power to rise from the dead. But I can truly claim that in coming into some of these more stable cities of the States I felt something quite sincerely of that historic emotion which is satisfied in the eternal cities of the Mediterranean. I felt in America what many Americans suppose can only be felt in Europe. I have seldom had that sentiment stirred more simply and directly than when I saw from afar off, above the vast grey labyrinth of Philadelphia, great Penn upon his pinnacle like the graven figure of a god who had fashioned a new world; and remembered that his body lay buried in a field at the turning of a lane, a league from my own door.

For this aspect of America is rather neglected in the talk about electricity and headlines. Needless to say, the modern vulgarity of avarice and advertisement sprawls all over Philadelphia or Boston; but so it does over Winchester or Canterbury. But most people know that there is something else to be found in Canterbury or Winchester; many people know that it is rather more interesting; and some people know that Alfred can still walk in Winchester and that St. Thomas at Canterbury was killed but did not die. It is at least as possible for a Philadelphian to feel the presence of Penn and Franklin as for an Englishman to see the ghosts of Alfred and of Becket. Tradition does not mean a dead town; it does not mean that the living are dead, but that the dead are alive. It means that it still matters what Penn did two hundred years ago or what Franklin did a hundred years ago; I never could feel in New York that it mattered what anybody did an hour ago. And these things did and do matter. Quakerism is not my favourite creed; but on that day when William Penn stood unarmed upon that spot and made his treaty with the Red Indians, his creed of humanity did have a triumph and a triumph that has not turned back. The praise given to him is not a priggish fiction of our conventional history, though such fictions have illogically curtailed it. The Nonconformists have been rather unfair to Penn even in picking their praises; and they generally forget that toleration cuts both ways, and that an open mind is open on all sides. Those who deify him for consenting to bargain with the savages cannot forgive him for consenting to bargain with the Stuarts. And the same is true of the other city, yet more closely connected with the tolerant experiment of the Stuarts. The state of Maryland was the first experiment in religious freedom in human history. Lord Baltimore and his Catholics were a long march ahead of William Penn and his Quakers on what is now called the path of progress. That the first religious toleration ever granted in the world was granted by Roman Catholics is one of those little informing details with which our Victorian histories did not exactly teem. But when I went into my hotel at Baltimore and found two priests waiting to see me, I was moved in a new fashion, for I felt that I touched the end of a living chain. Nor was the impression accidental; it will always remain with me with a mixture of gratitude and grief, for they brought a message of welcome from a great American whose name I had known from childhood and whose career was drawing to its close; for it was but a few days after I left the city that I learned that Cardinal Gibbons was dead.

On the top of a hill on one side of the town stood the first monument raised after the Revolution to Washington. Beyond it was a new monument saluting in the name of Lafayette the American soldiers who fell fighting in France in the Great War. Between them were steps and stone seats, and I sat down on one of them and talked to two children who were clambering about the bases of the monument. I felt a profound and radiant peace in the thought that they at any rate were not going to my lecture. It made me happy that in that talk neither they nor I had any names. I was full of that indescribable waking vision of the strangeness of life, and especially of the strangeness of locality; of how we find places and lose them; and see faces for a moment in a far-off land, and it is equally mysterious if we remember and mysterious if we forget. I had even stirring in my head the suggestion of some verses that I shall never finish—

If I ever go back to Baltimore
The city of Maryland.

But the poem would have to contain far too much; for I was thinking of a thousand things at once; and wondering what the children would be like twenty years after and whether they would travel in white goods or be interested in oil, and I was not untouched (it may be said) by the fact that a neighbouring shop had provided the only sample of the substance called "tea" ever found on the American continent; and in front of me soared up into the sky on wings of stone the column of all those high hopes of humanity a hundred years ago; and beyond there were lighted candles in the chapels and prayers in the ante-chambers, where perhaps already a Prince of the Church was dying. Only on a later page can I even attempt to comb out such a tangle of contrasts, which is indeed the tangle of America and this mortal life; but sitting there on that stone seat under that quiet sky, I had some experience of the thronging thousands of living thoughts and things, noisy and numberless as birds, that give its everlasting vivacity and vitality to a dead town.

Two other cities I visited which have this particular type of traditional character, the one being typical of the North and the other of the South. At least I may take as convenient anti-types the towns of Boston and St.Louis; and we might add Nashville as being a shade more truly southern than St.Louis. To the extreme South, in the sense of what is called the Black Belt, I never went at all. Now English travellers expect the South to be somewhat traditional; but they are not prepared for the aspects of Boston in the North which are even more so. If we wished only for an antic of antithesis, we might say that on one side the places are more prosaic than the names and on the other the names are more prosaic than the places. St.Louis is a fine town, and we recognize a fine instinct of the imagination that set on the hill over looking the river the statue of that holy horseman who has christened the city. But the city is not as beautiful as its name; it could not be. Indeed these titles set up a standard to which the most splendid spires and turrets could not rise, and below which the commercial chimneys and sky-signs conspicuously sink. We should think it odd if Belfast had borne the name of Joan of Arc. We should be slightly shocked if the town of Johannesburg happened to be called Jesus Christ. But few have noted a blasphemy, or even a somewhat challenging benediction, to be found in the very name of San Francisco.

But on the other hand a place like Boston is much more beautiful than its name. And, as I have suggested, an Englishman's general information, or lack of information, leaves him in some ignorance of the type of beauty that turns up in that type of place. He has heard so much about the purely commercial North as against the agricultural and aristocratic South, and the traditions of Boston and Philadelphia are rather too tenuous and delicate to be seen from across the Atlantic. But here also there are traditions and a great deal of traditionalism. The circle of old families, which still meets with a certain exclusiveness in Philadelphia, is the sort of thing that we in England should expect to find rather in New Orleans. The academic aristocracy of Boston, which Oliver Wendell Holmes called the Brahmins, is still a reality though it was always a minority and is now a very small minority. An epigram, invented by Yale at the expense of Harvard, describes it as very small indeed:—

> Here is to jolly old Boston, the home of the bean and the cod,
> Where Cabots speak only to Lowells, and Lowells speak only to God.

But an aristocracy must be a minority, and it is arguable that the smaller it is the better. I am bound to say, however, that the distinguished Dr. Cabot, the present representative of the family, broke through any taboo that may tie his affections to his Creator and to Miss Amy Lowell, and broadened his sympathies so indiscriminately as to show kindness and hospitality to so lost a being as an English lecturer. But if the thing is hardly a limit it is very living as a memory; and Boston on this side is very much a place of memories. It would be paying it a very poor compliment merely to say that parts of it reminded me of England; for indeed they reminded me of English things that have largely vanished from England. There are old brown houses in the corners of squares and streets that are like glimpses of a man's forgotten childhood; and when I saw the long path with posts where the Autocrat may be supposed to have walked with the schoolmistress, I felt I had come to the land where old tales come true. I pause in this place upon this particular aspect of America because it is very much missed in a mere contrast with England. I need not say that if I felt it even about slight figures of fiction, I felt it even more about solid figures of history. Such ghosts seemed particularly solid in the Southern States, precisely because of the comparative quietude and leisure of the atmosphere of the South. It was never more vivid to me than when coming, at a quiet hour of the night, into the comparatively quiet hotel at Nashville in Tennessee, and mounting to a dim and deserted upper floor where I found myself before a faded picture; and from the dark canvas looked forth the face of Andrew Jackson, watchful like a white eagle.

At that moment, perhaps, I was in more than one sense alone. Most Englishmen know a good deal of American fiction, and nothing whatever of American history. They know more about the autocrat of the breakfast-table than about the autocrat of the army and the people, the one great democratic despot of modern times; the Napoleon of the New World. The only notion the English public ever got about American politics they got from a novel, *Uncle Tom's Cabin*; and to say the least of it, it was no exception to the prevalence of fiction over fact. Hundreds of us have heard of Tom Sawyer for one who had heard of Charles Sumner; and it is probable that most of us could pass a more detailed examination about Toddy and Budge than about Lincoln and Lee. But in the case of Andrew Jackson it may be that I felt a special sense of individual isolation; for I believe that there are even fewer among Englishmen than among Americans who realize that the energy of that great man was largely directed towards saving us from the chief evil which destroys the nations today. He sought to cut down, as with a sword of simplicity, the new and nameless enormity of finance; and he must have known, as by a lightning flash, that the people were behind him, because all the politicians were against him. The end of that struggle is not yet; but if the bank is stronger than the sword or the sceptre of popular sovereignty, the end will be the end of democracy. It will have to choose between accepting an acknowledged dictator and accepting dictation which it dare not acknowledge. The process will have begun by giving power to people and refusing to give them their titles; and it will have ended by giving the power to people who refuse to give us their names.

But I have a special reason for ending this chapter on the name of the great popular dictator who made war on the politicians and the financiers. This chapter does not profess to touch on one in twenty of the interesting cities of America, even in this particular aspect of their relation to the history of America, which is so much neglected in England. If that were so, there would be a great deal to say even about the newest of them; Chicago, for instance, is certainly something more than the mere pork-packing yard that English tradition suggests; and it has been building a boulevard not unworthy of its splendid position on its splendid lake. But all these cities are defiled and even diseased with industrialism. It is due to the Americans to remember that they have deliberately preserved one of their cities from such defilement and such disease. And that is the presidential city, which stands in the American mind for the same ideal as the President; the idea of the Republic that rises above modern money getting and endures. There has really been an effort to keep the White House white. No factories are allowed in that town; no more than the necessary shops are tolerated. It is a beautiful city; and really retains something of that classical serenity of the eighteenth century in which the fathers of the Republic moved. With all respect to the colonial place of that name, I do not suppose that Wellington is particularly like Wellington. But Washington really is like Washington.

In this, as in so many things, there is no harm in our criticizing foreigners, if only we would also criticize ourselves. In other words, the world might need even less of its new charity, if it had a little more of the old humility. When we complain of American individualism, we forget that we have fostered it by ourselves having far less of this impersonal ideal of the Republic or commonwealth as a whole. When we complain, very justly, for instance, of great pictures passing into the possession of American magnates, we ought to remember that we paved the way for it by allowing them all to accumulate in the possession of English magnates. It is bad that a public treasure should be in the possession of a private man in America, but we took the first step in lightly letting it disappear into the private collection of a man in England. I know all about the genuine national tradition which treated the aristocracy as constituting the state; but these very foreign purchases go to prove that we ought to have had a state independent of the aristocracy. It is true that rich Americans do sometimes covet the monuments of our culture in a fashion that rightly revolts us as vulgar and irrational. They are said sometimes to want to take whole buildings away with them; and too many of such buildings are private and for sale. There were wilder stories of a millionaire wishing to transplant Glastonbury Abbey and similar buildings as if they were portable shrubs in pots. It is obvious that it is nonsense as well as vandalism to separate Glastonbury Abbey from Glastonbury. I can understand a man venerating it as a ruin; and I can understand a man despising it as a rubbish-heap. But it is senseless to insult a thing in order to idolatrize it; it is meaningless to desecrate the shrine in order to worship the stones. That sort of thing is the bad side of American appetite and ambition; and we are perfectly right to see it not only as a deliberate blasphemy but as an unconscious buffoonery. But there is another side to the American tradition, which is really too much lacking in our own tradition. And it is illustrated in this idea of preserving Washington as a sort of paradise of impersonal politics without personal commerce. Nobody could buy the White House or the Washington Monument; it may be hinted (as by an inhabitant of Glastonbury) that nobody wants to; but nobody could if he did want to. There is really a certain air of serenity and security about the place, lacking in every other American town. It is increased, of course, by the clear blue skies of that half-southern province, from which smoke has been banished. The effect is not so much in the mere buildings, though they are classical and often beautiful. But whatever else they have built, they have built a great blue dome, the largest dome in the world. And the place does express something in the inconsistent idealism of this strange people; and here at least they have lifted it higher than all the sky-scrapers, and set it in a stainless sky.

6

In the American Country

The sharpest pleasure of a traveller is in finding the things which he did not expect, but which he might have expected to expect. I mean the things that are at once so strange and so obvious that they must have been noticed, yet somehow they have not been noted. Thus I had heard a thousand things about Jerusalem before I ever saw it; I heard rhapsodies and disparagements of every description. Modern rationalistic critics, with characteristic consistency, had blamed it for its accumulated rubbish and its modern restoration, for its antiquated superstition and its up-to-date vulgarity. But somehow the one impression that had never pierced through their description was the simple and single impression of a city on a hill, with walls coming to the very edge of slopes that were almost as steep as walls; the turreted city which crowns a cone-shaped hill in so many mediaeval landscapes.

One would suppose that this was at once the plainest and most picturesque of all the facts; yet somehow, in my reading, I had always lost it amid a mass of minor facts that were merely details. We know that a city that is set upon a hill cannot be hid; and yet it would seem that it is exactly the hill that is hid; though perhaps it is only hid from the wise and the understanding. I had a similar and simple impression when I discovered America. I cannot avoid the phrase; for it would really seem that each man discovers it for himself.

Thus I had heard a great deal, before I saw them, about the tall and dominant buildings of New York. I agree that they have an instant effect on the imagination; which I think is increased by the situation in which they stand, and out of which they arose. They are all the more impressive because the building, while it is vertically so vast, is horizontally almost narrow. New York is an island, and has all the intensive romance of an island. It is a thing of almost infinite height upon very finite foundations. It is almost like a lofty lighthouse upon a lonely rock. But this story of the sky-scrapers, which I had often heard, would by itself give a curiously false impression of the freshest and most curious characteristic of American architecture. Told only in terms of these great towers of stone and brick in the big industrial cities, the story would tend too much to an impression of something cold and colossal like the monuments of Asia. It would suggest a modern Babylon altogether too Babylonian. It would imply that a man of the new world was a sort of new Pharaoh, who built not so much a pyramid as a pagoda of pyramids. It would suggest houses built by mammoths out of mountains; the cities reared by elephants in their own elephantine school of architecture. And New York does recall the most famous of all sky-scrapers—the tower of Babel. She recalls it none the less because there is no doubt about the confusion of tongues. But in truth the very reverse is true of most of the buildings in America. I had no sooner passed out into the suburbs of New York on the way to Boston than I began to see something else quite contrary and far more curious. I saw forests upon forests of small houses

70

stretching away to the horizon as literal forests do; villages and towns and cities. And they were, in another sense, literally like forests. They were all made of wood. It was almost as fantastic to an English eye as if they had been all made of cardboard. I had long outlived the silly old joke that referred to Americans as if they all lived in the backwoods. But, in a sense, if they do not live in the woods, they are not yet out of the wood.

I do not say this in any sense as a criticism. As it happens, I am particularly fond of wood. Of all the superstitions which our fathers took lightly enough to love, the most natural seems to me the notion it is lucky to touch wood. Some of them affect me the less as superstitions, because I feel them as symbols. If humanity had really thought Friday unlucky it would have talked about bad Friday instead of good Friday. And while I feel the thrill of thirteen at a table, I am not so sure that it is the most miserable of all human fates to fill the places of the Twelve Apostles. But the idea that there was something cleansing or wholesome about the touching of wood seems to me one of those ideas which are truly popular, because they are truly poetic. It is probable enough that the conception came originally from the healing of the wood of the Cross; but that only clinches the divine coincidence. It is like that other divine coincidence that the Victim was a carpenter, who might almost have made His own cross. Whether we take the mystical or the mythical explanation, there is obviously a very deep connection between the human working in wood and such plain and pathetic mysticism. It gives something like a touch of the holy childishness to the tale, as if that terrible engine could be a toy. In the same fashion a child fancies that mysterious and sinister horse, which was the downfall of Troy, as something plain and staring, and perhaps spotted, like his own rocking-horse in the nursery.

It might be said symbolically that Americans have a taste for rocking-horses, as they certainly have a taste for rocking-chairs. A flippant critic might suggest that they select rocking-chairs so that, even when they are sitting down, they need not be sitting still.

Something of this restlessness in the race may really be involved in the matter; but I think the deeper significance of the rocking-chair may still be found in the deeper symbolism of the rocking-horse. I think there is behind all this fresh and facile use of wood a certain spirit that is childish in the good sense of the word; something that is innocent, and easily pleased. It is not altogether untrue, still less is it unfriendly, to say that the landscape seems to be dotted with dolls' houses. It is the true tragedy of every fallen son of Adam that he has grown too big to live in a doll's house. These things seem somehow to escape the irony of time by not even challenging it; they are too temporary even to be merely temporal. These people are not building tombs; they are not, as in the fine image of Mrs. Meynell's poem, merely building ruins. It is not easy to imagine the ruins of a doll's house; and that is why a doll's house is an everlasting habitation. How far it promises a political permanence is a matter for further discussion; I am only describing the mood of discovery; in which all these cottages built of lath, like the palaces of a pantomime, really seemed coloured like the clouds of morning; which are both fugitive and eternal.

There is also in all this an atmosphere that comes in another sense from the nursery. We hear much of Americans being educated on English literature; but I think few Americans realize how much English children have been educated on American literature. It is true, and it is inevitable, that they can only be educated on rather old-fashioned American literature. Mr. Bernard Shaw, in one of his plays, noted truly the limitations of the young American millionaire, and especially the staleness of his English culture; but there is necessarily another side to it. If the American talked more of Macaulay than of Nietzsche, we should probably talk more of Emerson than of Ezra Pound. Whether this staleness is necessarily a disadvantage is, of course, a different question. But, in any case, it is true that the old American books were often the books of our childhood, even in the literal sense of the books of our nursery. I know few men in England who have not left their boyhood to some extent lost and entangled in the forests of

Huckleberry Finn. I know few women in England, from the most revolutionary Suffragette to the most carefully preserved Early Victorian, who will not confess to having passed a happy childhood with the *Little Women* of Miss Alcott. *Helen's Babies* was the first and by far the best book in the modern scriptures of baby-worship. And about all this old-fashioned American literature there was an undefinable savour that satisfied, and even fed, our growing minds. Perhaps it was the smell of growing things; but I am far from certain that it was not simply the smell of wood. Now that all the memory comes back to me, it seems to come back heavy in a hundred forms with the fragrance and the touch of timber. There was the perpetual reference to the wood-pile, the perpetual background of the woods. There was something crude and clean about everything; something fresh and strange about those far-off houses, to which I could not then have put a name. Indeed, many things become clear in this wilderness of wood, which could only be expressed in symbol and even in fantasy. I will not go so far as to say that it shortened the transition from Log Cabin to White House; as if the White House were itself made of white wood (as Oliver Wendell Holmes said), "that cuts like cheese, but lasts like iron for things like these." But I will say that the experience illuminates some other lines by Holmes himself:—

> Little I ask, my wants are few,
> I only ask a hut of stone.

I should not have known, in England, that he was already asking for a good deal even in asking for that. In the presence of this wooden world the very combination of words seems almost a contradiction, like a hut of marble, or a hovel of gold.

It was therefore with an almost infantile pleasure that I looked at all this promising expansion of fresh-cut timber and thought of the housing shortage at home. I know not by what incongruous movement of the mind there swept across me, at the same moment, the thought of things ancestral and hoary with the light of ancient dawns. The last war brought back body-armour; the next war may bring back bows and arrows. And I suddenly had a memory of old wooden houses in London; and a model of Shakespeare's town.

It is possible indeed that such Elizabethan memories may receive a check or a chill when the traveller comes, as he sometimes does, to the outskirts of one of these strange hamlets of new frame-houses, and is confronted with a placard inscribed in enormous letters, "Watch Us Grow." He can always imagine that he sees the timbers swelling before his eyes like pumpkins in some super-tropical summer. But he may have formed the conviction that no such proclamation could be found outside Shakespeare's town. And indeed there is a serious criticism here, to any one who knows history; since the things that grow are not always the things that remain; and pumpkins of that expansiveness have a tendency to burst. I was always told that Americans were harsh, hustling, rather rude and perhaps vulgar; but they were very practical and the future belonged to them. I confess I felt a fine shade of difference; I liked the Americans; I thought they were sympathetic, imaginative, and full of fine enthusiasms; the one thing I could not always feel clear about was their future. I believe they were happier in their frame-houses than most people in most houses; having democracy, good education, and a hobby of work; the one doubt that did float across me was something like, "Will all this be here at all in two hundred years?" That was the first impression produced by the wooden houses that seemed like the waggons of gipsies; it is a serious impression, but there is an answer to it. It is an answer that opens on the traveller more and more as he goes westward, and finds the little towns dotted about the vast central prairies. And the answer is agriculture. Wooden houses may or may not last; but farms will last; and farming will always last.

The houses may look like gipsy caravans on a heath or common; but they are not on a heath or common. They are on the most productive and prosperous land, perhaps, in the modern world. The houses might fall down like shanties, but the fields would remain; and whoever tills those fields will count for a great deal in the affairs of humanity. They are already counting for a great deal, and possibly for too much, in the affairs of America. The real criticism of the Middle West is concerned with two facts, neither of which has been yet adequately appreciated by the educated class in England. The first is that the turn of the world has come, and the turn of the agricultural countries with it. That is the meaning of the resurrection of Ireland; that is the meaning of the practical surrender of the Bolshevist Jews to the Russian peasants. The other is that in most places these peasant societies carry on what may be called the Catholic tradition. The Middle West is perhaps the one considerable place where they still carry on the Puritan tradition. But the Puritan tradition was originally a tradition of the town; and the second truth about the Middle West turns largely on its moral relation to the town. As I shall suggest presently, there is much in common between this agricultural society of America and the great agricultural societies of Europe. It tends, as the agricultural society nearly always does, to some decent degree of democracy. The agricultural society tends to the agrarian law. But in Puritan America there is an additional problem, which I can hardly explain without a periphrasis.

There was a time when the progress of the cities seemed to mock the decay of the country. It is more and more true, I think, to-day that it is rather the decay of the cities that seems to poison the progress and promise of the countryside. The cinema boasts of being a substitute for the tavern, but I think it a very bad substitute. I think so quite apart from the question about fermented liquor. Nobody enjoys cinemas more than I, but to enjoy them a man has only to look and not even to listen, and in a tavern he has to talk. Occasionally, I admit, he has to fight; but he need never move at the movies. Thus in the real village inn are the real village politics, while in the other are only the remote and unreal metropolitan politics. And those central city politics are not only cosmopolitan politics but corrupt politics. They corrupt everything that they reach, and this is the real point about many perplexing questions.

For instance, so far as I am concerned, it is the whole point about feminism and the factory. It is very largely the point about feminism and many other callings, apparently more cultured than the factory, such as the law court and the political platform. When I see women so wildly anxious to tie themselves to all this machinery of the modern city my first feeling is not indignation, but that dark and ominous sort of pity with which we should see a crowd rushing to embark in a leaking ship under a lowering storm. When I see wives and mothers going in for business government I not only regard it as a bad business but as a bankrupt business. It seems to me very much as if the peasant women, just before the French Revolution, had insisted on being made duchesses or (as is quite as logical and likely) on being made dukes.

It is as if those ragged women, instead of crying out for bread, had cried out for powder and patches. By the time they were wearing them they would be the only people wearing them. For powder and patches soon went out of fashion, but bread does not go out of fashion. In the same way, if women desert the family for the factory, they may find they have only done it for a deserted factory. It would have been very unwise of the lower orders to claim all the privileges of the higher orders in the last days of the French monarchy. It would have been very laborious to learn the science of heraldry or the tables of precedence when all suchthings were at once most complicated and most moribund. It would be tiresome to be taught all those tricks just when the whole bag of tricks was coming to an end. A French satirist might have written a fine apologue about Jacques Bonhomme coming up to Paris in his wooden shoes and demanding to be made Gold Stick in Waiting in the name of Liberty, Equality, and Fraternity; but I fear the stick in waiting would be waiting still.

One of the first topics on which I heard a conversation turning in America was that of a very interesting book called *Main Street*, which involves many of those questions of the modern industrial and the eternal feminine. It is simply the story, or perhaps rather the study than the story, of a young married woman in one of the multitudinous little towns on the great central plains of America; and of a sort of struggle between her own more restless culture and the provincial prosperity of her neighbours. There are a number of true and telling suggestions in the book, but the one touch which I found tingling in the memory of many readers was the last sentence, in which the master of the house, with unshaken simplicity, merely asks for the whereabouts of some domestic implement; I think it was a screw-driver. It seems to me a harmless request, but from the way people talked about it one might suppose he had asked for a screw-driver to screw down the wife in her coffin. And a great many advanced persons would tell us that the wooden house in which she lived really was like a wooden coffin. But this appears to me to be taking a somewhat funereal view of the life of humanity.

For, after all, on the face of it at any rate, this is merely the life of humanity, and even the life which all humanitarians have striven to give to humanity. Revolutionists have treated it not only as the normal but even as the ideal. Revolutionary wars have been waged to establish this; revolutionary heroes have fought, and revolutionary martyrs have died, only to build such a wooden house for such a worthy family. Men have taken the sword and perished by the sword in order that the poor gentleman might have liberty to look for his screw-driver. For there is here a fact about America that is almost entirely unknown in England. The English have not in the least realized the real strength of America. We in England hear a great deal, we hear far too much, about the economic energy of industrial America, about the money of Mr. Morgan, or the machinery of Mr. Edison. We never realize that while we in England suffer from the same sort of successes in capitalism and clockwork, we have not got what the Americans have got; something at least to balance it in the way of a free agriculture, a vast field of free farms dotted with small freeholders. For the reason I shall mention in a moment, they are not perhaps in the fullest and finest sense a peasantry. But they are in the practical and political sense a pure peasantry, in that their comparative equality is a true counterweight to the toppling injustice to the towns.

And, even in places like that described as Main Street, that comparative equality can immediately be felt. The men may be provincials, but they are certainly citizens; they consult on a common basis. And I repeat that in this, after all, they do achieve what many prophets and righteous men have died to achieve. This plain village, fairly prosperous, fairly equal, untaxed by tyrants and untroubled by wars, is after all the place which reformers have regarded as their aim; whenever reformers have used their wits sufficiently to have any aim. The march to Utopia, the march to the Earthly Paradise, the march to the New Jerusalem, has been very largely the march to Main Street. And the latest modern sensation is a book written to show how wretched it is to live there.

All this is true, and I think the lady might be more contented in her coffin, which is more comfortably furnished than most of the coffins where her fellow creatures live. Nevertheless, there is an answer to this, or at least a modification of it. There is a case for the lady and a case against the gentleman and the screw-driver. And when we have noted what it really is, we have noted the real disadvantage in a situation like that of modern America, and especially the Middle West. And with that we come back to the truth with which I started this speculation; the truth that—few have yet realized, but of which I, for one, am more and more convinced that industrialism is spreading because it is decaying; that only the dust and ashes of its dissolution are choking up the growth of natural things everywhere and turning the green world grey.

In this relative agricultural equality the Americans of the Middle West are far in advance of the English of the twentieth century. It is not their fault if they are still some centuries behind the English of the twelfth century. But the defect by which they fall short of being a true peasantry is that they do not produce their town spiritual food, in the same sense as their own material food. They do not, like some peasantries, create other kinds of culture besides the kind called agriculture. Their culture comes from the great cities; and that is where all the evil comes from.

If a man had gone across England in the Middle Ages, or even across Europe in more recent times, he would have found a culture which showed its vitality by its variety. We know the adventures of the three brothers in the old fairy tales who passed across the endless plain from city to city, and found one kingdom ruled by a wizard and another wasted by a dragon, one people living in castles of crystal and another sitting by fountains of wine. These are but legendary enlargements of the real adventures of a traveller passing from one patch of peasantry to another, and finding women wearing strange head-dresses and men singing new songs.

A traveller in America would be somewhat surprised if he found the people in the city of St. Louis all wearing crowns and crusading armour in honour of their patron saint. He might even feel some faint surprise if he found all the citizens of Philadelphia clad in a composite costume, combining that of a Quaker with that of a Red Indian, in honour of the noble treaty of William Penn. Yet these are the sort of local and traditional things that would really be found giving variety to the valleys of mediaeval Europe. I myself felt a perfectly genuine and generous exhilaration of freedom and fresh enterprise in new places like Oklahoma. But you would hardly find in Oklahoma what was found in Oberammergau. What goes to Oklahoma is not the peasant play, but the cinema. And the objection to the cinema is not so much that it goes to Oklahoma as that it does not come from Oklahoma. In other words, these people have on the economic side a much closer approach than we have to economic freedom. It is not for us, who have allowed our land to be stolen by squires and then vulgarized by sham squires, to sneer at such colonists as merely crude and prosaic. They at least have really kept something of the simplicity and, therefore, the dignity of democracy; and that democracy may yet save their country even from the calamities of wealth and science.

But, while these farmers do not need to become industrial in order to become industrious, they do tend to become industrial in so far as they become intellectual. Their culture, and to some great extent their creed, do come along the railroads from the great modern urban centres, and bring with them a blast of death and a reek of rotting things. It is that influence that alone prevents the Middle West from progressing towards the Middle Ages.

For, after all, linked up in a hundred legends of the Middle Ages, may be found a symbolic pattern of hammers and nails and saws; and there is no reason why they should not have also sanctified screw-drivers. There is no reason why the screw-driver that seemed such a trifle to the author should not have been borne in triumph down Main Street like a sword of state, in some pageant of the Guild of St. Joseph of the Carpenters or St. Dunstan of the Smiths. It was the Catholic poetry and piety that filled common life with something that is lacking in the worthy and virile democracy of the West. Nor are Americans of intelligence so ignorant of this as some may suppose. There is an admirable society called the Mediaevalists in Chicago; whose name and address will strike many as suggesting a certain struggle of the soul against the environment. With the national heartiness they blazon their note-paper with heraldry and the hues of Gothic windows; with the national high spirits they assume the fancy dress of friars; but any one who should essay to laugh at them instead of with them would find out his mistake. For many of them do really know a great deal about mediaevalism; much more than I do, or most other men brought up on an island that is crowded with its cathedrals. Something of the same spirit may be seen in the beautiful new plans and buildings of Yale, deliberately modelled not on classical harmony but on Gothic irregularity and surprise. The grace and energy of the mediaeval architecture resurrected by a man like Mr. R.A. Cram of Boston has behind it not merely artistic but historical and ethical enthusiasm; an enthusiasm for the Catholic creed which made mediaeval civilization. Even on the huge Puritan plains of the Middle West the influence strays in the strangest fashion. And it is notable that among the pessimistic epitaphs of the Spoon River Anthology, in that churchyard compared with which most churchyards are cheery, among the suicides and secret drinkers and monomaniacs and hideous hypocrites of that happy village, almost the only record of respect and a recognition of wider hopes is dedicated to the Catholic priest.

But Main Street is Main Street in the main. Main Street is Modern Street in its multiplicity of mildly half-educated people; and all these historic things are a thousand miles from them. They have not heard the ancient noise either of arts or arms; the building of the cathedral or the marching of the crusade. But at least they have not deliberately slandered the crusade and defaced the cathedral. And if they have not produced the peasant arts, they can still produce the peasant crafts. They can sow and plough and reap and live by these everlasting things; nor shall the foundations of their state be moved. And the memory of those colossal fields, of those fruitful deserts, came back the more readily into my mind because I finished these reflections in the very heart of a modern industrial city, if it can be said to have a heart. It was in fact an English industrial city, but it struck me that it might very well be an American one. And it also struck me that we yield rather too easily to America the dusty palm of industrial enterprise, and feel far too little apprehension about greener and fresher vegetables. There is a story of an American who carefully studied all the sights of London or Rome or Paris, and came to the conclusion that "it had nothing on Minneapolis." It seems to me that Minneapolis has nothing on Manchester. There were the same grey vistas of shops full of rubber tyres and metallic appliances; a man felt that he might walk a day without seeing a blade of grass; the whole horizon was so infinite with efficiency. The factory chimneys might have been Pittsburg; the sky-signs might have been New York. One looked up in a sort of despair at the sky, not for a sky-sign but in a sense for a sign, for some sentence of significance and judgment; by the instinct that makes any man in such a scene seek for the only thing that has not been made by men.

But even that was illogical, for it was night, and I could only expect to see the stars, which might have reminded me of Old Glory; but that was not the sign that oppressed me. All the ground was a wilderness of stone and all the buildings a forest of brick; I was far in the interior of a labyrinth of lifeless things. Only, looking up, between two black chimneys and a telegraph pole, I saw vast and far and faint, as the first men saw it, the silver pattern of the Plough.

7

The American Business Man

It is a commonplace that men are all agreed in using symbols, and all differ about the meaning of the symbols. It is obvious that a Russian republican might come to identify the eagle as a bird of empire and therefore a bird of prey. But when he ultimately escaped to the land of the free, he might find the same bird on the American coinage figuring as a bird of freedom. Doubtless, he might find many other things to surprise him in the land of the free, and many calculated to make him think that the bird, if not imperial, was at least rather imperious. But I am not discussing those exceptional details here. It is equally obvious that a Russian reactionary might cross the world with a vow of vengeance against the red flag. But that authoritarian might have some difficulties with the authorities if he shot a man for using the red flag on the railway between Willesden and Clapham Junction.

But, of course, the difficulty about symbols is generally much more subtle than in these simple cases. I have remarked elsewhere that the first thing which a traveller should write about is the thing which he has not read about. It may be a small or secondary thing, but it is a thing that he has seen and not merely expected to see.

I gave the example of the great multitude of wooden houses in America; we might say of wooden towns and wooden cities. But after he has seen such things, his next duty is to see the meaning of them; and here a great deal of complication and controversy is possible. The thing probably does not mean what he first supposes it to mean on the face of it; but even on the face of it, it might mean many different and even opposite things.

For instance, a wooden house might suggest an almost savage solitude; a rude shanty put together by a pioneer in a forest; or it might mean a very recent and rapid solution of the housing problem, conducted cheaply and therefore on a very large scale A wooden house might suggest the very newest thing in American or one of the very oldest things in England. It might mean a grey ruin at Stratford or a white exhibition at Earl's Court.

It is when we come to this interpretation of international symbols that we make most of the international mistakes. Without the smallest error of detail, I will promise to prove that Oriental women are independent because they wear trousers, or Oriental men subject because they wear skirts. Merely to apply it to this case, I will take the example of two very commonplace and trivial objects of modern life— a walking stick and a fur coat.

As it happened, I travelled about America with two sticks, like a Japanese nobleman with his two swords. I fear the simile is too stately. I bore more resemblance to a cripple with two crutches or a highly ineffectual version of the devil on two sticks. I carried them both because I valued them both, and did not wish to risk losing either of them in my erratic travels. One is a very plain grey stick from the woods of Buckinghamshire, but as I took it with me to Palestine it partakes of the character of a pilgrim's staff. When I can say that I have taken the same stick to Jerusalem and to Chicago, I think the stick and I may both have a rest. The other, which I value even more, was given me by the Knights of Columbus at Yale, and I wish I could think that their chivalric title allowed me to regard it as a sword.

Now, I do not know whether the Americans I met, struck by the fastidious foppery of my dress and appearance, concluded that it is the custom of elegant English dandies to carry two walking sticks. But I do know that it is much less common among Americans than among Englishmen to carry even one. The point, however, is not merely that more sticks are carried by Englishmen than by Americans; it is that the sticks which are carried by Americans stand for something entirely different.

In America a stick is commonly called a cane, and it has about it something of the atmosphere which the poet described as the nice conduct of the clouded cane. It would be an exaggeration to say that when the citizens of the United States see a man carrying a light stick, they deduce that if he does that he does nothing else. But there is about it a faint flavour of luxury and lounging, and most of the energetic citizens of this energetic society avoid it by instinct.

Now, in an Englishman like myself, carrying a stick may imply lounging, but it does not imply luxury, and I can say with some firmness that it does not imply dandyism. In a great many Englishmen it means the very opposite even of lounging. By one of those fantastic paradoxes which are the mystery of nationality, a walking stick often actually means walking. It frequently suggests the very reverse of the beau with his clouded cane; it does not suggest a town type, but rather specially a country type. It rather implies the kind of Englishman who tramps about in lanes and meadows and knocks the tops off thistles. It suggests the sort of man who has carried the stick through his native woods, and perhaps even cut it in his native woods.

There are plenty of these vigorous loungers, no doubt, in the rural parts of America, but the idea of a walking stick would not especially suggest them to Americans; it would not call up such figures like a fairy wand. It would be easy to trace back the difference to many English origins, possibly to aristocratic origins, to the idea of the old squire, a man vigorous and even rustic, but trained to hold a useless staff rather than a useful tool. It might be suggested that American citizens do at least so far love freedom as to like to have their hands free. It might be suggested, on the other hand, that they keep their hands for the handles of many machines. And that the hand on a handle is less free than the hand on a stick or even a tool. But these again are controversial questions and I am only noting a fact.

If an Englishman wished to imagine more or less exactly what the impression is, and how misleading it is, he could find something like a parallel in what he himself feels about a fur coat. When I first found myself among the crowds on the main floor of a New York hotel, my rather exaggerated impression of the luxury of the place was largely produced by the number of men in fur coats, and what we should consider rather ostentatious fur coats, with all the fur outside.

Now an Englishman has a number of atmospheric but largely accidental associations in connection with a fur coat. I will not say that he thinks a man in a fur coat must be a wealthy and wicked man; but I do say that in his own ideal and perfect vision a wealthy and wicked man would wear a fur coat. Thus I had the sensation of standing in a surging mob of American millionaires, or even African millionaires; for the millionaires of Chicago must be like the Knights of the Round Table compared with the millionaires of Johannesburg.

But, as a matter of fact, the man in the fur coat was not even an American millionaire, but simply an American. It did not signify luxury, but rather necessity, and even a harsh and almost heroic necessity. Orson probably wore a fur coat; and he was brought up by bears, but not the bears of Wall Street. Eskimos are generally represented as a furry folk; but they are not necessarily engaged in delicate financial operations, even in the typical and appropriate occupation called freezing out. And if the American is not exactly an arctic traveller rushing from pole to pole, at least he is often literally fleeing from ice to ice. He has to make a very extreme distinction between outdoor and indoor clothing. He has to live in an icehouse outside and a hothouse inside; so hot that he may be said to construct an icehouse inside that. He turns himself into an icehouse and warms himself against the cold until he is warm enough to eat ices. But the point is that the same coat of fur which in the England would indicate the sybarite life may here very well indicate the strenuous life; just as the same walking stick which would here suggest a lounger would in England suggest a plodder and almost a pilgrim.

And these two trifles are types which I should like to put, by way of proviso and apology, at the very beginning of any attempt at a record of any impressions of a foreign society. They serve merely to illustrate the most important impression of all, the impression of how false all impressions may be. I suspect that most of the very false impressions have come from the careful record of very true facts. They have come from the fatal power of observing the facts without being able to observe the truth. They came from seeing the symbol with the most vivid clarity and being blind to all that it symbolizes. It is as if a man who knew no Greek should imagine that he could read a Greek inscription because he took the Greek R for an English P or the Greek long E for an English H. I do not mention this merely as a criticism on other people's impressions of America, but as a criticism on my own. I wish it to be understood that I am well aware that all my views are subject to this sort of potential criticism, and that even when I am certain of the facts I do not profess to be certain of the deductions.

In this chapter I hope to point out how a misunderstanding of this kind affects the common impression, not altogether unfounded, that the Americans talk about dollars. But for the moment I am merely anxious to avoid a similar misunderstanding when I talk about Americans. About the dogmas of democracy, about the right of a people to its own symbols, whether they be coins or customs, I am convinced, and no longer to be shaken. But about the meaning of those symbols, in silver or other substances, I am always open to correction. That error is the price we pay for the great glory of nationality. And in this sense I am quite ready, at the start, to warn my own readers against my own opinions.

The fact without the truth is futile; indeed the fact without the truth is false. I have already noted that this is especially true touching our observations of a strange country; and it is certainly true touching one small fact which has swelled into a large fable. I mean the fable about America commonly summed up in the phrase about the Almighty Dollar. I do not think the dollar is almighty in America; I fancy many things are mightier, including many ideals and some rather insane ideals. But I think it might be maintained that the dollar has another of the attributes of deity. If it is not omnipotent it is in a sense omnipresent. Whatever Americans think about dollars, it is, I think, relatively true that they talk about dollars. If a mere mechanical record could be taken by the modern machinery of dictaphones and stenography, I do not think it probable that the mere word "dollars" would occur more often in any given number of American conversations than the mere word "pounds" or "shillings" in a similar number of English conversations. And these statistics, like nearly all statistics, would be utterly useless and even fundamentally false. It is as if we should calculate that the word "elephant" had been mentioned a certain number of times in a particular London street, or so many times more often than the word "thunderbolt" had been used in Stoke Poges. Doubtless there are statisticians capable of carefully collecting those statistics also; and doubtless there are scientific social reformers capable of legislating on the basis of them. They would probably argue from the elephantine imagery of the London street that such and such a percentage of the householders were megalomaniacs and required medical care and police coercion. And doubtless their calculations, like nearly all such calculations, would leave out the only important point; as that the street was in the immediate neighbourhood of the Zoo, or was yet more happily situated under the benignant shadow of the Elephant and Castle. And in the same way the mechanical calculation about the mention of dollars is entirely useless unless we have some moral understanding of why they are mentioned. It certainly does not mean merely a love of money; and if it did, a love of money may mean a great many very different and even contrary things. The love of money is very different in a peasant or in a pirate, in a miser or in a gambler, in a great financier or in a man doing some practical and productive work. Now this difference in the conversation of American and English business men arises, I think, from certain much deeper things in the American which are generally not understood by the Englishman. It also arises from much deeper things in the Englishman, of which the Englishman is even more ignorant.

To begin with, I fancy that the American, quite apart from any love of money, has a great love of measurement. He will mention the exact size or weight of things, in a way which appears to us as irrelevant. It is as if we were to say that a man came to see us carrying three feet of walking stick and four inches of cigar. It is so in cases that have no possible connection with any avarice or greed for gain. An American will praise the prodigal generosity of some other man in giving up his own estate for the good of the poor. But he will generally say that the philanthropist gave them a 200-acre park, where an Englishman would think it quite sufficient to say that he gave them a park. There is something about this precision which seems suitable to the American atmosphere; to the hard sunlight, and the cloudless skies, and the glittering detail of the architecture and the landscape; just as the vaguer English version is consonant to our mistier and more impressionist scenery. It is also connected perhaps with something more boyish about the younger civilization; and corresponds to the passionate particularity with which a boy will distinguish the uniforms of regiments, the rigs of ships, or even the colours of tram tickets. It is a certain godlike appetite for things, as distinct from thoughts.

But there is also, of course, a much deeper cause of the difference; and it can easily be deduced by noting the real nature of the difference itself. When two business men in a train are talking about dollars I am not so foolish as to expect them to be talking about the philosophy of St. Thomas Aquinas. But if they were two English business men I should not expect them to be talking about business. Probably it would be about some sport; and most probably some sport in which they themselves never dreamed of indulging. The approximate difference is that the American talks about his work and the Englishman about his holidays. His ideal is not labour but leisure. Like every other national characteristic, this is not primarily a point for praise or blame; in essence it involves neither and in effect it involves both. It is certainly connected with that snobbishness which is the great sin of English society. The Englishman does love to conceive himself as a sort of country gentleman; and his castles in the air are all castles in Scotland rather than in Spain. For, as an ideal, a Scotch castle is as English as a Welsh rarebit or an Irish stew. And if he talks less about money I fear it is sometimes because in one sense he thinks more of it. Money is a mystery in the old and literal sense of something too sacred for speech. Gold is a god; and like the god of some agnostics has no name and is worshipped only in his works. It is true in a sense that the English gentleman wishes to have enough money to be able to forget it. But it may be questioned whether he does entirely forget it. As against this weakness the American has succeeded, at the price of a great deal of crudity and clatter, in making general a very real respect for work. He has partly disenchanted the dangerous glamour of the gentleman, and in that sense has achieved some degree of democracy; which is the most difficult achievement in the world.

On the other hand, there is a good side to the Englishman's day-dream of leisure, and one which the American spirit tends to miss. It may be expressed in the word "holiday" or still better in the word "hobby." The Englishman, in his character of Robin Hood, really has got two strings to his bow. Indeed the Englishman really is well represented by Robin Hood; for there is always something about him that may literally be called outlawed, in the sense of being extra-legal or outside the rules. A Frenchman said of Browning that his centre was not in the middle; and it may be said of many an Englishman that his heart is not where his treasure is. Browning expressed a very English sentiment when he said:—

I like to know a butcher paints,
A baker rhymes for his pursuit,
Candlestick-maker much acquaints
His soul with song, or haply mute
Blows out his brains upon the flute.

Stevenson touched on the same insular sentiment when he said that many men he knew, who were meat-salesmen to the outward eye, might in the life of contemplation sit with the saints. Now the extraordinary achievement of the American meat-salesman is that his poetic enthusiasm can really be for meat sales; not for money but for meat. An American commercial traveller asked me, with a religious fire in his eye, whether I did not think that salesmanship could be an art. In England there are many salesmen who are sincerely fond of art; but seldom of the art of salesmanship. Art is with them a hobby; a thing of leisure and liberty. That is why the English traveller talks, if not of art, then of sport. That is why the two city men in the London train, if they are not talking about golf, may be talking about gardening. If they are not talking about dollars, or the equivalent of dollars, the reason lies much deeper than any superficial praise or blame touching the desire for wealth. In the English case, at least, it lies very deep in the English spirit. Many of the greatest English things have had this lighter and looser character of a hobby or a holiday experiment. Even a masterpiece has often been a by-product. The works of Shakespeare come out so casually that they can be attributed to the most improbable people; even to Bacon. The sonnets of Shakespeare are picked up after wards as if out of a wastepaper basket. The immortality of Dr. Johnson does not rest on the written leaves he collected, but entirely on the words he wasted, the words he scattered to the winds. So great a thing as Pickwick is almost a kind of accident; it began as something secondary and grew into something primary and pre-eminent. It began with mere words written to illustrate somebody else's pictures; and swelled like an epic expanded from an epigram. It might almost be said that in the case of Pickwick the author began as the servant of the artist. But, as in the same story of Pickwick, the servant became greater than the master. This incalculable and accidental quality, like all national qualities, has its strength and weakness; but it does represent a certain reserve fund of interests in the Englishman's life; and distinguishes him from the other extreme type, of the millionaire who works till he drops, or who drops because he stops working. It is the great achievement of American civilization that in that country it really is not cant to talk about the dignity of labour. There is something that might almost be called the sanctity of labour; but it is subject to the profound law that when anything less than the highest becomes a sanctity, it tends also to become a superstition. When the candlestick-maker does not blow out his brains upon the flute there is always a danger that he may blow them out somewhere else, owing to depressed conditions in the candlestick market.

Now certainly one of the first impressions of America, or at any rate of New York, which is by no means the same thing as America, is that of a sort of mob of business men, behaving in many ways in a fashion very different from that of the swarms of London city men who go up every day to the city. They sit about in groups with Red-Indian gravity, as if passing the pipe of peace; though, in fact, most of them are smoking cigars and some of them are eating cigars. The latter strikes me as one of the most peculiar of transatlantic tastes, more peculiar than that of chewing gum. A man will sit for hours consuming a cigar as if it were a sugar-stick; but I should imagine it to be a very disagreeable sugar-stick. Why he attempts to enjoy a cigar without lighting it I do not know; whether it is a more economical way of carrying a mere symbol of commercial conservation; or whether something of the same queer outlandish morality that draws such a distinction between beer and ginger beer draws an equally ethical distinction between touching tobacco and lighting it. For the rest, it would be easy to make a merely external sketch full of things equally strange; for this can always be done in a strange country. I allow for the fact of all foreigners looking alike; but I fancy that all those hard-featured faces, with spectacles and shaven jaws, do look rather alike, because they all like to make their faces hard. And with the mention of their mental attitude we realize the futility of any such external sketch. Unless we can see that these are something more than men smoking cigars and talking about dollars we had much better not see them at all.

It is customary to condemn the American as a materialist because of his worship of success. But indeed this very worship, like any worship, even devil-worship, proves him rather a mystic than a materialist. The Frenchman who retires from business when he has money enough to drink his wine and eat his omelette in peace might much more plausibly be called a materialist by those who do not prefer to call him a man of sense. But Americans do worship success in the abstract, as a sort of ideal vision. They follow success rather than money; they follow money rather than meat and drink. If their national life in one sense is a perpetual game of poker, they are playing excitedly for chips or counters as well as for coins. And by the ultimate test of material enjoyment, like the enjoyment of an omelette, even a coin is itself a counter. The Yankee cannot eat chips as the Frenchman can eat chipped potatoes; but neither can he swallow red cents as the Frenchman swallows red wine. Thus when people say of a Yankee that he worships the dollar, they pay a compliment to his fine spirituality more true and delicate than they imagine. The dollar is an idol because it is an image; but it is an image of success and not of enjoyment.

That this romance is also a religion is shown in the fact that there is a queer sort of morality attached to it. The nearest parallel to it is something like the sense of honour in the old duelling days. There is not a material but a distinctly moral savour about the implied obligation to collect dollars or to collect chips. We hear too much in England of the phrase about "making good"; for no sensible Englishman favours the needless interlarding of English with scraps of foreign languages. But though it means nothing in English, it means something very particular in American. There is a fine shade of distinction between succeeding and making good, precisely because there must always be a sort of ethical echo in the word good. America does vaguely feel a man making good as something analogous to a man being good or a man doing good. It is connected with his serious self-respect and his sense of being worthy of those he loves. Nor is this curious crude idealism wholly insincere even when it drives him to what some of us would call stealing; any more than the duellist's honour was insincere when it drove him to what some would call murder. A very clever American play which I once saw acted contained a complete working model of this morality. A girl was loyal to, but distressed by, her engagement to a young man on whom there was a sort of cloud of humiliation. The atmosphere was exactly what it would have been in England if he had been accused of cowardice or card-sharping. And there was nothing whatever the matter with the poor young man except that some rotten mine or other in Arizona had not "made good." Now in England we should either be below or above that ideal of good. If we were snobs, we should be content to know that he was a gentleman of good connections, perhaps too much accustomed to private means to be expected to be businesslike. If we were somewhat larger-minded people, we should know that he might be as wise as Socrates and as splendid as Bayard and yet be unfitted, perhaps one should say therefore be unfitted, for the dismal and dirty gambling of modern commerce. But whether we were snobbish enough to admire him for being an idler, or chivalrous enough to admire him for being an outlaw, in neither case should we ever really and in our hearts despise him for being a failure. For it is this inner verdict of instinctive idealism that is the point at issue. Of course there is nothing new, or peculiar to the new world, about a man's engagement practically failing through his financial failure. An English girl might easily drop a man because he was poor, or she might stick to him faithfully and defiantly although he was poor. The point is that this girl was faithful but she was not defiant; that is, she was not proud. The whole psychology of the situation was that she shared the weird worldly idealism of her family, and it was wounded as her patriotism would have been wounded if he had betrayed his country. To do them justice, there was nothing to show that they would have had any real respect for a royal duke who had inherited millions; what the simple barbarians wanted was a man who could "make good." That the process of making good would probably drag him through the mire of everything bad, that he would make good by bluffing, lying, swindling, and grinding the faces of the poor, did not seem to trouble them in the least. Against this fanaticism there is this shadow of truth even in the fiction of aristocracy; that a gentleman may at least be allowed to be good without being bothered to make it.

Another objection to the phrase about the almighty dollar is that it is an almighty phrase, and therefore an almighty nuisance. I mean that it is made to explain everything, and to explain everything much too well; that is, much too easily. It does not really help people to understand a foreign country; but it gives them the fatal illusion that they do understand it. Dollars stood for America as frogs stood for France; because it was necessary to connect particular foreigners with something, or it would be so easy to confuse a Moor with a Montenegrin or a Russian with a Red Indian. The only cure for this sort of satisfied familiarity is the shock of something really unfamiliar. When people can see nothing at all in American democracy except a Yankee running after a dollar, then the only thing to do is to trip them up as they run after the Yankee, or run away with their notion of the Yankee, by the obstacle of certain odd and obstinate facts that have no relation to that notion. And, as a matter of fact, there are a number of such obstacles to any such generalization; a number of notable facts that have to be reconciled somehow to our previous notions. It does not matter for this purpose whether the facts are favourable or unfavourable, or whether the qualities are merits or defects; especially as we do not even understand them sufficiently to say which they are. The point is that we are brought to a pause, and compelled to attempt to understand them rather better than we do. We have found the one thing that we did not expect; and therefore the one thing that we cannot explain. And we are moved to an effort, probably an unsuccessful effort, to explain it.

For instance, Americans are very unpunctual. That is the last thing that a critic expects who comes to condemn them for hustling and haggling and vulgar ambition. But it is almost the first fact that strikes the spectator on the spot. The chief difference between the humdrum English business man and the hustling American business man is that the hustling American business man is always late. Of course there is a great deal of difference between coming late and coming too late. But I noticed the fashion first in connection with my own lectures; touching which I could heartily recommend the habit of coming too late. I could easily understand a crowd of commercial Americans not coming to my lectures at all; but there was something odd about their coming in a crowd, and the crowd being expected to turn up some time after the appointed hour. The managers of these lectures (I continue to call them lectures out of courtesy to myself) often explained to me that it was quite useless to begin properly until about half an hour after time. Often people were still coming in three-quarters of an hour or even an hour after time. Not that I objected to that, as some lecturers are said to do; it seemed to me an agreeable break in the monotony; but as a characteristic of a people mostly engaged in practical business, it struck me as curious and interesting. I have grown accustomed to being the most unbusinesslike person in any given company; and it gave me a sort of dizzy exaltation to find I was not the most unpunctual person in that company. I was afterwards told by many Americans that my impression was quite correct; that American unpunctuality was really very prevalent, and extended to much more important things. But at least I was not content to lump this along with all sorts of contrary things that I did not happen to like, and call it America. I am not sure of what it really means, but I rather fancy that though it may seem the very reverse of the hustling, it has the same origin as the hustling. The American is not punctual because he is not punctilious. He is impulsive, and has an impulse to stay as well as an impulse to go. For, after all, punctuality belongs to the same order of ideas as punctuation; and there is no punctuation in telegrams. The order of clocks and set hours which English business has always observed is a good thing in its own way; indeed I think that in a larger sense it is better than the other way. But it is better because it is a protection against hustling, not a promotion of it. In other words, it is better because it is more civilized; as a great Venetian merchant prince clad in cloth of gold was more civilized; or an old English merchant drinking port in an oak-panelled room was more civilized; or a little French shopkeeper shutting up his shop to play dominoes is more civilized. And the reason is that the American has the romance of business and is monomaniac, while the Frenchman has the romance of life and is sane. But the romance of business really is a romance, and the Americans are really romantic about it. And that romance, though it revolves round pork or petrol, is really like a love-affair in this; that it involves not only rushing but also lingering.

The American is too busy to have business habits. He is also too much in earnest to have business rules. If we wish to understand him, we must compare him not with the French shopkeeper when he plays dominoes, but with the same French shopkeeper when he works the guns or mans the trenches as a conscript soldier. Everybody used to the punctilious Prussian standard of uniform and parade has noticed the roughness and apparent laxity of the French soldier, the looseness of his clothes, the unsightliness of his heavy knapsack, in short his inferiority in every detail of the business of war except fighting. There he is much too swift to be smart. He is much too practical to be precise.

By a strange illusion which can lift pork-packing almost to the level of patriotism, the American has the same free rhythm in his romance of business. He varies his conduct not to suit the clock but to suit the case. He gives more time to more important and less time to less important things; and he makes up his time-table as he goes along. Suppose he has three appointments; the first, let us say, is some mere trifle of erecting a tower twenty storeys high and exhibiting a sky-sign on the top of it; the second is a business discussion about the possibility of printing advertisements of soft drinks on the table-napkins at a restaurant; the third is attending a conference to decide how the populace can be prevented from using chewing-gum and the manufacturers can still manage to sell it. He will be content merely to glance at the sky-sign as he goes by in a trolley-car or an automobile; he will then settle down to the discussion with his partner about the table-napkins, each speaker indulging in long monologues in turn; a peculiarity of much American conversation. Now if in the middle of one of these monologues, he suddenly thinks that the vacant space of the waiter's shirt-front might also be utilized to advertize the Gee Whiz Ginger Champagne, he will instantly follow up the new idea in all its aspects and possibilities, in an even longer monologue; and will never think of looking at his watch while he is rapturously looking at his waiter. The consequence is that he will come late into the great social movement against chewing-gum, where an Englishman would probably have arrived at the proper hour. But though the Englishman's conduct is more proper, it need not be in all respects more practical. The Englishman's rules are better for the business of life, but not necessarily for the life of business. And it is true that for many of these Americans business is the business of life. It is really also, as I have said, the romance of life. We shall admire or deplore this spirit, accordingly as we are glad to see trade irradiated with so much poetry, or sorry to see so much poetry wasted on trade. But it does make many people happy, like any other hobby; and one is disposed to add that it does fill their imaginations like any other delusion. For the true criticism of all this commercial romance would involve a criticism of this historic phase of commerce. These people are building on the sand, though it shines like gold, and for them like fairy gold; but the world will remember the legend about fairy gold. Half the financial operations they follow deal with things that do not even exist; for in that sense all finance is a fairy tale. Many of them are buying and selling things that do nothing but harm; but it does them good to buy and sell them. The claim of the romantic salesman is better justified than he realizes. Business really is romance; for it is not reality.

There is one real advantage that America has over England, largely due to its livelier and more impressionable ideal. America does not think that stupidity is practical. It does not think that ideas are merely destructive things. It does not think that a genius is only a person to be told to go away and blow his brains out; rather it would open all its machinery to the genius and beg him to blow his brains in. It might attempt to use a natural force like Blake or Shelley for very ignoble purposes; it would be quite capable of asking Blake to take his tiger and his golden lions round as a sort of Barnum's show, or Shelley to hang his stars and haloed clouds among the lights of Broadway. But it would not assume that a natural force is useless, any more than that Niagara is useless. And there is a very definite distinction here touching the intelligence of the trader, whatever we may think of either course touching the intelligence of the artist. It is one thing that Apollo should be employed by Admetus, although he is a god. It is quite another thing that Apollo should always be sacked by Admetus, because he is a god. Now in England, largely owing to the accident of a rivalry and therefore a comparison with France, there arose about the end of the eighteenth century an extraordinary notion that there was some sort of connection between dullness and success. What the Americans call a bonehead became what the English call a hard-headed man. The merchants of London evinced their contempt for the fantastic logicians of Paris by living in a permanent state of terror lest somebody should set the Thames on fire. In this as in much else it is much easier to understand the Americans if we connect them with the French who were their allies than with the English who were their enemies. There are a great many Franco-American resemblances which the practical Anglo-Saxons are of course too hard-headed (or bone-headed) to see. American history is haunted with the shadow of the Plebiscitary President; they have a tradition of classical architecture for public buildings. Their cities are planned upon the squares of Paris and not upon the labyrinth of London. They call their cities Corinth and Syracuse, as the French called their citizens Epaminondas and Timoleon. Their soldiers wore the French kepi; and they make coffee admirably, and do not make tea at all. But of all the French elements in America the most French is this real practicality. They know that at certain times the most businesslike of all qualities is *l'audace, et encore de l'audace, et toujours de l'audace*. The publisher may induce the poet to do a pot-boiler; but the publisher would cheerfully allow the poet to set the Mississippi on fire, if it would boil his particular pot. It is not so much that Englishmen are stupid as that they are afraid of being clever; and it is not so much that Americans are clever as that they do not try to be any stupider than they are. The fire of French logic has burnt that out of America as it has burnt it out of Europe, and of almost every place except England. This is one of the few points on which English insularity really is a disadvantage. It is the fatal notion that the only sort of common sense is to be found in compromise, and that the only sort of compromise is to be found in confusion. This must be clearly distinguished from the commonplace about the utilitarian world not rising to the invisible values of genius. Under this philosophy the utilitarian does not see the utility of genius, even when it is quite visible. He does not see it, not because he is a utilitarian, but because he is an idealist whose ideal is dullness. For some time the English aspired to be stupid, prayed and hoped with soaring spiritual ambition to be stupid. But with all their worship of success, they did not succeed in being stupid. The natural talents of a great and traditional nation were always breaking out in spite of them. In spite of the merchants of

London, Turner did set the Thames on fire. In spite of our repeatedly explained preference for realism to romance, Europe persisted in resounding with the name of Byron. And just when we had made it perfectly clear to the French that we despised all their flamboyant tricks, that we were a plain prosaic people and there was no fantastic glory or chivalry about us, the very shaft we sent against them shone with the name of Nelson, a shooting and a falling star.

8

Presidents and Problems

All good Americans wish to fight the representatives they have chosen. All good Englishmen wish to forget the representatives they have chosen. This difference, deep and perhaps ineradicable in the temperaments of the two peoples, explains a thousand things in their literature and their laws. The American national poet praised his people for their readiness "to *rise* against the never-ending audacity of elected persons." The English national anthem is content to say heartily, but almost hastily, "Confound their politics," and then more cheerfully, as if changing the subject, "God save the King." For this is especially the secret of the monarch or chief magistrate in the two countries. They arm the President with the powers of a King, that he may be a nuisance in politics. We deprive the King even of the powers of a President, lest he should remind us of a politician. We desire to forget the never-ending audacity of elected persons; and with us therefore it really never does end. That is the practical objection to our own habit of changing the subject, instead of changing the ministry. The King, as the Irish wit observed, is not a subject; but in that sense the English crowned head is not a King. He is a popular figure intended to remind us of the England that politicians do not remember; the England of horses and ships and gardens and good fellowship. The Americans have no such purely social symbol; and it is rather the root than the result of this that their social luxury, and especially their sport, are a little lacking in humanity and humour. It is the American, much more than the Englishman, who takes his pleasures sadly, not to say savagely.

The genuine popularity of constitutional monarchs, in parliamentary countries, can be explained by any practical example. Let us suppose that great social reform, The Compulsory Haircutting Act, has just begun to be enforced. The Compulsory Haircutting Act, as every good citizen knows, is a statute which permits any person to grow his hair to any length, in any wild or wonderful shape, so long as he is registered with a hairdresser who charges a shilling. But it imposes a universal close shave (like that which is found so hygienic during a curative detention at Dartmoor) on all who are registered only with a barber who charges threepence. Thus, while the ornamental classes can continue to ornament the street with Piccadilly weepers or chin-beards if they choose, the working classes demonstrate the care with which the State protects them by going about in a fresher, cooler, and cleaner condition; a condition which has the further advantage of revealing at a glance that outline of the criminal skull, which is so common among them. The Compulsory Haircutting Act is thus in every way a compact and convenient example of all our current laws about education, sport, liquor and liberty in general. Well, the law has passed and the masses, insensible to its scientific value, are still murmuring against it. The ignorant peasant maiden is averse to so extreme a fashion of bobbing her hair; and does not see how she can even be a flapper with nothing to flap. Her father, his mind already poisoned by Bolshevists, begins to wonder who the devil does these things, and why. In proportion as he knows the world of to-day, he guesses that the real origin may be quite obscure, or the real motive quite corrupt. The pressure may have come from anybody who has gained power or money anyhow. It may come from the foreign millionaire who owns all the expensive hairdressing saloons; it may come from some swindler in the cutlery trade who has contracted to sell a million bad razors. Hence the poor man looks about him with suspicion in the street; knowing that the lowest sneak or the loudest snob he sees may be directing the government of his country. Anybody may have to do with politics; and this sort of thing is politics. Suddenly he catches sight of a crowd, stops, and begins wildly to cheer a carriage that is passing. The carriage contains the one person who has certainly not originated any great scientific reform. He is the only person in the commonwealth who is not allowed to cut off other people's hair, or to take away other people's liberties. He at least is kept out of politics; and men hold him up as they did an unspotted victim to appease the wrath of the gods. He is their King, and the only man they know is not their ruler. We need not be surprised that he is popular, knowing how they are ruled.

The popularity of a President in America is exactly the opposite. The American Republic is the last mediaeval monarchy. It is intended that the President shall rule, and take all the risks of ruling. If the hair is cut he is the haircutter, the magistrate that bears not the razor in vain. All the popular Presidents, Jackson and Lincoln and Roosevelt, have acted as democratic despots, but emphatically not as constitutional monarchs. In short, the names have become curiously interchanged; and as a historical reality it is the President who ought to be called a King.

But it is not only true that the President could correctly be called a King. It is also true that the King might correctly be called a President. We could hardly find a more exact description of him than to call him a President. What is expected in modern times of a modern constitutional monarch is emphatically that he should preside. We expect him to take the throne exactly as if he were taking the chair.

The chairman does not move the motion or resolution, far less vote it; he is not supposed even to favour it. He is expected to please everybody by favouring nobody. The primary essentials of a President or Chairman are that he should be treated with ceremonial respect, that he should be popular in his personality and yet impersonal in his opinions, and that he should actually be a link between all the other persons by being different from all of them. This is exactly what is demanded of the constitutional monarch in modern times. It is exactly the opposite to the American position; in which the President does not preside at all. He moves; and the things he moves may truly be called a motion; for the national idea is perpetual motion. Technically it is called a message; and might often actually be called a menace. Thus we may truly say that the King presides and the President reigns. Some would prefer to say that the President rules; and some Senators and members of Congress would prefer to say that he rebels. But there is no doubt that he moves; he does not take the chair or even the stool, but rather the stump.

Some people seem to suppose that the fall of President Wilson was a denial of this almost despotic ideal in America. As a matter of fact it was the strongest possible assertion of it The idea is that the President shall take responsibility and risk; and responsibility means being blamed, and risk means the risk of being blamed. The theory is that things are done by the President; and if things go wrong, or are alleged to go wrong, it is the fault of the President. This does not invalidate, but rather ratifies the comparison with true monarchs such as the mediaeval monarchs. Constitutional princes are seldom deposed; but despots were often deposed. In the simpler races of sunnier lands, such as Turkey, they were commonly assassinated. Even in our own history a King often received the same respectful tribute to the responsibility and reality of his office. But King John was attacked because he was strong, not because he was weak. Richard the Second lost the crown because the crown was a trophy, not because it was a trifle. And President Wilson was deposed because he had used a power which is such, in its nature, that a man must use it at the risk of deposition. As a matter of fact, of course, it is easy to exaggerate Mr. Wilson's real unpopularity, and still more easy to exaggerate Mr. Wilson's real failure. There are a great many people in America who justify and applaud him; and what is yet more interesting, who justify him not on pacifist and idealistic, but on patriotic and even military grounds. It is especially insisted by some that his demonstration, which seemed futile as a threat against Mexico, was a very far-sighted preparation for the threat against Prussia. But in so far as the democracy did disagree with him, it was but the occasional and inevitable result of the theory by which the despot has to anticipate the democracy.

Thus the American King and the English President are the very opposite of each other; yet they are both the varied and very national indications of the same contemporary truth. It is the great weariness and contempt that have fallen upon common politics in both countries. It may be answered, with some show of truth, that the new American President represents a return to common politics; and that in that sense he marks a real rebuke to the last President and his more uncommon politics. And it is true that many who put Mr. Harding in power regard him as the symbol of something which they call normalcy; which may roughly be translated into English by the word normality. And by this they do mean, more or less, the return to the vague capitalist conservatism of the nineteenth century. They might call Mr. Harding a Victorian if they had ever lived under Victoria. Perhaps these people do entertain the extraordinary notion that the nineteenth century was normal. But there are very few who think so, and even they will not think so long. The blunder is the beginning of nearly all our present troubles. The nineteenth century was the very reverse of normal. It suffered a most unnatural strain in the combination of political equality in theory with extreme economic inequality in practice. Capitalism was not a normalcy but an abnormalcy. Property is normal, and is more normal in proportion as it is universal. Slavery may be normal and even natural, in the sense that a bad habit may be a second nature.

But Capitalism was never anything so human as a habit; we may say it was never anything so good as a bad habit. It was never a custom; for men never grew accustomed to it. It was never even conservative; for before it was even created wise men had realized that it could not be conserved. It was from the first a problem; and those who will not even admit the Capitalist problem deserve to get the Bolshevist solution. All things considered, I cannot say anything worse of them than that.

The recent Presidential election preserved some trace of the old Party System of America; but its tradition has very nearly faded like that of the Party System of England. It is easy for an Englishman to confess that he never quite understood the American Party System. It would perhaps be more courageous in him, and more informing, to confess that he never really understood the British Party System. The planks in the two American platforms may easily be exhibited as very disconnected and ramshackle; but our own party was as much of a patchwork, and indeed, I think, even more so. Everybody knows that the two American factions were called "Democrat" and "Republican." It does not at all cover the case to identify the former with Liberals and the latter with Conservatives. The Democrats are the party of the South and have some true tradition from the Southern aristocracy and the defence of Secession and State Rights. The Republicans rose in the North as the party of Lincoln, largely condemning slavery. But the Republicans are also the party of Tariffs, and are at least accused of being the party of Trusts. The Democrats are the party of Free Trade; and in the great movement of twenty years ago the party of Free Silver. The Democrats are also the party of the Irish; and the stones they throw at Trusts are retorted by stones thrown at Tammany. It is easy to see all these things as curiously sporadic and bewildering; but I am inclined to think that they are as a whole more coherent and rational than our own old division of Liberals and Conservatives. There is even more doubt nowadays about what is the connecting link between the different items in the old British party programmes. I have never been able to understand why being in favour of Protection should have anything to do with being opposed to Home Rule; especially as most of the people who were to receive Home Rule were themselves in favour of Protection. I could never see what giving people cheap bread had to do with forbidding them cheap beer; or why the party which sympathizes with Ireland cannot sympathize with Poland. I cannot see why Liberals did not liberate public-houses or Conservatives conserve crofters. I do not understand the principle upon which the causes were selected on both sides; and I incline to think that it was with the impartial object of distributing nonsense equally on both sides. Heaven knows there is enough nonsense in American politics too; towering and tropical nonsense like a cyclone or an earthquake. But when all is said, I incline to think that there was more spiritual and atmospheric cohesion in the different parts of the American party than in those of the English party; and I think this unity was all the more real because it was more difficult to define. The Republican party originally stood for the triumph of the North, and the North stood for the nineteenth century; that is for the characteristic commercial expansion of the nineteenth century; for a firm faith in the profit and progress of its great and growing cities, its division of labour, its industrial science, and its evolutionary reform. The Democratic party stood more loosely for all the elements that doubted whether this development was democratic or was desirable; all that looked back to Jeffersonian idealism and the serene abstractions of the eighteenth century, or forward to Bryanite idealism and some simplified Utopia founded on grain rather than gold. Along with this went, not at all unnaturally, the last and lingering sentiment of the Southern squires, who remembered a more rural civilization that seemed by comparison romantic. Along with this went, quite logically, the passions and the pathos of the Irish themselves a rural civilization, whose basis is a religion or what the nineteenth century tended to call a superstition. Above all, it was perfectly natural that this tone of thought should favour local liberties, and even a revolt on behalf of local liberties, and should distrust the huge machine of centralized power called the Union. In short, something very near the truth was said by a suicidally silly Republican orator, who was running Blaine for the Presidency, when he denounced the Democratic party as supported by "Rome, rum, and rebellion." They seem to me to be three excellent things in their place; and that is why I suspect that I should have belonged to the Democratic party, if I had been born in America when there was a Democratic party. But I fancy that by this time even this general distinction has become very dim. If I had been an American twenty years ago, in the time of the great Free Silver campaign, I should certainly never have hesitated for an instant about my sympathies or my side. My feelings would have been exactly those that are nobly expressed by Mr. Vachell Lindsay, in a poem bearing the characteristic title of *Bryan, Bryan, Bryan, Bryan*. And, by the way, nobody can begin to sympathize with America whose soul does not to some extent begin to swing and dance to the drums and gongs of Mr. Vachell Lindsay's great orchestra; which has the note of his whole nation in this: that a refined person can revile it a hundred times over as violent and brazen and barbarous and absurd, but not as insincere; there is something in it, and that something is the soul of many million men. But the poet himself, in the political poem referred to, speaks of Bryan's fall over Free Silver as "defeat of my boyhood, defeat of my dream"; and it is only too probable that the cause has fallen as well as the candidate. The William Jennings Bryan of later years is not the man whom I should have seen in my youth, with the visionary eyes of Mr. Vachell Lindsay. He has become a commonplace Pacifist, which is in its nature the very opposite of a revolutionist; for if men will fight rather than sacrifice humanity on a golden cross, it cannot be wrong for them to resist its being sacrificed to an iron cross. I came into very indirect contact with Mr. Bryan when I was in America, in a fashion that made me realize how hard it has become to recover the illusions of a Bryanite. I believe that my lecture agent was anxious to arrange a debate, and I threw out a sort of loose challenge to the effect that woman's suffrage had weakened the position of woman; and while I was away in the wilds of Oklahoma my lecture agent (a man of blood-curdling courage and enterprise) asked Mr. Bryan to debate with me. Now Mr. Bryan is one of the greatest orators of modern history, and there is no conceivable reason why he should trouble to debate with a wandering lecturer. But as a matter of fact he expressed himself in the most magnanimous and courteous terms about my personal position, but said (as I understood) that it would be improper to debate on female suffrage as it was already a part of the political system. And when I heard that, I could not help a sigh; for I recognized something that I knew only too well on the front benches of my own beloved land. The great and glorious demagogue had degenerated into a statesman. I had never expected for a moment that the great orator could be bothered to debate with me at all; but it had never occurred to me, as a general moral principle, that two educated men were for ever forbidden to talk sense about a particular topic, because a lot of other people had already voted on it. What is the matter with that attitude is the loss of the freedom of the mind. There can be no liberty of thought unless it is ready to unsettle what has recently been settled as well as what has long been settled. We are perpetually being told in the papers that what is wanted is a strong man who will do things. What is wanted is a strong man who will undo things; and that will be a real test of strength.

Anyhow, we could have believed, in the time of the Free Silver fight, that the Democratic party was democratic with a small d. In Mr. Wilson it was transfigured, his friends would say into a higher and his foes into a hazier thing. And the Republican reaction against him, even where it has been healthy, has also been hazy. In fact, it has been not so much the victory of a political party as a relapse into repose after certain political passions; and in that sense there is a truth in the strange phrase about normalcy; in the sense that there is nothing more normal than going to sleep. But an even larger truth is this; it is most likely that America is no longer concentrated on these faction fights at all, but is considering certain large problems upon which those factions hardly troubled to take sides. They are too large even to be classified as foreign policy distinct from domestic policy. They are so large as to be inside as well as outside the state. From an English standpoint the most obvious example is the Irish; for the Irish problem is not a British problem, but also an American problem. And this is true even of the great external enigma of Japan. The Japanese question may be a part of foreign policy for America, but it is a part of domestic policy for California. And the same is true of that other intense and intelligent Eastern people, the genius and limitations of which have troubled the world so much longer. What the Japs are in California, the Jews are in America. That is, they are a piece of foreign policy that has become imbedded in domestic policy; something which is found inside but still has to be regarded from the outside. On these great international matters I doubt if Americans got much guidance from their party system; especially as most of these questions have grown very recently and rapidly to enormous size. Men are left free to judge of them with fresh minds. And that is the truth in the statement that the Washington Conference has opened the gates of a new world.

On the relations to England and Ireland I will not attempt to dwell adequately here. I have already noted that my first interview was with an Irishman, and my first impression from that interview a vivid sense of the importance of Ireland in Anglo-American relations; and I have said something of the Irish problem, prematurely and out of its proper order, under the stress of that sense of urgency. Here I will only add two remarks about the two countries respectively. A great many British journalists have recently imagined that they were pouring oil upon the troubled waters, when they were rather pouring out oil to smooth the downward path; and to turn the broad road to destruction into a butter-slide. They seem to have no notion of what to do, except to say what they imagine the very stupidest of their readers would be pleased to hear, and conceal whatever the most intelligent of their readers would probably like to know. They therefore informed the public that "the majority of Americans" had abandoned all sympathy with Ireland, because of its alleged sympathy with Germany; and that this majority of Americans was now adherently in sympathy with its English brothers across the sea. Now to begin with, such critics have no notion of what they are saying when they talk about the majority of Americans. To anybody who has happened to look in, let us say, on the city of Omaha, Nebraska, the remark will have something enormous and overwhelming about it. It is like saying that the majority of the inhabitants of China would agree with the Chinese Ambassador in a preference for dining at the Savoy rather than the Ritz. There are millions and millions of people living in those great central plains of the North American Continent of whom it would be nearer the truth to say that they have never heard of England, or of Ireland either, than to say that their first emotional movement is a desire to come to the rescue of either of them. It is perfectly true that the more monomaniac sort of Sinn Feiner might sometimes irritate this innocent and isolated American spirit by being pro-Irish. It is equally true that a traditional Bostonian or Virginian might irritate it by being pro-English. The only difference is that large numbers of pure Irishmen are scattered in those far places, and large numbers of pure Englishmen are not. But it is truest of all to say that neither England nor Ireland so much as crosses the mind of most of them once in six months. Painting up large notices of "Watch Us Grow," making money by farming with machinery, together with an occasional hold-up with six-shooters and photographs of a beautiful murderess or divorcée, fill up the round of their good and happy lives, and fleet the time carelessly as in the golden age.

But putting aside all this vast and distant democracy, which is the real "majority of Americans," and confining ourselves to that older culture on the eastern coast which the critics probably had in mind, we shall find the case more comforting but not to be covered with cheap and false comfort. Now it is perfectly true that any Englishman coming to this eastern coast, as I did, finds himself not only most warmly welcomed as a guest, but most cordially complimented as an Englishman. Men recall with pride the branches of their family that belong to England or the English counties where they were rooted; and there are enthusiasms for English literature and history which are as

113

spontaneous as patriotism itself. Something of this may be put down to a certain promptitude and flexibility in all American kindness, which is never sufficiently stodgy to be called good nature. The Englishman does sometimes wonder whether if he had been a Russian, his hosts would not have remembered remote Russian aunts and uncles and disinterred a Muscovite great-grandmother; or whether if he had come from Iceland, they would not have known as much about Icelandic sagas and been as sympathetic about the absence of Icelandic snakes. But with a fair review of the proportions of the case he will dismiss this conjecture, and come to the conclusion that a number of educated Americans are very warmly and sincerely sympathetic with England.

What I began to feel, with a certain creeping chill, was that they were only too sympathetic with England. The word sympathetic has sometimes rather a double sense. The impression I received was that all these chivalrous Southerners and men mellow with Bostonian memories were *rallying* to England. They were on the defensive; and it was poor old England that they were defending. Their attitude implied that somebody or something was leaving her undefended, or finding her indefensible. The burden of that hearty chorus was that England was not so black as she was painted; it seemed clear that somewhere or other she was being painted pretty black. But there was something else that made me uncomfortable; it was not only the sense of being somewhat boisterously forgiven; it was also something involving questions of power as well as morality. Then it seemed to me that a new sensation turned me hot and cold; and I felt something I have never before felt in a foreign land. Never had my father or my grandfather known that sensation; never during the great and complex and perhaps perilous expansion of our power and commerce in the last hundred years had an Englishman heard exactly that note in a human voice. England was being *pitied*. I, as an Englishman, was not only being pardoned but pitied. My country was beginning to be an object of compassion like Poland or Spain. My first emotion, full of the mood and movement of a hundred years, was one of furious anger.

But the anger has given place to anxiety; and the anxiety is not yet at an end.

It is not my business here to expound my view of English politics, still less of European politics or the politics of the world; but to put down a few impressions of American travel. On many points of European politics the impression will be purely negative; I am sure that most Americans have no notion of the position of France or the position of Poland. But if English readers want the truth, I am sure this is the truth about their notion of the position of England. They are wondering, or those who are watching are wondering, whether the term of her success is come and she is going down the dark road after Prussia. Many are sorry if this is so; some are glad if it is so; but all are seriously considering the probability of its being so. And herein lay especially the horrible folly of our Black-and-Tan terrorism over the Irish people. I have noted that the newspapers told us that America had been chilled in its Irish sympathies by Irish detachment during the war. It is the painful truth that any advantage we might have had from this we ourselves immediately proceeded to destroy. Ireland *might* have put herself wrong with America by her attitude about Belgium, if England had not instantly proceeded to put herself more wrong by her attitude towards Ireland. It is quite true that two blacks do not make a white; but you cannot send a black to reproach people with tolerating blackness; and this is quite as true when one is a Black Brunswicker and the other a Black-and-Tan. It is true that since then England has made surprisingly sweeping concessions; concessions so large as to increase the amazement that the refusal should have been so long. But unfortunately the combination of the two rather clinches the conception of our decline. If the concession had come before the terror, it would have looked like an attempt to emancipate, and would probably have succeeded. Coming so abruptly after the terror, it looked only like an attempt to tyrannize, and an attempt that failed. It was partly an inheritance from a stupid tradition, which tried to combine what it called firmness with what it called conciliation; as if when we

115

made up our minds to soothe a man with a five-pound note, we always took care to undo our own action by giving him a kick as well. The English politician has often done that; though there is nothing to be said of such a fool, except that he has wasted a fiver. But in this case he gave the kick first, received a kicking in return, and *then* gave up the money; and it was hard for the bystanders to say anything except that he had been badly beaten. The combination and sequence of events seems almost as if it were arranged to suggest the dark and ominous parallel. The first action looked only too like the invasion of Belgium, and the second like the evacuation of Belgium. So that vast and silent crowd in the West looked at the British Empire, as men look at a great tower that has begun to lean. Thus it was that while I found real pleasure, I could not find unrelieved consolation in the sincere compliments paid to my country by so many cultivated Americans; their memories of homely corners of historic counties from which their fathers came, of the cathedral that dwarfs the town, or the inn at the turning of the road. There was something in their voices and the look in their eyes which from the first disturbed me. So I have heard good Englishmen, who died afterwards the death of soldiers, cry aloud in 1914, "It seems impossible, of those jolly Bavarians!" or, "I will never believe it, when I think of the time I had at Heidelberg!"

But there are other things besides the parallel of Prussia or the problem of Ireland. The American press is much freer than our own; the American public is much more familiar with the discussion of corruption than our own; and it is much more conscious of the corruption of our politics than we are. Almost any man in America may speak of the Marconi Case; many a man in England does not even know what it means. Many imagine that it had something to do with the propriety of politicians speculating on the Stock Exchange. So that it means a great deal to Americans to say that one figure in that drama is ruling India and another is ruling Palestine. And this brings me to another problem, which is also dealt with much more openly in America than in England. I mention it here only because it is a perfect model of the misunderstandings in the modern world. If any one asks for an example of exactly how the important part of every story is left out, and even the part that is reported is not understood, he could hardly have a stronger case than the story of Henry Ford of Detroit.

When I was in Detroit I had the pleasure of meeting Mr. Ford, and it really was a pleasure. He is a man quite capable of views which I think silly to the point of insanity; but he is not the vulgar benevolent boss. It must be admitted that he is a millionaire; but he cannot really be convicted of being a philanthropist. He is not a man who merely wants to run people; it is rather his views that run him, and perhaps run away with him. He has a distinguished and sensitive face; he really invented things himself, unlike most men who profit by inventions; he is something of an artist and not a little of a fighter. A man of that type is always capable of being wildly wrong, especially in the sectarian atmosphere of America; and Mr. Ford has been wrong before and may be wrong now. He is chiefly known in England for a project which I think very preposterous; that of the Peace Ship, which came to Europe during the war. But he is not known in England at all in connection with a much more important campaign, which he has conducted much more recently and with much more success; a campaign against the Jews like one of the Anti-Semitic campaigns of the Continent. Now any one who knows anything of America knows exactly what the Peace Ship would be like. It was a national combination of imagination and ignorance, which has at least some of the beauty of innocence. Men living in those huge hedgeless inland plains know nothing about frontiers or the tragedy of a fight for freedom; they know nothing of alarum and armament or the peril of a high civilization poised like a precious statue within reach of a mailed fist. They are accustomed to a cosmopolitan citizenship, in which men of all bloods mingle and in which men of all creeds are counted equal. Their highest moral boast is humanitarianism; their highest mental boast is enlightenment. In a word, they are the very last men in the world who would seem likely to pride themselves on a prejudice against the Jews. They have no religion in particular, except a sincere sentiment which they would call "true Christianity," and which specially forbids an attack on the Jews. They have a patriotism which prides itself on assimilating all types, including the Jews. Mr. Ford is a pure product of this pacific world, as was sufficiently proved by his pacifism. If a man of that sort has discovered that there is a Jewish problem, it is because there is a Jewish problem. It is certainly not because there is an Anti-Jewish prejudice. For if there had been any amount of such racial and religious prejudice, he would have been about the very last sort of man to have it. His particular part of the world would have been the very last place to produce it. We may well laugh at the Peace Ship, and its wild course and inevitable shipwreck; but remember that its very wildness was an attempt to sail as far as possible from the castle of Front-de-Bœuf. Everything that made him Anti-War should have prevented him from being Anti-Semite. We may mock him for being mad on peace; but we can not say that he was so mad on peace that he made war on Israel.

It happened that, when I was in America, I had just published some studies on Palestine; and I was besieged by Rabbis lamenting my "prejudice". I pointed out that they would have got hold of the wrong word, even if they had not got hold of the wrong man. As a point of personal autobiography, I do not happen to be a man who dislikes Jews; though I believe that some men do. I have had Jews among my most intimate and faithful friends since my boyhood, and I hope to have them till I die. But even if I did have a dislike of Jews, it would be illogical to call that dislike a prejudice. Prejudice is a very lucid Latin word meaning the bias which a man has before he considers a case. I might be said to be prejudiced against a Hairy Ainu because of his name, for I have never been on terms of such intimacy with him as to correct my preconceptions. But if after moving about in the modern world and meeting Jews, knowing Jews, doing business with Jews, and reading and hearing about Jews, I came to the conclusion that I did not like Jews, my conclusion certainly would not be a prejudice. It would simply be an opinion; and one I should be perfectly entitled to hold;

though as a matter of fact I do not hold it. No extravagance of hatred merely following on *experience* of Jews can properly be called a prejudice.

Now the point is that this new American Anti-Semitism springs from experience and nothing but experience. There is no prejudice for it to spring from. Or rather the prejudice is all the other way. All the traditions of that democracy, and very creditable traditions too, are in favour of toleration and a sort of idealistic indifference. The sympathies in which these nineteenth-century people were reared were all against Front-de-Bœuf and in favour of Rebecca. They inherited a prejudice against Anti-Semitism; a prejudice of Anti-Anti-Semitism. These people of the plains have found the Jewish problem exactly as they might have struck oil; because it is *there*, and not even because they were looking for it. Their view of the problem, like their use of the oil, is not always satisfactory; and with parts of it I entirely disagree. But the point is that the thing which I call a problem, and others call a prejudice, has now appeared in broad daylight in a new country where there is no priestcraft, no *feudalism*, no ancient superstition to explain it. It has appeared because it is a problem; and those are the best friends of the Jews, including many of the Jews themselves, who are trying to find a solution. That is the meaning of the incident of Mr. Henry Ford of Detroit; and you will hardly hear an intelligible word about it in England.

The talk of prejudice against the Japs is not unlike the talk of prejudice against the Jews. Only in this case our indifference has really the excuse of ignorance. We used to lecture the Russians for oppressing the Jews, before we heard the word Bolshevist and began to lecture them for being oppressed by the Jews. In the same way we have long lectured the Californians for oppressing the Japs, without allowing for the possibility of their foreseeing that the oppression may soon be the other way. As in the other case, it may be a persecution but it is not a prejudice. The Californians know more about the Japanese than we do; and our own colonists when they are placed in the same position generally say the same thing. I will not attempt to deal adequately here with the vast international and diplomatic problems which arise with the name of the new power in the Far East. It is possible that Japan, having imitated European militarism, may imitate European pacificism. I cannot honestly pretend to know what the Japanese mean by the one any more than by the other. But when Englishmen, especially English Liberals like myself, take a superior and censorious attitude towards Americans and especially Californians, I am moved to make a final remark. When a considerable number of Englishmen talk of the grave contending claims of our friendship with Japan and our friendship with America, when they finally tend in a sort of summing up to dwell on the superior virtues of Japan, I may be permitted to make a single comment.

We are perpetually boring the world and each other with talk about the bonds that bind us to America. We are perpetually crying aloud that England and America are very much alike, especially England. We are always insisting that the two are identical in all the things in which they most obviously differ. We are always saying that both stand for democracy, when we should not consent to stand for their democracy for half a day. We are always saying that at least we are all Anglo-Saxons, when we are descended from Romans and Normans and Britons and Danes, and they are descended from Irishmen and Italians and Slavs and Germans. We tell a people whose very existence is a revolt against the British Crown that they are passionately devoted to the British Constitution. We tell a nation whose whole policy has been isolation and independence that with us she can bear safely the White Man's Burden of the universal empire. We tell a continent crowded with Irishmen to thank God that the Saxon can always rule the Celt. We tell a populace whose very virtues are lawless that together we up hold the Reign of Law. We recognize our own law-abiding character in people who make laws that neither they nor anybody else can abide. We congratulate them on clinging to all they have cast away, and on imitating everything which they came into existence to insult. And when we have established all these nonsensical analogies with a non-existent nation, we wait until there is a crisis in which we really are at one with America, and then we falter and threaten to fail her. In a battle where we really are of one blood, the blood of the great white race throughout the world, when we really have one language, the fundamental alphabet of Cadmus and the script of Rome, when we really do represent the same reign of law, the common conscience of Christendom and the morals of men baptized, when we really have an implicit faith and honour and type of freedom to summon up our souls as with trumpets—*then* many of us begin to weaken and waver and wonder whether there is not something very nice about little yellow men, whose heroic stories revolved round polygamy and suicide, and whose heroes wore two swords and worshipped the ancestors of the Mikado.

9

Prohibition in Fact and Fancy

I went to America with some notion of not discussing Prohibition. But I soon found that well-to-do Americans were only too delighted to discuss it over the nuts and wine. They were even willing, if necessary, to dispense with the nuts. I am far from sneering at this; having a general philosophy which need not here be expounded, but which may be symbolized by saying that monkeys can enjoy nuts but only men can enjoy wine. But if I am to deal with Prohibition, there is no doubt of the first thing to be said about it. The first thing to be said about it is that it does not exist. It is to some extent enforced among the poor; at any rate it was intended to be enforced among the poor; though even among them I fancy it is much evaded. It is certainly not enforced among the rich; and I doubt whether it was intended to be. I suspect that this has always happened whenever this negative notion has taken hold of some particular province or tribe. Prohibition never prohibits. It never has in history; not even in Moslem history; and it never will. Mahomet at least had the argument of a climate and not the interest of a class. But if a test is needed, consider what part of Moslem culture has passed permanently into our own modern culture. You will find the one Moslem poem that has really pierced is a Moslem poem in praise of wine. The crown of all the victories of the Crescent is that nobody reads the Koran and everybody reads the Rubaiyat.

Most of us remember with satisfaction an old picture in *Punch*, representing a festive old gentleman in a state of collapse on the pavement, and a philanthropic old lady anxiously calling the attention of a cabman to the calamity. The old lady says, "I'm sure this poor gentleman is ill," and the cabman replies with fervour, "Ill! I wish I 'ad 'alf 'is complaint."

We talk about unconscious humour; but there is such a thing as unconscious seriousness. Flippancy is a flower whose roots are often underground in the subconsciousness. Many a man talks sense when he thinks he is talking nonsense; touches on a conflict of ideas as if it were only a contradiction of language, or really makes a parallel when he means only to make a pun. Some of the *Punch* jokes of the best period are examples of this; and that quoted above is a very strong example of it. The cabman meant what he said; but he said a great deal more than he meant. His utterance contained fine philosophical doctrines and distinctions of which he was not perhaps entirely conscious. The spirit of the English language, the tragedy and comedy of the condition of the English people, spoke through him as the god spoke through a teraph-head or brazen mask of oracle. And the oracle is an omen; and in some sense an omen of doom.

Observe, to begin with, the sobriety of the cabman. Note his measure, his moderation; or to use the yet truer term, his temperance. He only wishes to have half the old gentleman's complaint. The old gentleman is welcome to the other half, along with all the other pomps and luxuries of his superior social station. There is nothing Bolshevist or even Communist about the temperance cabman. He might almost be called Distributist, in the sense that he wishes to distribute the old gentleman's complaint more equally between the old gentleman and himself. And, of course, the social relations there represented are very much truer to life than it is fashionable to suggest. By the realism of this picture Mr. Punch made amends for some more snobbish pictures, with the opposite social moral. It will remain eternally among his real glories that he exhibited a picture in which the cabman was sober and the gentleman was drunk. Despite many ideas to the contrary, it was emphatically a picture of real life. The truth is subject to the simplest of all possible tests. If the cabman were really and truly drunk he would not be a cabman, for he could not drive a cab. If he had the whole of the old gentleman's complaint, he would be sitting happily on the pavement beside the old gentleman; a symbol of social equality found at last, and the levelling of all classes of mankind. I do not say that there has never been such a monster known as a drunken cabman; I do not say that the driver may not sometimes have approximated imprudently to three-quarters of the complaint, instead of adhering to his severe but wise conception of half of it. But I do say that most men of the world, if they spoke sincerely, could testify to more examples of helplessly drunken gentlemen put inside cabs than of helplessly drunken drivers on top of them. Philanthropists and officials, who never look at people but only at papers, probably have a mass of social statistics to the contrary; founded on the simple fact that cabmen can be cross-examined about their habits and gentlemen cannot. Social workers probably have the whole thing worked out in sections and compartments showing how the extreme intoxication of cabmen compares with the parallel intoxication of costermongers; or measuring the drunkenness of a dustman against the drunkenness of a crossing-sweeper. But there is more practical experience embodied in the practical speech of the English; and in the proverb that says "as drunk as a lord."

Now Prohibition, whether as a proposal in England or a pretence in America, simply means that the man who has drunk less shall have no drink, and the man who has drunk more shall have all the drink. It means that the old gentleman shall be carried home in a cab drunker than ever; but that, in order to make it quite safe for him to drink to excess, the man who drives him shall be forbidden to drink even in moderation. That is what it means; that is all it means; that is all it ever will mean. It tends to that in Moslem countries; where the luxurious and advanced drink champagne, while the poor and fanatical drink water. It means that in modern America; where the wealthy are all at this moment sipping their cocktails, and discussing how much harder labourers can be made to work if only they can be kept from festivity. This is what it means and all it means; and men are divided about it according to whether they believe in a certain transcendental concept called "justice", expressed in a more mystical paradox as the equality of men. So long as you do not believe in justice, and so long as you are rich and really confident of remaining so, you can have Prohibition and be as drunk as you choose.

I see that some remarks by the Rev. R. J. Campbell, dealing with social conditions in America, are reported in the press. They include some observations about Sinn Fein in which, as in most of Mr. Campbell's allusions to Ireland, it is not difficult to detect his dismal origin, or the acrid smell of the smoke of Belfast. But the remarks about America are valuable in the objective sense, over and above their philosophy. He believes that Prohibition will survive and be a success, nor does he seem himself to regard the prospect with any special disfavour. But he frankly and freely testifies to the truth I have asserted; that Prohibition does not prohibit, so far as the wealthy are concerned. He testifies to constantly seeing wine on the table, as will any other grateful guest of the generous hospitality of America; and he implies humorously that he asked no questions about the story told him of the old stocks in the cellars. So there is no dispute about the facts; and we come back as before to the principles. Is Mr. Campbell content with a Prohibition which is another name for Privilege? If so, he has simply absorbed along with his new theology a new morality which is different from mine.

But he does state both sides of the inequality with equal logic and clearness; and in these days of intellectual fog that alone is like a ray of sunshine.

Now my primary objection to Prohibition is not based on any arguments against it, but on the one argument for it. I need nothing more for its condemnation than the only thing that is said in its defence. It is said by capitalists all over America; and it is very clearly and correctly reported by Mr. Campbell himself. The argument is that employees work harder, and therefore employers get richer. That this idea should be taken calmly, by itself, as the test or a problem of liberty, is in itself a final testimony to the presence of slavery. It shows that people have completely forgotten that there is any other test except the servile test. Employers are willing that workmen should have exercise, as it may help them to do more work. They are even willing that workmen should have leisure; for the more intelligent capitalists can see that this also really means that they can do more work. But they are not in any way willing that workmen should have fun; for fun only increases the happiness and not the utility of the worker. Fun is freedom; and in that sense is an end in itself. It concerns the man not as a worker but as a citizen, or even as a soul; and the soul in that sense is an end in itself. That a man shall have a reasonable amount of comedy and poetry and even fantasy in his life is part of his spiritual health, which is for the service of God; and not merely for his mechanical health, which is now bound to the service of man. The very test adopted has all the servile implication; the test of what we can get out of him, instead of the test of what he can get out of life.

Mr. Campbell is reported to have suggested, doubtless rather as a conjecture than a prophecy, that England may find it necessary to become teetotal in order to compete commercially with the efficiency and economy of teetotal America. Well, in the eighteenth and early nineteenth centuries there was in America one of the most economical and efficient of all forms of labour. It did not happen to be feasible for the English to compete with it by copying it. There were so many humanitarian prejudices about in those days. But economically there seems to be no reason why a man should not have prophesied that England would be forced to adopt American Slavery then, as she is urged to adopt American Prohibition now. Perhaps such a prophet would have prophesied rightly. Certainly it is not impossible that universal Slavery might have been the vision of Calhoun as universal Prohibition seems to be the vision of Campbell. The old England of 1830 would have said that such a plea for slavery was monstrous; but what would it have said of a plea for enforced water-drinking? Nevertheless, the nobler Servile State of Calhoun collapsed before it could spread to Europe. And there is always the hope that the same may happen to the far more materialistic Utopia of Mr. Campbell and Soft Drinks.

Abstract morality is very important; and it may well clear the mind to consider what would be the effect of Prohibition in America, if it were introduced there. It would, of course, be a decisive departure from the tradition of the Declaration of Independence. Those who deny that are hardly serious enough to demand attention. It is enough to say that they are reduced to minimizing that document in defence of Prohibition, exactly as the slave-owners were reduced to minimizing it in defence of Slavery. They are reduced to saying that the Fathers of the Republic meant no more than that they would not be ruled by a king. And they are obviously open to the reply which Lincoln gave to Douglas on the slavery question; that if that great charter was limited to certain events in the eighteenth century, it was hardly worth making such a fuss about in the nineteenth—or in the twentieth. But they are also open to another reply which is even more to the point, when they pretend that Jefferson's famous preamble only means to say that monarchy is wrong. They are maintaining that Jefferson only meant to say something that he does not say at all. The great preamble does not say that all monarchical government must be wrong; on the contrary, it rather implies that most government is right. It speaks of human governments in general as justified by the necessity of defending certain personal rights. I see no reason whatever to suppose that it would not include any royal government that does defend those rights. Still less do I doubt what it would say of a republican government that does destroy those rights.

But what are those rights? Sophists can always debate about their degree; but even sophists cannot debate about their direction. Nobody in his five wits will deny that Jeffersonian democracy wished to give the law a general control in more public things, but the citizens a more general liberty in private things. Wherever we draw the line, liberty can only be personal liberty; and the most personal liberties must at least be the last liberties we lose. But to-day they are the first liberties we lose. It is not a question of drawing the line in the right place, but of beginning at the wrong end. What are the rights of man, if they do not include the normal right to regulate his own health, in relation to the normal risks of diet and daily life? Nobody can pretend that beer is a poison as prussic acid is a poison; that all the millions of civilized men who drank it all fell down dead when they had touched it. Its use and abuse is obviously a matter of judgment; and there can be no personal liberty, if it is not a matter of private judgment. It is not in the least a question of drawing the line between liberty and licence. If this is licence, there is no such thing as liberty. It is plainly impossible to find any right more individual or intimate. To say that a man has a right to a vote, but not a right to a voice about the choice of his dinner, is like saying that he has a right to his hat but not a right to his head.

Prohibition, therefore, plainly violates the rights of man, if there are any rights of man. What its supporters really mean is that there are none. And in suggesting this, they have all the advantages that every sceptic has when he supports a negation. That sort of ultimate scepticism can only be retorted upon itself, and we can point out to them that they can no more prove the right of the city to be oppressive than we can prove the right of the citizen to be free. In the primary metaphysics of such a claim, it would surely be easier to make it out for a single conscious soul than for an artificial social combination. If there are no rights of men, what are the rights of nations? Perhaps a nation has no claim to self-government. Perhaps it has no claim to good government. Perhaps it has no claim to any sort of government or any sort of independence. Perhaps they will say *that* is not implied in the Declaration of Independence. But without going deep into my reasons for believing in natural rights, or rather in supernatural rights (and Jefferson certainly states them as supernatural), I am content here to note that a man's treatment of his own body in relation to tradition and ordinary opportunities for bodily excess, is as near to his self-respect as social coercion can possibly go; and that when that is gone there is nothing left. If coercion applies to that, it applies to everything; and in the future of this controversy it obviously will apply to everything. When I was in America, people were already applying it to tobacco. I never can see why they should not apply it to talking. Talking often goes with tobacco as it goes with beer; and what is more relevant, talking may often lead both to beer and tobacco. Talking often drives a man to drink, both negatively in the form of nagging and positively in the form of bad company. If the American Puritan is so anxious to be a *censor morum*, he should obviously put a stop to the evil communications that really corrupt good manners. He should reintroduce the Scold's Bridle among the other Blue Laws for a land of blue devils. He should gag all gay deceivers and plausible cynics; he should cut off all flattering lips and the tongue that speaketh proud things. Nobody can doubt that nine-tenths of the harm in the world is done simply by talking. Jefferson and the old democrats allowed people to talk, not because they were unaware of this fact, but because they were fettered by this old fancy of theirs about freedom and the rights of man. But since we have already abandoned that doctrine in a final fashion, I cannot see why the new principle should not be applied intelligently; and in that case it would be applied to the control of conversation. The State would provide us with forms already filled up with the subjects suitable for us to discuss at breakfast; perhaps allowing us a limited number of epigrams each. Perhaps we should have to make a formal application in writing, to be allowed to make a joke that had just occurred to us in conversation. And the committee would consider it in due course. Perhaps it would be effected in a more practical fashion, and the private citizens would be shut up as the public-houses were shut up. Perhaps they would all wear gags, which the policeman would remove at stated hours; and their mouths would be opened from one to three, as now in England even the public-houses are from time to time accessible to the public. To some this will sound fantastic; but not so fantastic as Jefferson would have thought Prohibition. But there is one sense in which it is indeed fantastic, for by hypothesis it leaves out the favouritism that is the fundamental of the whole matter. The only sense in which we can say that logic will never go so far as this is that logic will never go the length of equality. It is perfectly possible that the same forces that have forbidden beer may go on to forbid tobacco. But they will in a special and limited sense forbid tobacco—but not cigars. Or at any rate not expensive cigars. In America, where large numbers of ordinary men smoke rather ordinary cigars, there would be doubtless a good opportunity of penalizing a very ordinary pleasure. But the Havanas of the millionaire will be all right. So it will be if ever the Puritans bring back the Scold's Bridle and the statutory silence of the populace. It will only be the populace that is silent. The politicians will go on talking.

These I believe to be the broad facts of the problem of Prohibition; but it would not be fair to leave it without mentioning two other causes which, if not defences, are at least excuses. The first is that Prohibition was largely passed in a sort of fervour or fever of self-sacrifice, which was a part of the passionate patriotism of America in the war. As I have remarked elsewhere, those who have any notion of what that national unanimity was like will smile when they see America made a model of mere international idealism. Prohibition was partly a sort of patriotic renunciation; for the popular instinct, like every poetic instinct, always tends at great crises to great gestures of renunciation. But this very fact, while it makes the inhumanity far more human, makes it far less final and convincing. Men cannot remain standing stiffly in such symbolical attitudes; nor can a permanent policy be founded on something analogous to flinging a gauntlet or uttering a battle-cry. We might as well expect all the Yale students to remain through life with their mouths open, exactly as they were when they uttered the college yell. It would be as reasonable as to expect them to remain through life with their mouths shut while the wine-cup which has been the sacrament of all poets and lovers passed round among all the youth of the world. This point appeared very plainly in a discussion I had with a very thoughtful and sympathetic American critic, a clergyman writing in an Anglo-Catholic magazine. He put the sentiment of these healthier Prohibitionists, which had so much to do with the passing of Prohibition, by asking: "May not a man who is asked to give up his blood for his country be asked to give up his beer for his country?" And this phrase clearly illuminates all the limitations of the case. I have never denied, in principle, that it might in some abnormal crisis be lawful for a government to lock up the beer, or to lock up the bread. In that sense I am quite prepared to treat the sacrifice of beer in the same way as the sacrifice of blood. But is my American critic really ready to treat the sacrifice of blood in the same way as the sacrifice of beer? Is bloodshed to be as prolonged and protracted as Prohibition? Is the normal non-combatant to shed his gore as often as he misses his drink? I can imagine people submitting to a special regulation, as I can imagine them serving in a particular war. I do indeed despise the political knavery that deliberately passes drink regulations as war measures and then preserves them as peace measures. But that is not a question of whether drink and drunkenness are wrong, but of whether lying and swindling are wrong. But I never denied that there might need to be exceptional sacrifices for exceptional occasions; and war is in its nature an exception. Only, if war is the exception, why should Prohibition be the rule? If the surrender of beer is worthy to be compared to the shedding of blood, why then blood ought to be flowing for ever like a fountain in the public squares of Philadelphia and New York. If my critic wants to complete his parallel, he must draw up rather a remarkable programme for the daily life of the ordinary citizens. He must suppose that, through all their lives, they are paraded every day at lunch time and prodded with bayonets to show that they will shed their blood for their country. He must suppose that every evening, after a light repast of poison gas and shrapnel, they are made to go to sleep in a trench under a permanent drizzle of shell-fire. It is surely obvious that if this were the normal life of the citizen, the citizen would have no normal life. The common sense of the thing is that sacrifices of this sort are admirable but abnormal. It is not normal for the State to be perpetually regulating our days with the discipline of a fighting regiment; and it is not normal for the State to be perpetually regulating our diet with the discipline of a famine. To say that every citizen must be subject to control in such bodily things is like saying that every Christian ought to tear himself with red-hot pincers because the Christian Martyrs did their duty in time of persecution. A man has a right to control his body, though in a time of martyrdom he may give his body to be burned; and a man has a right to control his bodily health, though in a state of siege he may give his body to be starved. Thus, though the patriotic defence was a sincere defence, it is a defence that comes back on the defenders like a boomerang. For it proves only that Prohibition ought to be ephemeral, unless war ought to be eternal.

The other excuse is much less romantic and much more realistic. I have already said enough of the cause which is really realistic. The real power behind Prohibition is simply the plutocratic power of the pushing employers who wish to get the last inch of work out of their workmen. But before the progress of modern plutocracy had reached this stage, there was a predetermining cause for which there was a much better case. The whole business began with the problem of black labour. I have not attempted in this book to deal adequately with the question of the negro. I have refrained for a reason that may seem somewhat sensational; that I do not think I have anything particularly valuable to say or suggest. I do not profess to understand this singularly dark and intricate matter; and I see no use in men who have no solution filling up the gap with sentimentalism. The chief thing that struck me about the coloured people I saw was their charming and astonishing cheerfulness. My sense of pathos was appealed to much more by the Red Indians; and indeed I wish I had more space here to do justice to the Red Indians. They did heroic service in the war; and more than justified their glorious place in the day-dreams and nightmares of our boyhood. But the negro problem certainly demands more study than a sight-seer could give it; and this book is controversial enough about things that I have really considered, without permitting it to exhibit me as a sight-seer who shoots at sight. But I believe that it was always common ground to people of commonsense that the enslavement and importation of negroes had been the crime and catastrophe of American history. The only difference was originally that one side thought that the crime once committed, the only reparation was their freedom; while the other thought that, the crime once committed, the only safety was their slavery. It was only comparatively lately, by a process I shall have to indicate elsewhere, that anything like a positive case for slavery became possible. Now among the many problems of the presence of an alien and at least recently barbaric figure among the citizens, there was a very real problem of drink. Drink certainly has a very exceptionally destructive effect upon negroes in their native countries; and it was alleged to have a peculiarly demoralizing effect upon negroes in the United States; to call up the passions that are the particular temptation of the race and to lead to appalling outrages that are followed by appalling popular vengeance. However this may be, many of the states of the American Union, which first forbade liquor to citizens, meant simply to forbid it to negroes. But they had not the moral courage to deny that negroes are citizens. About all their political expedients necessarily hung the load that hangs so heavy on modern politics; hypocrisy. The superior race had to rule by a sort of secret society organized against the inferior. The American politicians dared not disfranchise the negroes; so they coerced everybody in theory and only the negroes in practice. The drinking of the white men became as much a conspiracy as the shooting by the white horsemen of the Ku-Klux Klan. And in that connection, it may be remarked in passing that the comparison illustrates the idiocy of supposing that the moral sense of mankind will ever support the prohibition of drinking as if it were something like the prohibition of shooting. Shooting in America is liable to take a free form, and sometimes a very horrible form; as when private bravos were hired to kill workmen in the capitalistic interests of that pure patron of disarmament, Carnegie. But when some of the rich Americans gravely tell us that their drinking cannot be interfered with, because they are only using up their existing stocks of wine, we may well be disposed to smile. When I was there, at any rate, they were using them up very fast; and with no apparent fears about the supply. But if the Ku-Klux Klan had started suddenly shooting everybody they didn't like in broad daylight, and had blandly explained that they were only using up the stocks of their ammunition, left over from the Civil War, it seems probable that there would at least have been a little curiosity about how much they had left. There might at least have been occasional inquiries about how long it was likely to go on. It is even conceivable that some steps might have been taken to stop it.

No steps are taken to stop the drinking of the rich, chiefly because the rich now make all the rules and therefore all the exceptions, but partly because nobody ever could feel the full moral seriousness of this particular rule. And the truth is, as I have indicated, that it was originally established as an exception and not as a rule. The emancipated negro was an exception in the community, and a certain plan was, rightly or wrongly, adopted to meet his case. A law was made professedly for everybody and practically only for him. Prohibition is only important as marking the transition by which the trick, tried successfully on black labour could be extended to all labour. We in England have no right to be Pharisaic at the expense of the Americans in this matter; for we have tried the same trick in a hundred forms. The true philosophical defence of the modern oppression of the poor would be to say frankly that we have ruled them so badly that they are unfit to rule themselves. But no modern oligarch is enough of a man to say this. For like all virile cynicism it would have an element of humility; which would not mix with the necessary element of hypocrisy. So we proceed, just as the Americans do, to make a law for everybody and then evade it for ourselves. We have not the honesty to say that the rich may bet because they can afford it; so we forbid any man to bet in any place; and then say that a place is not a place. It is exactly as if there were an American law allowing a negro to be murdered because he is not a man within the meaning of the Act. We have not the honesty to drive the poor to school because they are ignorant; so we pretend to drive everybody; and then send inspectors to the slums but not to the smart streets. We apply the same ingenuous principle; and are quite as undemocratic as Western democracy. Nevertheless there is an element in the American case which cannot be present in ours; and this chapter may well conclude upon so important a change.

America can now say with pride that she has abolished the colour bar. In this matter the white labourer and the black labourer have at last been put upon an equal social footing. White labour is every bit as much enslaved as black labour; and is actually enslaved by a method and a model only intended for black labour. We might think it rather odd if the exact regulations about flogging negroes were reproduced as a plan for punishing strikers; or if industrial arbitration issued its reports in the precise terminology of the Fugitive Slave Law. But this is in essentials what has happened; and one could almost fancy some negro orgy of triumph, with the beating of gongs and all the secret violence of Voodoo, crying aloud to some ancestral Mumbo Jumbo that the Poor White Trash was being treated according to its name.

10

Fads and Public Opinion

A foreigner is a man who laughs at everything except jokes. He is perfectly entitled to laugh at anything, so long as he realizes, in a reverent and religious spirit, that he himself is laughable. I was a foreigner in America; and I can truly claim that the sense of my own laughable position never left me. But when the native and the foreigner have finished with seeing the fun of each other in things that are meant to be serious, they both approach the far more delicate and dangerous ground of things that are meant to be funny. The sense of humour is generally very national; perhaps that is why the internationalists are so careful to purge themselves of it. I had occasion during the war to consider the rights and wrongs of certain differences alleged to have arisen between the English and American soldiers at the front. And, rightly or wrongly, I came to the conclusion that they arose from the failure to understand when a foreigner is serious and when he is humorous. And it is in the very nature of the best sort of joke to be the worst sort of insult if it is not taken as a joke.

The English and the American types of humour are in one way directly contrary. The most American sort of fun involves a soaring imagination, piling one house on another in a tower like that of a skyscraper. The most English humour consists of a sort of bathos, of a man returning to the earth his mother in a homely fashion; as when he sits down suddenly on a butter-slide. English farce describes a man as being in a hole. American fantasy, in its more aspiring spirit, describes a man as being up a tree. The former is to be found in the cockney comic songs that concern themselves with hanging out the washing or coming home with the milk. The latter is to be found in those fantastic yarns about machines that turn live pigs into pig-skin purses or burning cities that serve to hatch an egg. But it will be inevitable, when the two come first into contact, that the bathos will sound like vulgarity and the extravagance will sound like boasting.

Suppose an American soldier said to an English soldier in the trenches, "The Kaiser may want a place in the sun; I reckon he won't have a place in the solar system when we begin to hustle". The English soldier will very probably form the impression that this is arrogance; an impression based on the extraordinary assumption that the American means what he says. The American has merely indulged in a little art for art's sake, and abstract adventure of the imagination; he has told an American short story. But the Englishman, not understanding this, will think the other man is boasting, and reflecting on the insufficiency of the English effort. The English soldier is very likely to say something like, "Oh, you'll be wanting to get home to your old woman before that, and asking for a kipper with your tea." And it is quite likely that the American will be offended in his turn at having his arabesque of abstract beauty answered in so personal a fashion. Being an American, he will probably have a fine and chivalrous respect for his wife; and may object to her being called an old woman. Possibly he in turn may be under the extraordinary delusion that talking of the old woman really means that the woman is old. Possibly he thinks the mysterious demand for a kipper carries with it some charge of ill-treating his wife; which his national sense of honour swiftly resents. But the real cross-purposes come from the contrary direction of the two exaggerations, the American making life more wild and impossible than it is, and the Englishman making it more flat and farcical than it is; the one escaping the house of life by a skylight and the other by a trap-door.

This difficulty of different humours is a very practical one for practical people. Most of those who profess to remove all international differences are not practical people. Most of the phrases offered for the reconciliation of severally patriotic peoples are entirely serious and even solemn phrases. But human conversation is not conducted in those phrases. The normal man on nine occasions out of ten is rather a flippant man. And the normal man is almost always the national man. Patriotism is the most popular of all the virtues. The drier sort of democrats who despise it have the democracy against them in every country in the world. Hence their international efforts seldom go any farther than to effect an international reconciliation of all internationalists. But we have not solved the normal and popular problem until we have an international reconciliation of all nationalists.

It is very difficult to see how humour can be translated at all. When Sam Weller is in the Fleet Prison and Mrs. Weller and Mr. Stiggins sit on each side of the fireplace and weep and groan with sympathy, old Mr. Weller observes, "Veil, Sammy, I hope you find your spirits rose by this 'ere lively visit." I have never looked up this passage in the popular and successful French version of *Pickwick*; but I confess I am curious as to what French past-participle conveys the precise effect of the word "rose." A translator has not only to give the right translation of the right word but the right translation of the wrong word. And in the same way I am quite prepared to suspect that there are English jokes which an Englishman must enjoy in his own rich and romantic solitude, without asking for the sympathy of an American. But Englishmen are generally only too prone to claim this fine perception, without seeing that the fine edge of it cuts both ways. I have begun this chapter on the note of national humour because I wish to make it quite clear that I realize how easily a foreigner may take something seriously that is not serious. When I think something in America is really foolish, it may be I that am made a fool of. It is the first duty of a traveller to allow for this; but it seems to be the very last thing that occurs to some travellers. But when I seek to say something of what may be called the fantastic side of America, I allow beforehand that some of it may be meant to be fantastic. And indeed it is very difficult to believe that some of it is meant to be serious. But whether or no there is a joke, there is certainly an inconsistency, and it is an inconsistency in the moral make-up of America which both puzzles and amuses me.

The danger of democracy is not anarchy but convention. There is even a sort of double meaning in the word "convention"; for it is also used for the most informal and popular sort of parliament; a parliament not summoned by any king. The Americans come together very easily without any king; but their coming together is in every sense a convention, and even a very conventional convention. In a democracy riot is rather the exception and respectability certainly the rule. And though a superficial sight-seer should hesitate about all such generalizations, and certainly should allow for enormous exceptions to them, he does receive a general impression of unity verging on uniformity. Thus Americans all dress well; one might almost say that American women all look well; but they do not, as compared with Europeans, look very different. They are in the fashion; too much in the fashion even to be conspicuously fashionable. Of course there are patches, both Bohemian and Babylonian, of which this is not true, but I am talking of the general tone of a whole democracy. I have said there is more respectability than riot; but indeed in a deeper sense the same spirit is behind both riot and respectability. It is the same social force that makes it possible for the respectable to boycott a man and for the riotous to lynch him. I do not object to it being called "the herd instinct," so long as we realize that it is a metaphor and not an explanation.

Public opinion can be a prairie fire. It eats up everything that opposes it; and there is the grandeur as well as the grave disadvantages of a natural catastrophe in that national unity. Pacifists who complained in England of the intolerance of patriotism have no notion of what patriotism can be like. If they had been in America, after America had entered the war, they would have seen something which they would have always perhaps subconsciously dreaded, and would then have beyond all their worse dreams detested; and the name of it is democracy. They would have found that there are disadvantages in birds of a feather flocking together; and that one of them follows on a too complacent display of the white feather. The truth is that a certain flexible sympathy with eccentrics of this kind is rather one of the advantages of an aristocratic tradition. The imprisonment of Mr. Debs, the American Pacifist, which really was prolonged and oppressive, would probably have been shortened in England where his opinions were shared by aristocrats like Mr. Bertrand Russell and Mr. Ponsonby. A man like Lord Hugh Cecil could be moved to the defence of conscientious objectors, partly by a true instinct of chivalry; but partly also by the general feeling that a gentleman may very probably have aunts and uncles who are quite as mad. He takes the matter personally, in the sense of being able to imagine the psychology of the persons. But democracy is no respecter of persons. It is no respecter of them, either in the bad and servile or in the good and sympathetic sense. And Debs was nothing to democracy. He was but one of the millions. This is a real problem, or question in the balance, touching different forms of government; which is of course, quite neglected by the idealists who merely repeat long words. There was during the war a society called the Union of Democratic Control, which would have been instantly destroyed anywhere where democracy had any control, or where there was any union. And in this sense the United States have most emphatically got a union. Nevertheless I think there is something rather more subtle than this simple popular solidity behind the assimilation of American citizens to each other. There is something even in the individual ideals that drives towards this social sympathy. And it is here that we have to remember that biological fancies like the herd instinct are only figures of speech, and cannot really cover anything human. For the Americans are in some ways a very self-conscious people. To compare their social enthusiasm to a stampede of cattle is to ask us to believe in a bull writing a diary or a cow looking in a looking-glass. Intensely sensitive by their very vitality, they are certainly conscious of criticism and not merely of a blind and brutal appetite. But the peculiar point about them is that it is this very vividness in the self that often produces the similarity. It may be that when they are unconscious they are like bulls and cows. But it is when they are self-conscious that they are like each other.

Individualism is the death of individuality. It is so, if only because it is an "ism." Many Americans become almost impersonal in their worship of personality. Where their natural selves might differ, their ideal selves tend to be the same. Anybody can see what I mean in those strong self-conscious photographs of American business men that can be seen in any American magazine. Each may conceive himself to be a solitary Napoleon brooding at St. Helena; but the result is a multitude of Napoleons brooding all over the place. Each of them must have the eyes of a mesmerist; but the most weak-minded person cannot be mesmerized by more than one millionaire at a time. Each of the millionaires must thrust forward his jaw, offering (if I may say so) to fight the world with the same weapon as Samson. Each of them must accentuate the length of his chin, especially, of course, by always being completely clean-shaven. It would be obviously inconsistent with Personality to prefer to wear a beard. These are of course fantastic examples on the fringe of American life; but they do stand for a certain assimilation, not through brute gregariousness, but rather through isolated dreaming. And though it is not always carried so far as this, I do think it is carried too far. There is not quite enough unconsciousness to produce real individuality. There is a sort of worship of will-power in the abstract so that people are actually thinking about how they can will, more than about what they want. To this I do think a certain corrective could be found in the nature of English eccentricity. Every man in his humour is most interesting when he is unconscious of his humour; or at least when he is in an intermediate stage between humour in the old sense of oddity and in the new sense of irony. Much is said in these days against negative morality; and certainly most Americans would show a positive preference for positive morality. The virtues they venerate collectively are very active virtues; cheerfulness and courage and vim, otherwise zip, also pep and similar things. But it is sometimes forgotten that negative morality is freer than positive morality. Negative morality is a net of a larger and more open pattern, of which the lines or cords constrict at longer intervals. A man like Dr. Johnson could grow in his own way to his own stature in the net of the Ten Commandments; precisely because he was convinced there were only ten of them. He was not compressed into the mould of positive beauty, like that of the Apollo Belvedere or the American citizen.

This criticism is sometimes true even of the American woman, who is certainly a much more delightful person than the mesmeric millionaire with his shaven jaw. Interviewers in the United States perpetually asked me what I thought of American women, and I confessed a distaste for such generalizations which I have not managed to lose. The Americans, who are the most chivalrous people in the world, may perhaps understand me; but I can never help feeling that there is something polygamous about talking of women in the plural at all; something unworthy of any American except a Mormon. Nevertheless, I think the exaggeration I suggest does extend in a less degree to American women fascinating as they are. I think they too tend too much to this cult of impersonal personality. It is a description easy to exaggerate even by the faintest emphasis; for all these things are subtle and subject to striking individual exceptions. To complain of people for being brave and bright and kind and intelligent may not unreasonably appear unreasonable. And yet there is something in the background that can only be expressed by a symbol, something that is not shallowness but a neglect of the subconsciousness and the vaguer and slower impulses; something that can be missed amid all that laughter and light, under those starry candelabra of the ideals of the happy virtues. Sometimes it came over me, in a wordless wave, that I should like to see a sulky woman. How she would walk in beauty like the night, and reveal more silent spaces full of older stars! These things can not be conveyed in their delicate proportion even in the most detached description. But the same thing was in the mind of a white-bearded old man I met in New York, an Irish exile and a wonderful talker, who stared up at the tower of gilded galleries of the great hotel, and said with that spontaneous movement of style which is hardly heard except from Irish talkers: "And I have been in a village in the mountains where the people could hardly read or write; but all the men were like soldiers, and all the women had pride."

It sounds like a poem about an Earthly Paradise to say that in this land the old women can be more beautiful than the young. Indeed, I think Walt Whitman, the national poet, has a line somewhere almost precisely to that effect. It sounds like a parody upon Utopia, and the image of the lion lying down with the lamb, to say it is a place where a man might almost fall in love with his mother-in-law. But there is nothing in which the finer side of American gravity and good feeling does more honourably exhibit itself than in a certain atmosphere around the older women. It is not a cant phrase to say that they grow old gracefully; for they do really grow old gracefully; for they do really grow old. In this the national optimism really has in it the national courage. The old women do not dress like young women; they only dress better. There is another side to this feminine dignity in the old, sometimes a little lost in the young, with which I shall deal presently. The point for the moment is that even Whitman's truly poetic vision of the beautiful old women suffers a little from that bewildering multiplicity and recurrence that is indeed the whole theme of Whitman. It is like the green eternity of "Leaves of Grass." When I think of the eccentric spinsters and incorrigible grandmothers of my own country, I cannot imagine that any one of them could possibly be mistaken for another, even at a glance. And in comparison I feel as if I had been travelling in an Earthly Paradise of more decorative harmonies; and I remember only a vast cloud of grey and pink as of the plumage of cherubim in an old picture. But on second thoughts, I think this may be only the inevitable effect of visiting any country in a swift and superficial fashion; and that the grey and pink cloud is probably an illusion, like the spinning prairies scattered by the wheel of the train.

Anyhow there is enough of this equality, and of a certain social unity favourable to sanity, to make the next point about America very much of a puzzle. It seems to me a very real problem, to which I have never seen an answer even such as I shall attempt here, why a democracy should produce fads; and why, where there is so genuine a sense of human dignity, there should be so much of an impossible petty tyranny. I am not referring solely or even specially to Prohibition, which I discuss elsewhere. Prohibition is at least a superstition, and therefore next door to a religion; it has some imaginable connection with moral questions, as have slavery or human sacrifice. But those who ask us to model ourselves on the States which punish the sin of drink forget that there are States which punish the equally shameless sin of smoking a cigarette in the open air. The same American atmosphere that permits Prohibition permits of people being punished for kissing each other. In other words, there are States psychologically capable of making a man a convict for wearing a blue neck-tie or having a green front-door, or anything else that anybody chooses to fancy. There is an American atmosphere in which people may some day be shot for shaking hands, or hanged for writing a post-card.

As for the sort of thing to which I refer, the American newspapers are full of it and there is no name for it but mere madness. Indeed it is not only mad, but it calls itself mad. To mention but one example out of many, it was actually boasted that some lunatics were teaching children to take care of their health. And it was proudly added that the children were "health-mad." That it is not exactly the object of all mental hygiene to make people mad did not occur to them; and they may still be engaged in their earnest labours to teach babies to be valetudinarians and hypochondriacs in order to make them healthy. In such cases, we may say that the modern world is too ridiculous to be ridiculed. You cannot caricature a caricature. Imagine what a satirist of saner days would have made of the daily life of a child of six, who was actually admitted to be mad on the subject of his own health. These are not days in which that great extravaganza could be written; but I dimly see some of its episodes like uncompleted dreams. I see the child pausing in the middle of a cart-wheel, or when he has performed three-quarters of a cart-wheel, and consulting a little note-book about the amount of exercise per diem. I see him pausing half-way up a tree, or when he has climbed exactly one-third of a tree; and then producing a clinical thermometer to take his own temperature. But what would be the good of imaginative logic to prove the madness of such people, when they themselves praise it for being mad?

There is also the cult of the Infant Phenomenon, of which Dickens made fun and of which educationalists make fusses. When I was in America another newspaper produced a marvellous child of six who had the intellect of a child of twelve. The only test given, and apparently one on which the experiment turned, was that she could be made to understand and even to employ the word "annihilate." When asked to say something proving this, the happy infant offered the polished aphorism, "When common sense comes in, superstition is annihilated." In reply to which, by way of showing that I also am as intelligent as a child of twelve, and there is no arrested development about me, I will say in the same elegant diction, "When psychological education comes in, common sense is annihilated." Everybody seems to be sitting round this child in an adoring fashion. It did not seem to occur to anybody that we do not particularly want even a child of twelve to talk about annihilating superstition; that we do not want a child of six to talk like a child of twelve, or a child of twelve to talk like a man of fifty, or even a man of fifty to talk like a fool. And on the principle of hoping that a little girl of six will have a massive and mature brain, there is every reason for hoping that a little boy of six will grow a magnificent and bushy beard.

Now there is any amount of this nonsense cropping up among American cranks. Anybody may propose to establish coercive Eugenics; or enforce psychoanalysis—that is, enforce confession without absolution. And I confess I cannot connect this feature with the genuine democratic spirit of the mass. I can only suggest, in concluding this chapter, two possible causes rather peculiar to America, which may have made this great democracy so unlike all other democracies, and in this so manifestly hostile to the whole democratic idea.

The first historical cause is Puritanism; but not Puritanism merely in the sense of Prohibitionism. The truth is that prohibitions might have done far less harm as prohibitions, if a vague association had not arisen, on some dark day of human unreason, between prohibition and progress. And it was the progress that did the harm, not the prohibition. Men can enjoy life under considerable limitations, if they can be sure of their limited enjoyments; but under Progressive Puritanism we can never be sure of anything. The curse of it is not limitation; it is unlimited limitation. The evil is not in the restriction; but in the fact that nothing can ever restrict the restriction. The prohibitions are bound to progress point by point; more and more human rights and pleasures must of necessity be taken away; for it is of the nature of this futurism that the latest fad is the faith of the future, and the most fantastic fad inevitably makes the pace. Thus the worst thing in the seventeenth-century aberration was not so much Puritanism as sectarianism. It searched for truth not by synthesis but by subdivision. It not only broke religion into small pieces, but it was bound to choose the smallest piece. There is in America, I believe, a large religious body that has felt it right to separate itself from Christendom, because it cannot believe in the morality of wearing buttons. I do not know how the schism arose; but it is easy to suppose, for the sake of argument, that there had originally existed some Puritan body which condemned the frivolity of ribbons though not of buttons, I was going to say of badges but not buttons; but on reflection I cannot bring myself to believe that any American however insane, would object to wearing badges. But the point is that as the holy spirit of progressive prophesy rested on the first sect because it had invented a new objection to ribbons, so that holy spirit would then pass from it to the new sect who invented a further objection to buttons. And from them it must inevitably pass to any rebel among them who shall choose to rise and say that he disapproves of trousers because of the existence of trouser-buttons. Each secession in turn must be right because it is recent, and progress must progress by growing smaller and smaller. That is the progressive theory, the legacy of seventeenth-century sectarianism, the dogma implied in much modern politics, and the evident enemy of democracy. Democracy is reproached with saying that the majority is always right. But progress says that the minority is always right. Progressives are prophets; and fortunately not all the people are prophets. Thus in the atmosphere of this slowly dying sectarianism anybody who chooses to prophesy and prohibit can tyrannize over the people. If he chooses to say that drinking is always wrong, or that kissing is always wrong, or that wearing buttons is always wrong, people are afraid to contradict him for fear they should be contradicting their own great-grandchild. For their superstition is an inversion of the ancestor-worship of China; and instead of vainly appealing to something that is dead, they appeal to something that may never be born.

There is another cause of this strange servile disease in American democracy. It is to be found in American feminism, and feminist America is an entirely different thing from feminine America. I should say that the overwhelming majority of American girls laugh at their female politicians at least as much as the majority of American men despise their male politicians. But though the aggressive feminists are a minority, they are in this atmosphere which I have tried to analyse;

the atmosphere in which there is a sort of sanctity about the minority. And it is this superstition of seriousness that constitutes the most solid obstacle and exception to the general and almost conventional pressure of public opinion. When a fad is frankly felt to be anti-national, as was Abolitionism before the Civil War, or Pro-Germanism in the Great War, or the suggestion of racial admixture in the South at all times, then the fad meets far less mercy than anywhere else in the world; it is snowed under and swept away. But when it does not thus directly challenge patriotism or popular ideas, a curious halo of hopeful solemnity surrounds it, merely because it is a fad, but above all if it is a feminine fad. The earnest lady-reformer who really utters a warning against the social evil of beer or buttons is seen to be walking clothed in light, like a prophetess. Perhaps it is something of the holy aureole which the East sees shining around an idiot.

But I think there is another explanation, feminine rather than feminist, and proceeding from normal women and not from abnormal idiots. It is something that involves an old controversy, but one upon which I have not, like so many politicians, changed my opinion. It concerns the particular fashion in which women tend to regard, or rather to disregard, the formal and legal rights of the citizen. In so far as this is a bias, it is a bias in the directly opposite direction from that now lightly alleged. There is a sort of underbred history going about, according to which women in the past have always been in the position of slaves. It is much more to the point to note that women have always been in the position of despots. They have been despotic, because they ruled in an area where they had too much common sense to attempt to be constitutional. You cannot grant a constitution to a nursery; nor can babies assemble like barons and extort a Great Charter. Tommy cannot plead a Habeas Corpus against going to bed; and an infant cannot be tried by twelve other infants before he is put in the corner. And as there can be no laws or liberties in a nursery, the extension of feminism means that there shall be no more laws or liberties in a state than there are in a nursery. The woman does not really regard men as citizens but as children. She may, if she is a humanitarian, love all mankind; but she does not respect it. Still less does she respect its votes. Now a man must be very blind nowadays not to see that there is a danger of a sort of amateur science or pseudo-science being made the excuse for every trick of tyranny and interference. Anybody who is not an anarchist agrees with having a policeman at the corner of the street; but the danger at present is that of finding the policeman half-way down the chimney or even under the bed. In other words, it is a danger of turning the policeman into a sort of benevolent burglar. Against this protests are already being made, and will increasingly be made, if men retain any instinct of independence or dignity at all. But to complain of the woman interfering in the home will always sound like the complaining of the oyster intruding into the oyster-shell. To object that she has too much power over education will seem like objecting to a hen having too much to do with eggs. She has already been given an almost irresponsible power over a limited region in these things; and if that power is made infinite it will be even more irresponsible. If she adds to her own power in the family all these alien fads external to the family, her power will not only be irresponsible but insane. She will be something which may well be called a nightmare of the nursery; a mad mother. But the point is that she will be mad about other nurseries as well as her own, or possibly instead of her own. The results will be interesting; but at least it is certain that under this softening influence government of the people, by the people, for the people, will most assuredly perish from the earth.

But there is always another possibility. Hints of it may be noted here and there like muffled gongs of doom. The other day some people preaching some low trick or other, for running away from the glory of motherhood, were suddenly silenced in New York; by a voice of deep and democratic volume. The prigs who potter about the great plains are pygmies dancing round a sleeping giant. That which sleeps, so far as they are concerned, is the huge power of human unanimity and intolerance in the soul of America. At present the masses in the

Middle West are indifferent to such fancies or faintly attracted by them, as fashions of culture from the great cities. But any day it may not be so; some lunatic may cut across their economic rights or their strange and buried religion; and then he will see something. He will find himself running like a nigger who has wronged a white woman or a man who has set the prairie on fire. He will see something which the politicians fan in its sleep and flatter with the name of the people, which many reactionaries have cursed with the name of the mob, but which in any case has had under its feet the crowns of many kings. It was said that the voice of the people is the voice of God; and this at least is certain, that it can be the voice of God to the wicked. And the last antics of their arrogance shall stiffen before something enormous, such as towers in the last words that Job heard out of the whirlwind; and a voice they never knew shall tell them that his name is Leviathan, and he is lord over all the children of pride.

11

The Extraordinary American

When I was in America I had the feeling that it was far more foreign than France or even than Ireland. And by foreign I mean fascinating rather than repulsive. I mean that element of strangeness which marks the frontier of any fairyland, or gives to the traveller himself the almost eerie title of the stranger. And I saw there more clearly than in countries counted as more remote from us, in race or religion, a paradox that is one of the great truths of travel.

We have never even begun to understand a people until we have found something that we do not understand. So long as we find the character easy to read, we are reading into it our own character. If when we see an event we can promptly provide an explanation, we may be pretty certain that we had ourselves prepared the explanation before we saw the event. It follows from this that the best picture of a foreign people can probably be found in a puzzle picture. If we can find an event of which the meaning is really dark to us, it will probably throw some light on the truth. I will therefore take from my American experiences one isolated incident, which certainly could not have happened in any other country I have ever clapped eyes on. I have really no notion of what it meant. I have heard even from Americans about five different conjectures about its meaning. But though I do not understand it, I do sincerely believe that if I did understand it, I should understand America.

It happened in the city of Oklahoma, which would require a book to itself, even considered as a background. The State of Oklahoma is a district in the south-west recently reclaimed from the Red Indian territory. What many, quite incorrectly, imagine about all America is really true of Oklahoma. It is proud of having no history. It is glowing with the sense of having a great future—and nothing else. People are just as likely to boast of an old building in Nashville as in Norwich; people are just as proud of old families in Boston as in Bath. But in Oklahoma the citizens do point out a colossal structure, arrogantly affirming that it wasn't there last week. It was against the colours of this crude stage scenery, as of a pantomime city of pasteboard, that the fantastic figure appeared which still haunts me like a walking note of interrogation. I was strolling down the main street of the city, and looking in at a paper-stall vivid with the news of crime, when a stranger addressed me; and asked me, quite politely but with a curious air of having authority to put the question, what I was doing in that city.

He was a lean brown man, having rather the look of a shabby tropical traveller, with a grey moustache and a lively and alert eye. But the most singular thing about him was that the front of his coat was covered with a multitude of shining metallic emblems made in the shape of stars and crescents. I was well accustomed by this time to Americans adorning the lapels of their coats with little symbols of various societies; it is a part of the American passion for the ritual of comradeship. There is nothing that an American likes so much as to have a secret society and to make no secret of it. But in this case, if I may put it so, the rash of symbolism seemed to have broken out all over the man, in a fashion that indicated that the fever was far advanced. Of this minor mystery, however, his first few sentences offered a provisional explanation. In answer to his question, touching my business in Oklahoma, I replied with restraint that I was lecturing. To which he replied without restraint, but rather with an expansive and radiant pride, "I also am lecturing. I am lecturing on astronomy."

So far a certain wild rationality seemed to light up the affair. I knew it was unusual, in my own country, for the Astronomer Royal to walk down the Strand with his coat plastered all over with the Solar System. Indeed, it was unusual for any English astronomical lecturer to advertize the subject of his lectures in this fashion. But though it would be unusual, it would not necessarily be unreasonable. In fact, I think it might add to the colour and variety of life, if specialists did adopt this sort of scientific heraldry. I should like to be able to recognize an entomologist at sight by the decorative spiders and cockroaches crawling all over his coat and waistcoat. I should like to see a conchologist in a simple costume of shells. An osteopath, I suppose, would be agreeably painted so as to resemble a skeleton, while a botanist would enliven the street with the appearance of a Jack-in-the-Green. So while I regarded the astronomical lecturer in the astronomical coat as a figure distinguishable, by a high degree of differentiation, from the artless astronomers of my island home (enough their simple loveliness for me) I saw in him nothing illogical, but rather an imaginative extreme of logic. And then came another turn of the wheel of topsy-turvydom and all the logic was scattered to the wind.

Expanding his starry bosom and standing astraddle, with the air of one who owned the street, the strange being continued, "Yes, I am lecturing on astronomy, anthropology, archaeology, palaeontology, embryology, eschatology," and so on in a thunderous roll of theoretical sciences apparently beyond the scope of any single university, let alone any single professor. Having thus introduced himself, however, he got to business. He apologized with true American courtesy for having questioned me at all, and excused it on the ground of his own exacting responsibilities. I imagined him to mean the responsibility of simultaneously occupying the chairs of all the faculties already mentioned. But these apparently were trifles to him, and something far more serious was clouding his brow.

"I feel it to be my duty," he said, "to acquaint myself with any stranger visiting this city; and it is an additional pleasure to welcome here a member of the Upper Ten." I assured him earnestly that I knew nothing about the Upper Ten, except that I did not belong to them; I felt, not without alarm, that the Upper Ten might be another secret society. He waved my abnegation aside and continued, "I have a great responsibility in watching over this city. My friend the mayor and I have a great responsibility." And then an extraordinary thing happened. Suddenly diving his hand into his breast-pocket, he flashed something before my eyes like a hand-mirror; something which disappeared again almost as soon as it appeared. In that flash I could only see that it was some sort of polished metal plate, with some letters engraved on it like a monogram. But the reward of a studious and virtuous life, which has been spent chiefly in the reading of American detective stories, shone forth for me in that hour of trial; I received at last the prize of a profound scholarship in the matter of imaginary murders in tenth-rate magazines. I remembered who it was who in the Yankee detective yarn flashes before the eyes of Slim Jim or the Lone Hand Crook a badge of metal sometimes called a shield. Assuming all the desperate composure of Slim Jim himself, I replied, "You mean you are connected with the police authorities here, don't you? Well, if I commit a murder here, I'll let you know." Whereupon that astonishing man waved a hand in deprecation, bowed in farewell with the grace of a dancing master; and said, "Oh, those are not things we expect from members of the Upper Ten."

Then that moving constellation moved away, disappearing in the dark tides of humanity, as the vision passed away down the dark tides from Sir Galahad and, starlike, mingled with the stars.

That is the problem I would put to all Americans, and to all who claim to understand America. Who and what was that man? Was he an astronomer? Was he a detective? Was he a wandering lunatic? If he was a lunatic who thought he was an astronomer, why did he have a badge to prove he was a detective? If he was a detective pretending to be an astronomer, why did he tell a total stranger that he was a detective two minutes after saying he was an astronomer? If he wished to watch over the city in a quiet and unobtrusive fashion, why did he blazon himself all over with all the stars of the sky, and profess to give public lectures on all the subjects of the world? Every wise and well-conducted student of murder stories is acquainted with the notion of a policeman in plain clothes. But nobody could possibly say that this gentleman was in plain clothes. Why not wear his uniform, if he was resolved to show every stranger in the street his badge? Perhaps after all he had no uniform; for these lands were but recently a wild frontier rudely ruled by vigilance committees. Some Americans suggested to me that he was the Sheriff; the regular hard-riding, free-shooting Sheriff of Bret Harte and my boyhood's dreams. Others suggested that he was an agent of the Ku-Klux Klan, that great nameless revolution of the revival of which there were rumours at the time; and that the symbol he exhibited was theirs. But whether he was a sheriff acting for the law, or a conspirator against the law, or a lunatic entirely outside the law, I agree with the former conjectures upon one point. I am perfectly certain he had something else in his pocket besides a badge. And I am perfectly certain that under certain circumstances he would have handled it instantly, and shot me dead between the gay bookstall and the crowded trams. And that is the last touch to the complexity; for though in that country it often seems that the law is made by a lunatic, you never know when the lunatic may not shoot you for keeping it. Only in the presence of that citizen of Oklahoma I feel I am confronted with the fullness and depth of the mystery of America. Because I understand nothing, I recognize the thing that we call a nation; and I salute the flag.

But even in connection with this mysterious figure there is a moral which affords another reason for mentioning him. Whether he was a sheriff or an outlaw, there was certainly something about him that suggested the adventurous violence of the old border life of America; and whether he was connected with the police or no, there was certainly violence enough in his environment to satisfy the most ardent policeman. The posters in the paper-shop were placarded with the verdict in the Hamon trial; a *cause célèbre* which reached its crisis in Oklahoma while I was there. Senator Hamon had been shot by a girl whom he had wronged, and his widow demanded justice, or what might fairly be called vengeance. There was very great excitement culminating in the girl's acquittal. Nor did the Hamon case appear to be entirely exceptional in that breezy borderland. The moment the town had received the news that Clara Smith was free, newsboys rushed down the street shouting, "Double stabbing outrage near Oklahoma," or "Banker's throat cut on Main Street," and otherwise resuming their regular mode of life. It seemed as much as to say, "Do not imagine that our local energies are exhausted in shooting a Senator," or "Come, now, the world is young, even if Clara Smith is acquitted, and the enthusiasm of Oklahoma is not yet cold."

But my particular reason for mentioning the matter is this. Despite my friend's mystical remarks about the Upper Ten, he lived in an atmosphere of something that was at least the very reverse of a respect for persons. Indeed, there was something in the very crudity of his social compliment that smacked, strangely enough, of that egalitarian soil. In a vaguely aristocratic country like England, people would never dream of telling a total stranger that he was a member of the Upper Ten. For one thing, they would be afraid that he might be. Real snobbishness is never vulgar; for it is intended to please the refined. Nobody licks the boots of a duke, if only because the duke does not like his boots cleaned in that way. Nobody embraces the knees of a marquis, because it would embarrass that nobleman. And nobody tells him he is a member of the Upper Ten, because everybody is expected to know it? But there is a much more subtle kind of snobbishness pervading the atmosphere of any society trial in England. And the first thing that struck me was the total absence of that atmosphere in the trial at Oklahoma. Mr. Hamon was presumably a member of the Upper Ten, if there is such a thing. He was a member of the Senate or Upper House in the American Parliament; he was a millionaire and a pillar of the Republican party, which might be called the respectable party; he is said to have been mentioned as a possible President. And the speeches of Clara Smith's counsel, who was known by the delightfully Oklahomite title of Wild Bill McLean, were wild enough in all conscience; but they left very little of my friend's illusion that members of the Upper Ten could not be accused of crimes. Nero and Borgia were quite presentable people compared with Sentor Hamon when Wild Bill McLean had done with him. But the difference was deeper, and even in a sense more delicate than this. There is a certain tone about English trials, which does at least begin with a certain scepticism about people prominent in public life being abominable in private life. People do vaguely doubt the criminality of "a man in that position"; that is, the position of the Marquise de Brinvilliers or the Marquis de Sade. *Prima facie*, it would be an advantage to the Marquis de Sade that he was a marquis. But it was certainly against Hamon that he was a millionaire. Wild Bill did not minimize him as a bankrupt or an adventurer; he insisted on the solidity and size of his fortune, he made mountains out of the "Hamon millions," as if they made the matter much worse; as indeed I think they do. But that is because I happen to share a certain political philosophy with Wild Bill and other wild buffaloes of the prairies. In other words, there is really present here a democratic instinct against the domination of wealth. It does not prevent wealth from dominating; but it does prevent the domination from being regarded with any affection or loyalty. Despite the man in the starry coat, the Americans have not really any illusions about the Upper Ten. McLean was appealing to an implicit public opinion when he pelted the Senator with his gold.

But something more is involved. I became conscious, as I have been conscious in reading the crime novels of America, that the millionaire was taken as a type and not an individual. This is the great difference; that America recognizes rich crooks as a *class*. Any Englishman might recognize them as individuals. Any English romance may turn on a crime in high life; in which the baronet is found to have poisoned his wife, or the elusive burglar turns out to be the bishop. But the English are not always saying, either in romance or reality, "What's to be done, if our food is being poisoned by all these baronets?" They do not murmur in indignation, "If bishops will go on burgling like this, something must be done." The whole point of the English romance is the exceptional character of a crime in high life. That is not the tone of American novels or American newspapers or American trials like the trial in Oklahoma. Americans may be excited when a millionaire crook is caught, as when any other crook is caught; but it is at his being caught, not at his being discovered. To put the matter shortly, England recognizes a criminal class at the bottom of the social scale. America also recognizes a criminal class at the top of the social scale. In both, for various reasons, it may be difficult for the criminals to be convicted; but in America the upper class of criminals is recognized. In both America and England, of course, it exists.

This is an assumption at the back of the American mind which makes a great difference in many ways; and in my opinion a difference for the better. I wrote merely fancifully just now about bishops being burglars; but there is a story in New York, illustrating this, which really does in a sense attribute a burglary to a bishop. The story was that an Anglican Lord Spiritual, of the pompous and now rather antiquated school, was pushing open the door of a poor American tenement with all the placid patronage of the squire and rector visiting the cottagers, when a gigantic Irish policeman came round the corner and hit him a crack over the head with a truncheon on the assumption that he was a house-breaker. I hope that those who laugh at the story see that the laugh is not altogether against the policeman; and that it is not only the policeman, but rather the bishop, who had failed to recognize some fine logical distinctions. The bishop, being a learned man, might well be called upon (when he had sufficiently recovered from the knock on the head) to define what is the exact difference between a house-breaker and a home-visitor; and why the home-visitor should not be regarded as a house-breaker when he will not behave as a guest. An impartial intelligence will be much less shocked at the policeman's disrespect for the home-visitor than by the home-visitor's disrespect for the home.

But that story smacks of the western soil, precisely because of the element of brutality there is in it. In England snobbishness and social oppression are much subtler and softer; the manifestations of them at least are more mellow and humane. In comparison there is indeed something which people call ruthless about the air of America, especially the American cities. The bishop may push open the door without an apology, but he would not break open the door with a truncheon; but the Irish policeman's truncheon hits both ways. It may be brutal to the tenement dweller as well as to the bishop; but the difference and distinction is that it might really be brutal to the bishop. It is because there is after all, at the back of all that barbarism, a sort of a negative belief in the brotherhood of men, a dark democratic sense that men are really men and nothing more, that the coarse and even corrupt bureaucracy is not resented exactly as oligarchic bureaucracies are resented. There is a sense in which corruption is not so narrow as nepotism. It is upon this queer cynical charity, and even humility, that it has been possible to rear so high and uphold so long that tower of brass, Tammany Hall. The modern police system is in spirit the most inhuman in history, and its evil belongs to an age and not to a nation. But some American police methods are evil past all parallel; and the detective can be more crooked than a hundred crooks. But in the States it is not only possible that the policeman is worse than the convict, it is by no means certain that he thinks that he is any better. In the popular stories of O. Henry there are light allusions to tramps being kicked out of hotels which will make any Christian seek relief in strong language and a trust in heaven—not to say in hell. And yet books even more popular than O. Henry's are those of the "sob-sisterhood" who swim in lachrymose lakes after love-lorn spinsters, who pass their lives in reclaiming and consoling such tramps. There are in this people two strains of brutality and sentimentalism which I do not understand, especially where they mingle; but I am fairly sure they both work back to the dim democratic origin. The Irish policeman does not confine himself fastidiously to bludgeoning bishops; his truncheon finds plenty of poor people's heads to hit; and yet I believe on my soul he has a sort of sympathy with poor people not to be found in the police of more aristocratic states. I believe he also reads and weeps over the stories of the spinsters and the reclaimed tramps; in fact, there is much of such pathos in an American magazine (my sole companion on many happy railway journeys) which is not only devoted to detective stories, but apparently edited by detectives. In these stories also there is the honest popular astonishment at the Upper Ten expressed by the astronomical detective, if indeed he was a detective and not a demon from the dark Red-Indian forests that faded to the horizon behind him. But I have set him as the head and text of this chapter because with these elements of the Third Degree of devilry and the Seventh Heaven of sentimentalism I touch on elements that I do not understand; and when I do not understand, I say so.

12

The Republican in the Ruins

The heathen in his blindness bows down to wood and stone; especially to a wood-cut or a lithographic stone. Modern people put their trust in pictures, especially scientific pictures, as much as the most superstitious ever put it in religious pictures. They publish a portrait of the Missing Link as if he were the Missing Man, for whom the police are always advertising; for all the world as if the anthropoid had been photographed before he absconded. The scientific diagram may be the hypothesis; it may be a fancy; it may be a forgery. But it is always an idol in the true sense of an image; and an image in the true sense of the thing mastering the imagination and not the reason. The power of these talismanic pictures is almost hypnotic to modern humanity. We can never forget that we have seen a portrait of the Missing Link; though we should instantly detect the lapse of logic into superstition, if we were told that the old Greek agnostics had made a statue of the Unknown God. But there is a still stranger fashion in which we fall victims to the same trick of fancy. We accept in a blind and literal spirit, not only images of speculation, but even figures of speech. The nineteenth century prided itself on having lost its faith in myths, and proceeded to put all its faith in metaphors. It dismissed the old doctrines about the way of life and the light of the world; and then it proceeded to speak as if the light of truth were really and literally a light, that could be absorbed by merely opening our eyes; or as if the path of progress were really and truly a path, to be found by merely following our noses. Thus the purpose of God is an idea, true or false; but the purpose of Nature is merely a metaphor; for obviously if there is no God there is no purpose. Yet while men, by an imaginative instinct, spoke of the purpose of God with a grand agnosticism, as something too large to be seen, something reaching out to worlds and to eternities, they speak of the purpose of Nature in particular and practical problems of curing babies or cutting up rabbits. The power of the modern metaphor must be understood, by way of an introduction, if we are to understand one of the chief errors, at once evasive and pervasive, which perplex the problem of America.

America is always spoken of as a young nation; and whether or no this be a valuable and suggestive metaphor, very few people notice that it is a metaphor at all. If somebody said that a certain deserving charity had just gone into trousers, we should recognize that it was a figure of speech, and perhaps a rather surprising figure of speech. If somebody said that a daily paper had recently put its hair up, we should know it could only be a metaphor, and possible a rather strained metaphor. Yet these phrases would mean the only thing that can possibly be meant by calling a corporate association of all sorts of people "young"; that is, that a certain institution has only existed for a certain time. I am not now denying that such a corporate nationality may happen to have a psychology comparatively analogous to the psychology of youth. I am not even denying that America has it. I am only pointing out, to begin with, that we must free ourselves from the talismanic tyranny of a metaphor which we do recognize as a metaphor. Men realized that the old mystical doctrines were mystical; they do not realize that the new metaphors are metaphorical. They have some sort of hazy notion that American society must be growing, must be promising, must have the virtues of hope or the faults of ignorance, merely *because* it has only had a separate existence since the eighteenth century. And that is exactly like saying that a new chapel must be growing taller, or that a limited liability company will soon have its second teeth.

Now in truth this particular conception of American hopefulness would be anything but hopeful for America. If the argument really were, as it is still vaguely supposed to be, that America must have a long life before it, because it only started in the eighteenth century, we should find a very fatal answer by looking at the other political systems that did start in the eighteenth century. The eighteenth century was called the Age of Reason; and there is a very real sense in which the other systems were indeed started in a spirit of reason. But starting from reason has not saved them from ruin. If we survey the Europe of to-day with real clarity and historic comprehension, we shall see that it is precisely the most recent and the most rationalistic creations that have been ruined. The two great states which did most definitely and emphatically deserve to be called modern states were Prussia and Russia. There was no real Prussia before Frederick the Great; no real Russian Empire before Peter the Great. Both those innovators recognized themselves as rationalists bringing a new reason and order into an indeterminate barbarism; and doing for the barbarians what the barbarians could not do for themselves. They did not, like the kings of England or France or Spain or Scotland, inherit a sceptre that was the symbol of a historic and patriotic people. In this sense there was no Russia but only an Emperor of Russia. In this sense Prussia was a kingdom before it was a nation; if it ever was a nation. But anyhow both men were particularly modern in their whole mood and mind. They were modern to the extent of being not only anti-traditional, but almost anti-patriotic. Peter forced the science of the West on Russia to the regret of many Russians. Frederick talked the French of Voltaire and not the German of Luther. The two experiments were entirely in the spirit of Voltairean rationalism; they were built in broad daylight by men who believed in nothing but the light of common day; and already their day is done.

If then the promise of America were in the fact that she is one of the latest births of progress, we should point out that it is exactly the latest born that were the first to die. If in this sense she is praised as young, it may be answered that the young have died young, and have not lived to be old. And if this be confused with the argument that she came in an age of clarity and scepticism, uncontaminated by old superstitions, it could still be retorted that the works of superstition have survived the works of scepticism. But the truth is, of course, that the real quality of America is much more subtle and complex than this; and is mixed not only of good and bad, and rational and mystical, but also of old and new. That is what makes the task of tracing the true proportions of American life so interesting and so impossible.

To begin with, such a metaphor is always as distracting as a mixed metaphor. It is a double-edged tool that cuts both ways; and consequently opposite ways. We use the same word "young" to mean two opposite extremes. We mean something at an early stage of growth, and also something having the latest fruits of growth. We might call a commonwealth young if it conducted all its daily conversation by wireless telegraphy; meaning that it was progressive. But we might also call it young if it conducted all its industry with chipped flints; meaning that it was primitive. These two meanings of youth are hopelessly mixed up when the word is applied to America. But what is more curious, the two elements really are wildly entangled in America. America is in some ways what is called in advance of the times, and in some ways what is called behind the times; but it seems a little confusing to convey both notions by the same word.

On the one hand, Americans often are successful in the last inventions. And for that very reason they are often neglectful of the last but one. It is true of men in general, dealing with things in general, that while they are progressing in one thing, such as science, they are going back in another thing, such as art. What is less fully realized is that this is true even as between different methods of science. The perfection of wireless telegraphy might well be followed by the gross imperfection of wires. The very enthusiasm of American science brings this out very vividly. The telephone in New York works miracles all day long. Replies from remote places come as promptly as in a private talk; nobody cuts anybody off; nobody says, "Sorry you've been troubled." But then the postal service of New York does not work at all. At least I could never discover it working. Letters lingered in it for days and days, as in some wild village of the Pyrenees. When I asked a taxi-driver to drive me to a post-office, a look of far-off vision and adventure came into his eyes, and he said he had once heard of a post-office somewhere near West Ninety-Seventh Street. Men are not efficient in everything, but only in the fashionable thing. This may be a mark of the march of science; it does certainly in one sense deserve the description of youth. We can imagine a very young person forgetting the old toy in the excitement of a new one.

But on the other hand, American manners contain much that is called young in the contrary sense; in the sense of an earlier stage of history. There are whole patches and particular aspects that seem to me quite Early Victorian. I cannot help having this sensation for instance, about the arrangement for smoking in the railway carriages. There are no smoking carriages as a rule; but a corner of each of the great cars is curtained off mysteriously, that a man may go behind the curtain and smoke. Nobody thinks of a woman doing so. It is regarded as a dark, bohemian, and almost brutally masculine indulgence; exactly as it was regarded by the dowagers in Thackeray's novels. Indeed, this is one of the many such cases in which extremes meet; the extremes of stuffy antiquity and cranky modernity. The American dowager is sorry that tobacco was ever introduced; and the American suffragette and social reformer is considering whether tobacco ought not to be abolished. The tone of American society suggests some sort of compromise, by which women will be allowed to smoke, but men forbidden to do so.

In one respect, however, America is very old indeed. In one respect America is more historic than England; I might almost say more archaeological than England. The record of one period of the past, morally remote and probably irrevocable, is there preserved in a more perfect form as a pagan city is preserved at Pompeii. In a more general sense, of course, it is easy to exaggerate the contrast as a mere contrast between the old world and the new. There is a superficial satire about the millionaire's daughter who has recently become the wife of an aristocrat; but there is a rather more subtle satire in the question of how long the aristocrat has been aristocratic. There is often much misplaced mockery of a marriage between an upstart's daughter and a decayed relic of feudalism; when it is really a marriage between an upstart's daughter and an upstart's grandson. The sentimental socialist often seems to admit the blue blood of the nobleman, even when he wants to shed it; just as he seems to admit the marvellous brains of the millionaire, even when he wants to blow them out. Unfortunately (in the interests of social science, of course) the sentimental socialist never does go so far as bloodshed or blowing out brains; otherwise the colour and quality of both blood and brains would probably be a disappointment to him. There are certainly more American families that really came over in the *Mayflower* than English families that really came over with the Conqueror; and an English county family clearly dating from the time of the *Mayflower* would be considered a very traditional and historic house. Nevertheless, there are ancient things in England, though the aristocracy is hardly one of them. There are buildings, there are institutions, there are even ideas in England which do preserve, as in a perfect pattern, some particular epoch of the past, and even of the remote past. A man could study the Middle Ages in Lincoln as well as in Rouen; in Canterbury as well as in Cologne. Even of the Renaissance the same is true, at least on the literary side;

if Shakespeare was later he was also greater than Ronsard. But the point is that the spirit and philosophy of the periods were present in fullness and in freedom. The guildsmen were as Christian in England as they were anywhere; the poets were as pagan in England as they were anywhere. Personally I do not admit that the men who served patrons were freer than those who served patron saints. But each fashion has its own kind of freedom; and the point is that the English, in each case, had the fullness of that kind of freedom. But there was another ideal of freedom which the English never had at all; or, anyhow, never expressed at all. There was another ideal, the soul of another epoch, round which we built no monuments and wrote no masterpieces. You will find no traces of it in England; but you will find them in America.

The thing I mean was the real religion of the eighteenth century. Its religion, in the more defined sense, was generally Deism, as in Robespierre or Jefferson. In the more general way of morals and atmosphere it was rather Stoicism, as in the suicide of Wolfe Tone. It had certain very noble and, as some would say, impossible ideals; as that a politician should be poor, and should be proud of being poor. It knew Latin; and therefore insisted on the strange fancy that the Republic should be a public thing. Its Republican simplicity was anything but a silly pose; unless all martyrdom is a silly pose. Even of the prigs and fanatics of the American and French Revolutions we can often say, as Stevenson said of an American, that "thrift and courage glowed in him." And its virtue and value for us is that it did remember the things we now most tend to forget; from the dignity of liberty to the danger of luxury. It did really believe in self-determination, in the self-determination of the self, as well as of the state. And its determination was really determined. In short, it believed in self-respect; and it is strictly true even of its rebels and regicides that they desired chiefly to be respectable. But there were in it the marks of religion as well as respectability; it had a creed; it had a crusade. Men died singing its songs; men starved rather than write against its principles. And its principles were liberty, equality and fraternity, or the dogmas of the Declaration of Independence. This was the idea that redeemed the dreary negations of the eighteenth century; and there are still corners of Philadelphia or Boston or Baltimore where we can feel so suddenly in the silence its plain garb and formal manners, that the walking ghost of Jefferson would hardly surprise us.

There is not the ghost of such a thing in England. In England the real religion of the eighteenth century never found freedom or scope. It never cleared a space in which to build that cold and classic building called the Capitol. It never made elbow-room for that free if sometimes frigid figure called the Citizen.

In eighteenth-century England he was crowded out, partly perhaps by the relics of better things of the past, but largely at least by the presence of much worse things in the present. The worst things kept out the best things of the eighteenth century. The ground was occupied by legal fictions; by a godless Erastian church and a powerless Hanoverian king. Its realties were an aristocracy of Regency dandies, in costumes made to match Brighton Pavilion; a paganism not frigid but florid. It was a touch of this aristocratic waste in Fox that prevented that great man from being a glorious exception. It is therefore well for us to realize that there is something in history which we did not experience; and therefore probably something in Americans that we do not understand. There was this idealism at the very beginning of their individualism. There was a note of heroic publicity and honourable poverty which lingers in the very name of Cincinnati.

But I have another and special reason for noting this historical fact; the fact that we English never made anything upon the model of a capitol, while we can match anybody with the model of a cathedral. It is far from improbable that the latter model may again be a working model. For I have myself felt, naturally and for a long time, a warm sympathy with both those past ideals, which seem to some so incompatible. I have felt the attraction of the red cap as well as the red cross, of the Marseillaise as well as the Magnificat. And even when they were in furious conflict I have never altogether lost my sympathy for either. But in the conflict between the Republic[1] and the Church, the point often made against the Church seems to me much more of a point against the Republic. It is emphatically the Republic and not the Church that I venerate as something beautiful but belonging to the past. In fact I feel exactly the same sort of sad respect for the republican ideal that many mid-Victorian free-thinkers felt for the religious ideal. The most sincere poets of that period were largely divided between those who insisted, like Arnold and Clough, that Christianity might be a ruin, but after all it must be treated as a picturesque ruin; and those like Swinburne, who insisted that it might be a picturesque ruin, but after all it must be treated as a ruin. But surely their own pagan temple of political liberty is now much more of a ruin than the other; and I fancy I am one of the few who still take off their hats in that ruined temple. That is why I went about looking for the fading traces of that lost cause, in the old-world atmosphere of the new world.

But I do not, as a fact, feel that the cathedral is a ruin; I doubt if I should feel it even if I wished to lay it in ruins. I doubt if Mr. M'Cabe really thinks that Catholicism is dying, though he might deceive himself into saying so. Nobody could be naturally moved to say that the crowded cathedral of St. Patrick in New York was a ruin, or even that the unfinished Anglo-Catholic Cathedral at Washington was a ruin, though it is not yet a church; or that there is anything lost or lingering about the splendid and spirited Gothic churches springing up under the inspiration of Mr. Cram of Boston. As a matter of feeling, as a matter of fact, as a matter quite apart from theory or opinion, it is not in the religious centres that we now have the feeling of something beautiful but receding, of something loved but lost. It is exactly in the spaces cleared and levelled by America for the large and sober religion of the eighteenth century; it is where an old house in Philadelphia

[1] In the conclusion of this chapter I mean by the Republic not merely the American Republic, but the whole modern representative system, as in France or even in England.

contains an old picture of Franklin, or where the men of Maryland raised above their city the first monument of Washington. It is there that I feel like one who treads alone some banquet hall deserted, whose lights are fled, whose garlands dead, and all save he departed. It is then that I feel as if I were the last Republican.

But when I say that the Republic of the Age of Reason is now a ruin, I should rather say that at its best it is a ruin. At its worst it has collapsed into a death-trap or is rotting like a dunghill. What is the real Republic of our day as distinct from the ideal Republic of our fathers, but a heap of corrupt capitalism crawling with worms; with those parasites, the professional politicians? I was re-reading Swinburne's bitter but not ignoble poem, "Before a Crucifix," in which he bids Christ, or the ecclesiastical image of Christ, stand out of the way of the onward march of political idealism represented by United Italy or the French Republic. I was struck by the strange and ironic exactitude with which every taunt he flings at the degradation of the old divine ideal would now fit the degradation of his own human ideal. The time has already come when we can ask his Goddess of Liberty, as represented by the actual Liberals, "Have *you* filled full men's starved-out souls; have *you* brought freedom on the earth?" For every engine in which these old free-thinkers firmly and confidently trusted has itself become an engine of oppression and even of class oppression. Its free Parliament has become an oligarchy. Its free press has become a monopoly. If the pure Church has been corrupted in the course of two thousand years, what about the pure Republic that has rotted into a filthy plutocracy in less than a hundred?

O hidden face of man, whereover
The years have woven a viewless veil,
If thou wert verily man's lover
What did thy love or blood avail?
Thy blood the priests make poison of;
And in gold shekels coin thy love.

172

Which has most to do with shekels to-day, the priests or the politicians? Can we say in any special sense nowadays that clergymen, as such, make a poison out of the blood of the martyrs? Can we say it in anything like the real sense, in which we do say that yellow journalists make a poison out of the blood of the soldiers?

But I understand how Swinburne felt when confronted by the image of the carven Christ, and, perplexed by the contrast between its claims and its consequences, he said his strange farewell to it, hastily indeed, but not without regret, not even really without respect. I felt the same myself when I looked for the last time on the Statue of Liberty.

13

Is the Atlantic Narrowing?

A certain kind of question is asked very earnestly in our time. Because of a certain logical quality in it, connected with premises and data, it is very difficult to answer. Thus people will ask what is the hidden weakness in the Celtic race that makes them everywhere fail or fade away; or how the Germans contrived to bring all their organization into a state of such perfect efficiency; and what was the significance of the recent victory of Prussia. Or they will ask by what stages the modern world has abandoned all belief in miracles; and the modern newspapers ceased to print any news of murders. They will ask why English politics are free from corruption; or by what mental and moral training certain millionaires were enabled to succeed by sheer force of character; in short they will ask why plutocrats govern well and how it is that pigs fly, spreading their pink pinions to the breeze or delighting us as they twitter and flutter from tree to tree. The logical difficulty of answering these questions is connected with an old story about Charles the Second and a bowl of goldfish, and with another anecdote about a gentleman who was asked, "When did you leave off beating your wife?" But there is something analogous to it in the present discussions about the forces drawing England and America together. It seems as if the reasoners hardly went far enough back in their argument, or took trouble enough to disentangle their assumptions. They are still moving with the momentum of the peculiar nineteenth century notion of progress; of certain very simple tendencies perpetually increasing and needing no special analysis. It is so with the international *rapprochement* I have to consider here.

In other places I have ventured to express a doubt about whether nations can be drawn together by an ancient rumour about races; by a sort of prehistoric chit-chat or the gossip of the Stone Age. I have ventured farther; and even expressed a doubt about whether they ought to be drawn together, or rather dragged together, by the brute violence of the engines of science and speed. But there is yet another horrible doubt haunting my morbid mind, which it will be better for my constitution to confess frankly. And that is the doubt about whether they are being drawn together at all.

It has long been a conversational commonplace among the enlightened that all countries are coming closer and closer to each other. It was a conversational commonplace among the enlightened, somewhere about the year 1913, that all wars were receding farther and farther into a barbaric past. There is something about these sayings that seems simple and familiar and entirely satisfactory when we say them; they are of that consoling sort which we can say without any of the mental pain of thinking what we are saying. But if we turn our attention from the phrases we use to the facts that we talk about, we shall realize at least that there are a good many facts on the other side and examples pointing the other way. For instance, it does happen occasionally, from time to time, that people talk about Ireland. He would be a very hilarious humanitarian who should maintain that Ireland and England have been more and more assimilated during the last hundred years. The very name of Sinn Fein is an answer to it, and the very language in which that phrase is spoken. Curran and Sheil would no more have dreamed of uttering the watchword of "Repeal" in Gaelic than of uttering it in Zulu. Grattan could hardly have brought himself to believe that the real repeal of the Union would actually be signed in London in the strange script as remote as the snaky ornament of the Celtic crosses. It would have seemed like Washington signing the Declaration of Independence in the picture-writing of the Red Indians. Ireland has clearly grown away from England; and her language, literature, and type of patriotism are far less English than they were. On the other hand, no one will pretend that the mass of modern Englishmen are much nearer to talking Gaelic or decorating Celtic crosses. A hundred years ago it was perfectly natural that Byron and Moore should walk down the street arm in arm. Even the sight of Mr. Rudyard Kipling and Mr. W. B. Yeats walking down the street arm in arm would now arouse some remark.

I could give any number of other examples of the same new estrangement of nations. I could cite the obvious facts that Norway and Sweden parted company not very long ago, that Austria and Hungary have again become separate states. I could point to the mob of new nations that have started up after the war; to the fact that the great empires are now nearly all broken up; that the Russian Empire no longer directs Poland, that the Austrian Empire no longer directs Bohemia, that the Turkish Empire no longer directs Palestine. Sinn Fein is the separatism of the Irish. Zionism is the separatism of the Jews. But there is one simple and sufficing example, which is here more to my purpose, and is at least equally sufficient for it. And that is the deepening national difference between the Americans and the English.

Let me test it first by my individual experience in the matter of literature. When I was a boy I read a book like *The Autocrat of the Breakfast-Table* exactly as I read another book like *The Book of Snobs*.

I did not think of it as an American book, but simply as a book. Its wit and idiom were like those of the English literary tradition; and its few touches of local colour seemed merely accidental, like those of an Englishman who happened to be living in Switzerland or Sweden. My father and my father's friends were rightly enthusiastic for the book; so that it seemed to come to me by inheritance *like Gulliver's Travels or Tristram Shandy. Its* language was as English as Ruskin, and a great deal more English than Carlyle. Well, I have seen in later years an almost equally wide and well-merited popularity of the stories of O. Henry. But never for one moment could I or any one else reading them forget that they were stories by an American about America. The very first fact about them is that they are told with an American accent, that is, in the unmistakable tones of a brilliant and fascinating foreigner. And the same is true of every other recent work of which the fame has managed to cross the Atlantic. We did not say that *The Spoon River Anthology* was a new book, but that it was a new book from America. It was exactly as if a remarkably realistic novel was reported from Russia or Italy. We were in no danger of confusing it with the "Elegy in a Country Churchyard." People in England who heard of Main Street were not likely to identify it with a High Street; with the principal thoroughfare in any little town in Berkshire or Buckinghamshire. But when I was a boy I practically identified the boarding-house of the Autocrat with any boarding-house I happened to know in Brompton or Brighton. No doubt there were differences; but the point is that the differences did not pierce the consciousness or prick the illusion. I said to myself, "People are like this in boarding-houses," not "People are like this in Boston."

This can be seen even in the simple matter of language, especially in the sense of slang. Take, for instance, the delightful sketch in the causerie of Oliver Wendell Holmes; the character of the young man called John. He is a very modern type in every modern country who does specialize in slang. He is the young fellow who is something in the City; the everyday young man of the Gilbertian song, with a stick and a pipe and a half-bred black-and-tan. In every country he is at once witty and commonplace. In every country, therefore, he tends both to the vivacity and the vulgarity of slang. But when he appeared in Holmes's book, his language was not very different from what it would have been in a Brighton instead of a Boston boarding-house; or, in short, if the young man called John had more commonly been called 'Arry. If he had appeared in a modern American book, his language would have been almost literally unintelligible. At the least an Englishman would have had to read some of the best sentences twice, as he sometimes has to read the dizzy and involved metaphors of O. Henry. Nor is it an answer that this depended on the personalities of the particular writers. A comparison between the real journalism of the time of Holmes and the real journalism of the time of Henry reveals the same thing. It is the expansion of a slight difference of style into a luxuriant difference of idiom; and the process continued indefinitely would certainly produce a totally different language. After a few centuries the signatures of American ambassadors would look as fantastic as Gaelic, and the very name of the Republic be as strange as Sinn Fein.

It is true that there has been on the surface a certain amount of give and take; or at least, as far as the English are concerned, of take rather than give. But it is true that it was once all the other way; and indeed the one thing is something like a just nemesis of the other. Indeed, the story of the reversal is somewhat singular, when we come to think of it. It began in a certain atmosphere and spirit of certain well-meaning people who talked about the English-speaking race; and were apparently indifferent to how the English was spoken, whether in the accent of a Jamaican negro or a convict from Botany Bay. It was their logical tendency to say that Dante was a Dago. It was their logical punishment to say that Disraeli was an Englishman. Now there may have been a period when this Anglo-American amalgamation included more or less equal elements from England and America. It never included the larger elements, or the more valuable elements of either. But, on the whole, I think it true to say that it was not an allotment but an interchange of parts; and that things first went all one way and then all the other. People began by telling the Americans that they owed all their past triumphs to England; which was false. They ended up by telling the English that they would owe all their future triumphs to America; which is, if possible, still more false. Because we chose to forget that New York had been New Amsterdam, we are now in danger of forgetting that London is not New York. Because we insisted that Chicago was only a pious imitation of Chiswick, we may yet see Chiswick an inferior imitation of Chicago. Our Anglo-Saxon historians attempted that conquest in which Howe and Burgoyne had failed, and with infinitely less justification on their side. They attempted the great crime of the Anglicization of America. They have called down the punishment of the Americanization of England. We must not murmur; but it is a heavy punishment.

It may lift a little of its load, however, if we look at it more closely; we shall then find that though it is very much on top of us, it is only on top. In that sense such Americanization as there is very superficial. For instance, there is a certain amount of American slang picked up at random; it appears in certain pushing types of journalism and drama. But we may easily dwell too much on this tragedy; of people who have never spoken English beginning to speak American. I am far from suggesting that American, like any other foreign language, may not frequently contribute to the common culture of the world phrases for which there is no substitute; there are French phrases so used in England and English phrases in France. The word "high-brow," for instance, is a real discovery and revelation, a new and necessary name for something that walked nameless but enormous in the modern world, a shaft of light and a stroke of lightning. That comes from America and belongs to the world, as much as "The Raven" or *The Scarlet Letter* or the novels of Henry James belong to the world. In fact, I can imagine Henry James originating it in the throes of self-expression, and bringing out a word like "high-browed," with a sort of gentle jerk, at the end of searching sentences which groped sensitively until they found the phrase. But most of the American slang that is borrowed seems to be borrowed for no particular reason. It either has no point or the point is lost by translation into another context and culture. It is either something which does not need any grotesque and exaggerative description, or of which there already exists a grotesque and exaggerative description more native to our tongue and soil. For instance, I cannot see that the strong and simple expression "Now it is for you to pull the police magistrate's nose" is in any way strengthened by saying, "Now it is up to you to pull the police magistrate's nose." When Tennyson says of the men of the Light Brigade "Theirs but to do and die," the expression seems to me perfectly lucid. "Up to them to do and die" would alter the metre without especially clarifying the meaning. This is an example of ordinary language being quite adequate; but there is a further difficulty that even wild slang comes to sound like ordinary language. Very often the English have already as humorous and fanciful idiom of their own, only that through habit it has lost its humour. When Keats wrote the line, "What pipes and timbrels, what wild ecstasy!" I am willing to believe that the American humorist would have expressed the same sentiment by beginning the sentence with "Some pipe!" When that was first said, somewhere in the wilds of Colorado, it was really funny; involving a powerful understatement and the suggestion of a mere sample. If a spinster has informed us that she keeps a bird, and we find it is an ostrich, there will be considerable point in the Colorado satirist saying inquiringly, "Some bird?" as if he were offering us a small slice of a small plover. But if we go back to this root and rationale of a joke, the English language already contains quite as good a joke. It is not necessary to say "Some bird"; there is a far finer irony in the old expression, "Something like a bird." It suggests that the speaker sees something faintly and strangely birdlike about a bird; that it remotely and almost irrationally reminds him of a bird; and that there is about ostrich plumes a yard long something like the faint and delicate traces of a feather. It has every quality of imaginative irony, except that nobody even imagines it to be ironical.

All that happens is that people get tired of that turn of phrase, take up a foreign phrase and get tired of that, without realizing the point of either. All that happens is that a number of weary people who used to say "Something like a bird," now say, "Some bird," with undiminished weariness. But they might just as well use dull and decent English; for in both cases they are only using jocular language without seeing the joke.

There is indeed a considerable trade in the transplantation of these American jokes to England just now. They generally pine and die in our climate, or they are dead before their arrival; but we cannot be certain that they were never alive. There is a sort of unending frieze or scroll of decorative designs unrolled ceaselessly before the British public, about a hen-pecked husband, which is indistinguishable to the eye from an actual self-repeating pattern like that of the Greek Key, but which is imported as if it were as precious and irreplaceable as the Elgin Marbles. Advertisement and syndication make mountains out of the most funny little molehills; but no doubt the molehills are picturesque enough in their own landscape. In any case there is nothing so national as humour; and many things, like many people, can be humorous enough when they are at home. But these American jokes are boomed as solemnly as American religions; and their supporters gravely testify that they are funny, without seeing the fun of it for a moment. This is partly perhaps the spirit of spontaneous institutionalism in American democracy, breaking out in the wrong place. They make humour an institution; and a man will be set to tell an anecdote as if to play the violin. But when the story is told in America it really is amusing; and when these jokes are reprinted in England they are often not even intelligible. With all the stupidity of the millionaire and the monopolist, the enterprising proprietor prints jokes in England which are necessarily unintelligible to nearly every English person; jokes referring to domestic and local conditions quite peculiar to America. I saw one of these narrative caricatures the other day in which the whole of the joke (what there was of it) turned on the astonishment of a housewife at the absurd notion of not having an ice-box. It is perfectly true that nearly every ordinary American housewife possesses an ice-box. An ordinary English housewife would no more expect to possess an ice-box than to possess an iceberg. And it would be about as sensible to tow an iceberg to an English port all the way from the North Pole, as to trail that one pale and frigid joke to Fleet Street all the way from the New York papers. It is the same with a hundred other advertisements and adaptations. I have already confessed that I took a considerable delight in the dancing illuminations of Broadway—in Broadway. Everything there is suitable to them, the vast interminable thoroughfare, the toppling houses, the dizzy and restless spirit of the whole city. It is a city of dissolving views, and one may almost say a city in everlasting dissolution. But I do not especially admire a burning fragment of Broadway stuck up opposite the old Georgian curve of Regent Street. I would as soon express sympathy with the Republic of Switzerland by erecting a small Alp, with imitation snow, in the middle of St. James's Park.

But all this commercial copying is very superficial; and above all, it never copies anything that is, really worth copying. Nations never *learn* anything from each other in this way. We have many things to learn from America; but we only listen to those Americans who have still to learn them. Thus, for instance, we do not import the small farm but only the big shop. In other words, we hear nothing of the democracy of the Middle West, but everything of the plutocracy of the middleman, who is probably as unpopular in the Middle West as the miller in the Middle Ages. If Mr. Elihu K. Pike could be transplanted bodily from the neighbourhood of his home town of Marathon, Neb., with his farm and his frame-house and all its fittings, and they could be set down exactly in the spot now occupied by Selfridge's (which could be easily cleared away for the purpose), I think we could really get a great deal of good by watching him, even if the watching were inevitably a little too like watching a wild beast in a cage or an insect under a glass case. Urban crowds could collect every day behind a barrier or railing, and gaze at Mr. Pike pottering about all day in his ancient and autochthonous occupations. We could see him growing Indian corn with all the gravity of an Indian; though it is impossible to imagine Mrs. Pike blessing the cornfield in the manner of Minnehaha. As I have said, there is a certain lack of humane myth and mysticism about this Puritan peasantry. But we could see him transforming the maize into pop-corn, which is a very pleasant domestic ritual and pastime, and is the American equivalent of the glory of roasting chestnuts. Above all, many of us would learn for the first time that a man can really live and walk about upon something more productive than a pavement; and that when he does so he can really be a free man, and have no lord but the law. Instead of that, America can give nothing to London but those multiple modern shops, of which it has too many already. I know that many people entertain the innocent illusion that big shops are more efficient than small ones; but that is only because the big combinations have the monopoly of advertisement as well as trade. The big shop is not in the least remarkable for efficiency; it is only too big to be blamed for its inefficiency. It is secure in its reputation for always sacking the wrong man. A big shop, considered as a place to shop in, is simply a village of small shops roofed in to keep out the light and air; and one in which none of the shopkeepers are really responsible for their shops. If any one has any doubts on this matter, since I have mentioned it, let him consider this fact: that in practice we never do apply this method of commercial combination to anything that matters very much. We do not go to the surgical department of the Stores to have a portion of our brain removed by a delicate operation; and then pass on to the advocacy department to employ one or any of its barristers, when we are in temporary danger of being hanged. We go to men who own their own tools and are responsible for the use of their own talents. And the same truth applies to that other modern method of advertisement, which has also so largely fallen across us like the gigantic shadow of America. Nations do not arm themselves for a mortal struggle by remembering which sort of submarine they have seen most often on the hoardings. They can do it about something like soap, precisely because a nation will not perish by having a second-rate sort of soap, as it might by having a second-rate sort of submarine. A nation may indeed perish slowly by having a second-rate sort of food or drink or medicine; but that is another and much longer story, and the story is not ended yet. But nobody wins a great battle at a great crisis because somebody has told him that Cadgerboy's Cavalry Is The Best. It may be that commercial enterprise will eventually cover these fields also, and advertisement-agents will provide the instruments of the surgeon and the weapons of the soldier. When that happens, the armies will be defeated and the patients will die. But though we modern people are indeed patients, in the sense of being merely receptive and accepting things with astonishing patience, we are not dead yet; and we have lingering gleams of sanity.

For the best things do not travel. As I appear here as a traveller, I may say with all modesty that the best people do not travel, either. Both in England and America the normal people are the national people; and I repeat that I think they are growing more and more national. I do not think the abyss is being bridged by cosmopolitan theories; and I am sure I do not want it bridged by all this slang journalism and blatant advertisement. I have called all that commercial publicity the gigantic shadow of America. It may be the shadow of America, but it is not the light of America. The light lies far beyond, a level light upon the lands of sunset, where it shines upon wide places full of a very simple and a very happy people; and those who would see it must seek for it.

14

Lincoln and Lost Causes

It has already been remarked here that the English know a great deal about past American literature, but nothing about past American history. They do not know either, of course, as well as they know the present American advertising, which is the least important of the three. But it is worth noting once more how little they know of the history, and how illogically that little is chosen. They have heard, no doubt, of the fame and the greatness of Henry Clay. He is a cigar. But it would be unwise to cross-examine any Englishman, who may be consuming that luxury at the moment, about the Missouri Compromise or the controversies with Andrew Jackson. And just as the statesman of Kentucky is a cigar, so the state of Virginia is a cigarette. But there is perhaps one exception, or half-exception, to this simple plan. It would perhaps be an exaggeration to say that Plymouth Rock is a chicken. Any English person keeping chickens, and chiefly interested in Plymouth Rocks considered as chickens, would nevertheless have a hazy sensation of having seen the word somewhere before. He would feel subconsciously that the Plymouth Rock had not always been a chicken. Indeed, the name connotes something not only solid but antiquated; and is not therefore a very tactful name for a chicken. There would rise up before him something memorable in the haze that he calls his history; and he would see the history books of his boyhood and old engravings of men in steeple-crowned hats struggling with sea-waves or Red Indians. The whole thing would suddenly become clear to him if (by a simple reform) the chickens were called Pilgrim Fathers.

Then he would remember all about it. The Pilgrim Fathers were champions of religious liberty; and they discovered America. It is true that he has also heard of a man called Christopher Columbus; but that was in connection with an egg. He has also heard of somebody known as Sir Walter Raleigh; and though his principal possession was a cloak, it is also true that he had a potato, not to mention a pipe of tobacco. Can it be possible that he brought it from Virginia, where the cigarettes come from? Gradually the memories will come back and fit themselves together for the average hen-wife who learnt history at the English elementary schools, and who has now something better to do. Even when the narrative becomes consecutive, it will not necessarily become correct. It is not strictly true to say that the Pilgrim Fathers discovered America. But it is quite as true as saying that they were champions of religious liberty. If we said that they were martyrs who would have died heroically in torments rather than tolerate any religious liberty, we should be talking something like sense about them, and telling the real truth that is their due. The whole Puritan movement, from the Solemn League and Covenant to the last stand of the last Stuarts, was a struggle *against* religious toleration, or what they would have called religious indifference. The first religious equality on earth was established by a Catholic cavalier in Maryland. Now there is nothing in this to diminish any dignity that belongs to any real virtues and virilities in the Pilgrim

Fathers; on the contrary, it is rather to the credit of their consistency and conviction. But there is no doubt that the note of their whole experiment in New England was intolerance, and even inquisition. And there is no doubt that New England was then only the newest and not the oldest of these colonial experiments. At least two cavaliers had been in the field before any Puritans. And they had carried with them much more of the atmosphere and nature of the normal Englishman than any Puritan could possibly carry. They had established it especially in Virginia, which had been founded by a great Elizabethan and named after the great Elizabeth. Before there was any New England in the North, there was something very like Old England in the South. Relatively speaking, there is still.

Whenever the anniversary of the *Mayflower* comes round, there is a chorus of Anglo-American congratulation and comradeship, as if this at least were a matter on which all can agree. But I knew enough about America, even before I went there, to know that there are a good many people there at any rate who do not agree with it. Long ago I wrote a protest in which I asked why Englishmen had forgotten the great state of Virginia, the first in foundation and long the first in leadership; and why a few crabbed Nonconformists should have the right to erase a record that begins with Raleigh and ends with Lee, and incidentally includes Washington. The great state of Virginia was the backbone of America until it was broken in the Civil War. From Virginia came the first great Presidents and most of the Fathers of the Republic. Its adherence to the Southern side in the war made it a great war, and for a long time a doubtful war. And in the leader of the Southern armies it produced what is perhaps the one modern figure that may come to shine like St. Louis in the lost battle, or Hector dying before holy Troy.

Again, it is characteristic that while the modern English know nothing about Lee they do know something about Lincoln; and nearly all that they know is wrong. They know nothing of his Southern connections, nothing of his considerable Southern sympathy, nothing of the meaning of his moderation in face of the problem of slavery, now lightly treated as self-evident. Above all, they know nothing about the respect in which Lincoln was quite un-English, was indeed the very reverse of English; and can be understood better if we think of him as a Frenchman, since it seems so hard for some of us to believe that he was an American. I mean his lust for logic for its own sake, and the way he kept mathematical truths in his mind like the fixed stars. He was so far from being a merely practical man, impatient of academic abstractions, that he reviewed and revelled in academic abstractions, even while he could not apply them to practical life. He loved to repeat that slavery was intolerable while he tolerated it, and to prove that something ought to be done while it was impossible to do it. This was probably very bewildering to his brother-politicians; for politicians always whitewash what they do not destroy. But for all that this inconsistent consistency beat the politicians at their own game, and this abstracted logic proved the most practical of all. For when the chance did come to do something, there was no doubt about the thing to be done. The thunderbolt fell from the clear heights of heaven; it had not been tossed about and lost like a common missile in the market-place. The matter is worth mentioning, because it has a moral for a much larger modern question. A wise man's attitude towards industrial capitalism will be very like Lincoln's attitude towards slavery. That is, he will manage to endure capitalism; but he will not endure a defence of capitalism. He will recognize the value, not only of knowing what he is doing, but of knowing what he would like to do. He will recognize the importance of having a thing clearly labelled in his own mind as bad, long before the opportunity comes to abolish it. He may recognize the risk of even worse things in immediate abolition, as Lincoln did in abolitionism. He will not call all business men brutes, any more than Lincoln would call all planters demons; because he knows they are not. He will regard many alternatives to capitalism as crude and inhuman, as Lincoln regarded John Brown's raid; because they are. But he will clear his *mind* from cant about capitalism; he will have no doubt of what is the truth about Trusts and Trade Combines and the concentration of capital; and it is the truth that they endure under one of the ironic silences of heaven, over the pageants and the passing triumphs of hell.

But the name of Lincoln has a more immediate reference to the international matters I am considering here. His name has been much invoked by English politicians and journalists in connection with the quarrel with Ireland. And if we study the matter, we shall hardly admire the tact and sagacity of those journalists and politicians.

History is an eternal tangle of cross-purposes; and we could not take a clearer case, or rather a more complicated case, of such a tangle, than the facts lying behind a political parallel recently mentioned by many politicians. I mean the parallel between the movement for Irish independence and the attempted secession of the Southern Confederacy in America. Superficially any one might say that the comparison is natural enough; and that there is much in common between the quarrel of the North and South in Ireland and the quarrel of the North and South in America. In both cases the South was on the whole agricultural, the North on the whole industrial. True, the parallel exaggerates the position of Belfast; to complete it we must suppose the whole Federal system to have consisted of Pittsburg. In both the side that was more successful was felt by many to be less attractive. In both the same political terms were used, such as the term "Union" and "Unionism." An ordinary Englishman comes to America, knowing these main lines of American history, and knowing that the Americans know the similar main lines of Irish history. He knows that there are strong champions of Ireland in America; possibly he also knows that there are very genuine champions of England in America. By every possible historical analogy, he would naturally expect to find the pro-Irish in the South and the pro-English in the North. As a matter of fact, he finds almost exactly the opposite. He finds Boston governed by Irishmen, and Nashville containing people more pro-English than Englishmen. He finds Virginians not only of British blood, like George Washington, but of British opinions almost worthy of George the Third.

But I do not say this, as will be seen in a moment, as a criticism of the comparative Toryism of the South. I say it as a criticism of the superlative stupidity of English propaganda. On another page, I remark on the need for a new sort of English propaganda; a propaganda that should be really English and have some remote reference to England. Now if it were a matter of making foreigners feel the real humours and humanities of England, there are no Americans so able or willing to do it as the Americans of the Southern States. As I have already hinted, some of them are so loyal to the English humanities, that they think it their duty to defend even the English inhumanities. New England is turning into New Ireland. But Old England can still be faintly traced in Old Dixie. It contains some of the best things that England herself has had, and therefore (of course) the things that England herself has lost, or is trying to lose. But above all, as I have said, there are people in these places whose historic memories and family traditions really hold them to us, not by alliance but by affection. Indeed, they have the affection in spite of the alliance. They love us in spite of our compliments and courtesies and hands across the sea; all our ambassadorial salutations and speeches cannot kill their love. They manage even to respect us in spite of the shady Jew stockbrokers we send them as English envoys, or the "efficient" men, who are sent out to be tactful with foreigners because they have been too tactless with trades unionists. This type of traditional American, North or South, really has some traditions connecting him with England; and though he is now in a very small minority, I cannot imagine why England should wish to make it smaller. England once sympathized with the South. The South still sympathizes with England. It would seem that the South, or some elements in the South, had rather the advantage of us in political firmness and fidelity; but it does not follow that fidelity will stand every shock. And at this moment, and in this matter, of all things in the world, our political propagandists must try to bolster British Imperialism up, by kicking Southern Secession when it is down. The English politicians eagerly point out that we shall be justified in crushing Ireland exactly as

Sumner and Stevens crushed the most English part of America. It does not seem to occur to them that this comparison between the Unionist triumph in America and a Unionist triumph in Britain is rather hard upon our particular sympathizers, who did not triumph. When England exults in Lincoln's victory over his foes, she is exulting in his victory over her own friends. If her diplomacy continues as delicate and chivalrous as it is at present, they may soon be her only friends. England will be defending herself at the expense of her only defenders. But however this may be, it is as well to bear witness to some of the elements of my own experience; and I can answer for it, at least, that there are some people in the South who will not be pleased at being swept into the rubbish heap of history as rebels and ruffians; and who will not, I regret to say, by any means enjoy even being classed with Fenians and Sinn Feiners.

Now touching the actual comparison between the conquest of the Confederacy and the conquest of Ireland, there are, of course, a good many things to be said which politicians cannot be expected to understand. Strange to say, it is not certain that a lost cause was never worth winning; and it would be easy to argue that the world lost very much indeed when that particular cause was lost. These are not days in which it is exactly obvious that an agricultural society was more dangerous than an industrial one. And even Southern slavery had this one moral merit, that it was decadent; it has this one historic advantage, that it is dead. The Northern slavery, industrial slavery, or what is called wage slavery, is not decaying but increasing; and the end of it is not yet. But in any case, it would be well for us to realize that the reproach of resembling the Confederacy does not ring in all ears as an unanswerable condemnation. It is scarcely a self-evident or sufficient argument, to some hearers, even to prove that the English are as delicate and philanthropic as Sherman, still less that the Irish are as criminal and lawless as Lee. Nor will it soothe every single soul on the American continent to say that the English victory in Ireland will be followed by a reconstruction, like the reconstruction exhibited in the film called

"The Birth of a Nation." And, indeed, there is a further inference from that fine panorama of the exploits of the Ku-Klux Klan. It would be easy, as I say, to turn the argument entirely in favour of the Confederacy. It would be easy to draw the moral, not that the Southern Irish are as wrong as the Southern States, but that the Southern States were as right as the Southern Irish. But upon the whole, I do not incline to accept the parallel in that sense any more than in the opposite sense. For reasons I have already given elsewhere, I do believe that in the main Abraham Lincoln was right. But right in what?

If Lincoln was right, he was right in guessing that there was not really a Northern nation and a Southern nation, but only one American nation. And if he has been proved right, he has been proved right by the fact that men in the South, as well as the North, do now feel a patriotism for that American nation. His wisdom, if it really was wisdom, was justified not by his opponents being conquered, but by their being converted. Now, if the English politicians must insist on this parallel, they ought to see that the parallel is fatal to themselves. The very test which proved Lincoln right has proved them wrong. The very judgment which may have justified him quite unquestionably condemns them. We have again and again conquered Ireland, and have never come an inch nearer to converting Ireland. We have had not one Gettysburg, but twenty Gettysburgs; but we have had no Union. And that is where, as I have remarked, it is relevant to remember that flying fantastic vision on the films that told so many people what no histories have told them. I occasionally heard in America rumours of the local reappearance of the Ku-Klux Klan; but the smallness and mildness of the manifestation, as compared with the old Southern or the new Irish case, is alone a sufficient example of the exception that proves the rule. To approximate to any resemblance to recent Irish events, we must imagine the Ku-Klux Klan riding again in more than the terrors of that vision, wild as the wind, white as the moon, terrible as an army with banners. If there were really such a revival of the Southern action, there would equally be a revival of the Southern argument. It would be clear that Lee was right and Lincoln was wrong; that the Southern States were national and were as indestructible as nations. If the South were as rebellious as Ireland, the North would be as wrong as England.

But I desire a new English diplomacy that will exhibit, not the things in which England is wrong but the things in which England is right. And England is right in England, just as she is wrong in Ireland; and it is exactly that rightness of a real nation in itself that it is at once most difficult and most desirable to explain to foreigners. Now the Irishman, and to some extent the American, has remained alien to England, largely because he does not truly realize that the Englishman loves England, still less can he really imagine why the Englishman loves England. That is why I insist on the stupidity of ignoring and insulting the opinions of those few Virginians and other Southerners who really have some inherited notion of why Englishmen love England; and even love it in something of the same fashion themselves. Politicians who do not know the English spirit when they see it at home, cannot of course be expected to recognize it abroad. Publicists are eloquently praising Abraham Lincoln, for all the wrong reasons; but fundamentally for that worst and vilest of all reasons—that he succeeded. None of them seems to have the least notion of how to look for England in England; and they would see something fantastic in the figure of a traveller who found it elsewhere, or anywhere but in New England. And it is well, perhaps, that they have not yet found England where it is hidden in England; for if they found it, they would kill it.

All I am concerned to consider here is the inevitable failure of this sort of Anglo-American propaganda to create a friendship. To praise Lincoln as an Englishman is about as appropriate as if we were praising Lincoln as an English town. We are talking about something totally different. And indeed the whole conversation is rather like some such cross-purposes about some such word as "Lincoln"; in which one party should be talking about the President and the other about the cathedral. It is like some wild bewilderment in a farce, with one man wondering how a President could have a church-spire, and the other wondering how a church could have a chin-beard. And the moral is the moral on which I would insist everywhere in this book; that the remedy is to be found in disentangling the two and not in entangling them further. You could not produce a democrat of the logical type of Lincoln merely out of the moral materials that now make up an English cathedral town, like that on which Old Tom of Lincoln looks down. But on the other hand, it is quite certain that a hundred Abraham Lincolns, working for a hundred years, could not build Lincoln Cathedral. And the farcical allegory of an attempt to make Old Tom and Old Abe embrace to the glory of the illogical Anglo-Saxon language is but a symbol of something that is always being attempted, and always attempted in vain. It is not by mutual imitation that the understanding can come. It is not by erecting New York sky-scrapers in London that New York can learn the sacred significance of the towers of Lincoln. It is not by English dukes importing the daughters of American millionaires that England can get any glimpse of the democratic dignity of American men. I have the best of all reasons for knowing that a stranger can be welcomed in America; and just as he is courteously treated in the country as a stranger, so he should always be careful to treat it as a strange land. That sort of imaginative respect, as for something different and even distant, is the only beginning of any attachment between patriotic peoples. The English traveller may carry with him at least one word of his own great language and literature; and whenever he is inclined to say of anything "This is passing strange," he may remember that it was no inconsiderable Englishman who appended to it the answer, "And therefore as a stranger give it welcome."

15

Wells and the World State

There was recently a highly distinguished gathering to celebrate the past, present, and especially future triumphs of aviation. Some of the most brilliant men of the age, such as Mr. H. G. Wells and Mr. J. L. Garvin, made interesting and important speeches, and many scientific aviators luminously discussed the new science. Among their graceful felicitations and grave and quiet analyses a word was said, or a note was struck, which I myself can never hear, even in the most harmless after-dinner speech, without an impulse to leap up and yell, and smash the decanters and wreck the dinner-table.

Long ago, when I was a boy, I heard it with fury; and never since have I been able to understand any free man hearing it without fury. I heard it when Bloch, and the old prophets of pacifism by panic, preached that war would become too horrible for patriots to endure.

It sounded to me like saying that an instrument of torture was being prepared by my dentist, that would finally cure me of loving my dog. And I felt it again when all these wise and well-meaning persons began to talk about the inevitable effect of aviation in bridging the Atlantic, and establishing alliance and affection between England and America.

I resent the suggestion that a machine can make me bad. But I resent quite equally the suggestion that a machine can make me good. It might be the unfortunate fact that a coolness had arisen between myself and Mr. Fitzarlington Blenkinsop, inhabiting the suburban villa and garden next to mine; and I might even be largely to blame for it. But if somebody told me that a new kind of lawn-mower had just been invented, of so cunning a structure that I should be forced to become a bosom-friend of Mr. Blenkinsop whether I liked it or not, I should be very much annoyed. I should be moved to say that if that was the only way of cutting my grass I would not cut my grass, but continue to cut my neighbour. Or suppose the difference were even less defensible; suppose a man had suffered from a trifling shindy with his wife. And suppose somebody told him that the introduction of an entirely new vacuum-cleaner would compel him to a reluctant reconciliation with his wife. It would be found, I fancy, that human nature abhors that vacuum. Reasonably spirited human beings will not be ordered about by bicycles and sewing-machines; and a sane man will not be made good, let alone bad, by the things he has himself made. I have occasionally dictated to a typewriter, but I will not be dictated to by a typewriter, even of the newest and most complicated mechanism; nor have I ever met a typewriter, however complex, that attempted such a tyranny.

Yet this and nothing else is what is implied in all such talk of the aeroplane annihilating distinctions as well as distances; and an international aviation abolishing nationalities. This and nothing else was really implied in one speaker's prediction that such aviation will almost necessitate an Anglo-American friendship. Incidentally, I may remark, it is not a true suggestion even in the practical and materialistic sense; and the speaker's phrase refuted the speaker's argument. He said that international relations must be more friendly when men can get from England to America in a day. Well, men can already get from England to Germany in a day; and the result was a mutual invitation of which the formalities lasted for five years. Men could get from the coast of England to the coast of France very quickly, through nearly all the ages during which those two coasts were bristling with arms against each other. They could get there very quickly when Nelson went down by that Burford Inn to embark for Trafalgar; they could get there very quickly when Napoleon sat in his tent in that camp at Boulogne that filled England with alarums of invasion. Are these the amiable and pacific relations which will unite England and America, when Englishmen can get to America in a day? The shortening of the distance seems quite as likely, so far as that argument goes, to facilitate that endless guerilla warfare which raged across the narrow seas in the Middle Ages; when French invaders carried away the bells of Rye, and the men of those flats of East Sussex gloriously pursued and recovered them. I do not know whether American privateers, landing at Liverpool, would carry away a few of the more elegant factory chimneys as a substitute for the superstitious symbols of the past. I know not if the English, on ripe reflection, would essay with any enthusiasm to get them back. But anyhow it is anything but self-evident that people cannot fight each other because they are near to each other; and if it were true, there would never have been any such thing as border warfare in the world. As a fact, border warfare has often been the one sort of warfare which it was most difficult to bring under control. And our own traditional position in face of this new logic is somewhat disconcerting. We have always supposed ourselves safer because we were insular and therefore isolated. We have been congratulating ourselves for centuries on having enjoyed peace because we were cut off from our neighbours. And now they are telling us that we shall only enjoy peace when we are joined up with our neighbours. We have pitied the poor nations with frontiers, because a frontier only produces fighting; and now we are trusting to a frontier as the only thing that will produce friendship. But, as a matter of fact, and for a far deeper and more spiritual reason, a frontier will not produce friendship. Only friendliness produces friendship. And we must look far deeper into the soul of man for the thing that produces friendliness.

But apart from this fallacy about the facts, I feel, as I say, a strong abstract anger against the idea, or what some would call the ideal. If it were true that men could be taught and tamed by machines, even if they were taught wisdom or tamed to amiability, I should think it the most tragic truth in the world. A man so improved would be, in an exceedingly ugly sense, losing his soul to save it. But in truth he cannot be so completely coerced into good; and in so far as he is incompletely coerced, he is quite as likely to be coerced into evil. Of the financial characters who figure as philanthropists and philosophers in such cases, it is strictly true to say that their good is evil. The light in their bodies is darkness, and the highest objects of such men are the lowest objects of ordinary men. Their peace is mere safety, their friendship is mere trade; their international friendship is mere international trade. The best we can say of that school of capitalism is that it will be unsuccessful. It has every other vice, but it is not practical. It has at least the impossibility of idealism; and so far as remoteness can carry it, that Inferno is indeed a Utopia. All the visible manifestations of these men are materialistic; but at least their visions will not materialize. The worse we suffer; but the best we shall at any rate escape. We may continue to endure the realities of cosmopolitan capitalism; but we shall be spared its ideals.

But I am not primarily interested in the plutocrats whose vision takes so vulgar a form. I am interested in the same thing when it takes a far more subtle form, in men of genius and genuine social enthusiasm like Mr. H. G. Wells. It would be very unfair to a man like Mr. Wells to suggest that in his vision the Englishman and the American are to embrace only in the sense of clinging to each other in terror. He is a man who understands what friendship is, and who knows how to enjoy the motley humours of humanity. But the political reconstruction which he proposes is too much determined by this old nightmare of necessitarianism. He tells us that our national dignities and differences must be melted into the huge mould of a World State, or else (and I think these are almost his own words) we shall be destroyed by the instruments and machinery we have ourselves made. In effect, men must abandon patriotism or they will be murdered by science. After this, surely no one can accuse Mr. Wells of an undue tenderness for scientific over other types of training. Greek may be a good thing or no; but nobody says that if Greek scholarship is carried past a certain point, everybody will be torn in pieces like Orpheus, or burned up like Semele, or poisoned like Socrates. Philosophy, theology and logic may or may not be idle academic studies; but nobody supposes that the study of philosophy, or even of theology, ultimately forces its students to manufacture racks and thumb-screws against their will; or that even logicians need be so alarmingly logical as all that. Science seems to be the only branch of study in which people have to be waved back from perfection as from a pestilence. But my business is not with the scientific dangers which alarm Mr. Wells, but with the remedy he proposes for them; or rather with the relation of that remedy to the foundation and the future of America. Now it is not too much to say that Mr. Wells finds his model in America. The World State is to be the United States of the World. He answers almost all objections to the practicability of such a peace among states, by pointing out that the American States have such a peace, and by adding, truly enough, that another turn of history might easily have seen them broken up by war. The pattern of the World State is to be found in the New World.

Oddly enough, as it seems to me, he proposes almost cosmic conquests for the American Constitution, while leaving out the most successful thing in that Constitution. The point appeared in answer to a question which many, like myself, must have put in this matter; the question of despotism and democracy. I cannot understand any democrat not seeing the danger of so distant and indirect a system of government. It is hard enough anywhere to get representatives to represent. It is hard enough to get a little town council to fulfil the wishes of a little town, even when the townsmen meet the town councillors every day in the street, and could kick them down the street if they liked. What the same town councillors would be like if they were ruling all their fellow-creatures from the North Pole or the New Jerusalem, is a vision of Oriental despotism beyond the towering fancies of Tamberlane. This difficulty in all representative government is felt everywhere, and not least in America. But I think that if there is one truth apparent in such a choice of evils, it is that monarchy is at least better than oligarchy; and that where we have to act on a large scale, the most genuine popularity can gather round a particular person like a Pope or a President of the United States, or even a dictator like Cæsar or Napoleon, rather than round a more or less corrupt committee which can only be defined as an obscure oligarchy. And in that sense any oligarchy is obscure. For people to continue to trust twenty-seven men it is necessary, as a preliminary formality, that people should have heard of them. And there are no twenty-seven men of whom everybody has heard as everybody in France had heard of Napoleon, as all Catholics have heard of the Pope or all Americans have heard of the President. I think the mass of ordinary Americans do really elect their President; and even where they cannot control him at least they watch him, and in the long run they judge him. I think, therefore, that the American Constitution has a real popular institution in the Presidency. But Mr. Wells would appear to want the American Constitution without the Presidency. If I understand his words rightly, he seems to want the great democracy without its popular institution. Alluding to this danger, that the World State might be a world tyranny, he seems to take tyranny entirely in the sense of autocracy. He asks whether the President of the World State would not be rather too tremendous a person and seems to suggest in answer that there need not even be any such a person. He seems to imply that the committee controlling the planet could meet almost without anyone in the chair, certainly without anyone on the throne. I cannot imagine anything more manifestly made to be a tyranny than such an acephalous aristocracy. But while Mr. Wells's decision seems to me strange, his reason for it seems to me still more extraordinary.

He suggests that no such dictator will be needed in his World State because "there will be no wars and no diplomacy." A World State ought doubtless to go round the world; and going round the world seems to be a good training for arguing in a circle. Obviously there will be no wars and no war-diplomacy if something has the power to prevent them; and we cannot deduce that the something will not want any power. It is rather as if somebody, urging that the Germans could only be defeated by uniting the Allied commands under Marshal Foch, had said that after all it need not offend the British Generals because the French supremacy need only be a fiction, the Germans being defeated. We should naturally say that the German defeat would only be a reality because the Allied command was not a fiction. So the universal peace would only be a reality if the World State were not a fiction. And it could not be even a state if it were not a government. This argument amounts to saying, first that the World State will be needed because it is strong, and then that it may safely be weak because it will not be needed.

Internationalism is in any case hostile to democracy. I do not say it is incompatible with it; but any combination of the two will be a compromise between the two. The only purely popular government is local, and founded on local knowledge. The citizens can rule the city because they know the city; but it will always be an exceptional sort of citizen who has or claims the right to rule over ten cities, and these remote and altogether alien cities. All Irishmen may know roughly the same sort of things about Ireland; but it is absurd to say they all know the same things about Iceland, when they may include a scholar steeped in Icelandic sagas or a sailor who has been to Iceland. To make all politics cosmopolitan is to create an aristocracy of globe-trotters. If your political outlook really takes in the Cannibal Islands, you depend of necessity upon a superior and picked minority of the people who have been to the Cannibal Islands; or rather of the still smaller and more select minority who have come back.

Given this difficulty about quite direct democracy over large areas, I think the nearest thing to democracy is despotism. At any rate I think it is some sort of more or less independent monarchy, such as Andrew Jackson created in America. And I believe it is true to say that the two men whom the modern world really and almost reluctantly regards with impersonal respect, as clothed by their office with something historic and honourable, are the Pope and the President of the United States.

But to admire the United States as the United States is one thing. To admire them as the World State is quite another. The attempt of Mr. Wells to make America a sort of model for the federation of all the free nations of the earth, though it is international in intention, is really as narrowly national, in the bad sense, as the desire of Mr. Kipling to cover the world with British Imperialism, or of Professor Treitschke to cover it with Prussian Pan-Germanism. Not being schoolboys, we no longer believe that everything can be settled by painting the map red. Nor do I believe it can be done by painting it blue with white spots, even if they are called stars. The insufficiency of British Imperialism does not lie in the fact that it has always been applied by force of arms. As a matter of fact, it has not. It has been effected largely by commerce, by colonization of comparatively empty places, by geographical discovery and diplomatic bargain. Whether it be regarded as praise or blame, it is certainly the truth that among all the things that have called themselves empires, the British has been perhaps the least purely military, and has least both of the special guilt and the special glory that goes with militarism. The insufficiency of British Imperialism is not that it is imperial, let alone military. The insufficiency of British Imperialism is that it is British; when it is not merely Jewish. It is that just as a man is no more than a man, so a nation is no more than a nation; and any nation is inadequate as an international model. Any state looks small when it occupies the whole earth. Any polity is narrow as soon as it is as wide as the world. It would be just the same if Ireland began to paint the map green or Montenegro were to paint it black. The objection to spreading anything all over the world is that, among other things, you have to spread it very thin.

But America, which Mr Wells takes as a model, is in another sense rather a warning. Mr. Wells says very truly that there was a moment in history when America might well have broken up into independent states like those of Europe. He seems to take it for granted that it was in all respects an advantage that this was avoided. Yet there is surely a case, however mildly we put it, for a certain importance in the world still attaching to Europe. There are some who find France as interesting as Florida; and who think they can learn as much about history and humanity in the marble cities of the Mediterranean as in the wooden towns of the Middle West. Europe may have been divided, but it was certainly not destroyed; nor has its peculiar position in the culture of the world been destroyed. Nothing has yet appeared capable of completely eclipsing it, either in its extension in America or its imitation in Japan. But the immediate point here is perhaps a more important one. There is now no creed accepted as embodying the common sense of all Europe, as the Catholic creed was accepted as embodying it in mediaeval times. There is no culture broadly superior to all others, as the Mediterranean culture was superior to that of the barbarians in Roman times. If Europe were united in modern times, it would probably be by the victory of one of its types over others, possibly over all the others. And when America was united finally in the nineteenth century, it *was* by the victory of one of its types over others. It is not yet certain that this victory was a good thing. It is not yet certain that the world will be better for the triumph of the North over the Southern traditions of America. It may yet turn out to be as unfortunate as a triumph of the North Germans over the Southern traditions of Germany and of Europe.

The men who will not face this fact are men whose minds are not free. They are more crushed by Progress than any pietists by Providence. They are not allowed to question that whatever has recently happened was all for the best. Now Progress is Providence without God. That is, it is a theory that everything has always perpetually gone right by accident. It is a sort of atheistic optimism, based on an everlasting coincidence far more miraculous than a miracle. If there be no purpose, or if the purpose permits of human free will, then in either case it is almost insanely unlikely that there should be in history a period of steady and uninterrupted progress; or in other words a period in which poor bewildered humanity moves amid a chaos of complications, without making a single mistake. What has to be hammered into the heads of most normal newspaper-readers to-day is that Man has made a great many mistakes. Modern Man has made a great many mistakes. Indeed, in the case of that progressive and pioneering character, one is sometimes tempted to say that he has made nothing but mistakes. Calvinism was a mistake, and Capitalism was a mistake, and Teutonism and the flattery of the Northern tribes were mistakes. In the French the persecution of Catholicism by the politicians was a mistake, as they found out in the Great War; when the memory gave Irish or Italian Catholics an excuse for hanging back. In England the loss of agriculture and therefore of food-supply in war, and the power to stand a siege, was a mistake. And in America the introduction of the negroes was a mistake; but it may yet be found that the sacrifice of the Southern white man to them was even more of a mistake.

The reason of this doubt is in one word. We have not yet seen the end of the whole industrial experiment; and there are already signs of it coming to a bad end. It may end in Bolshevism. It is more likely to end in the Servile State. Indeed, the two things are not so different as some suppose, and they grow less different every day. The Bolshevists have already called in Capitalists to help them to crush the free peasants. The Capitalists are quite likely to call in Labour Leaders to whitewash their compromise as social reform or even Socialism. The cosmopolitan Jews who are the Communists in the East will not find it so very hard to make a bargain with the cosmopolitan Jews who are Capitalists in the West. The Western Jews would be willing to admit a nominal Socialism. The Eastern Jews have already admitted that their Socialism is nominal. It was the Bolshevist leader himself who said, "Russia is again a Capitalist country." But whoever makes the bargain, and whatever is its precise character, the substance of it will be servile.

It will be servile in the only rational and reliable sense; that is, an arrangement by which a mass of men are ensured shelter and livelihood, in return for being subjected to a law which obliges them to continue to labour. Of course it will not be called the Servile State; it is very probable that it will be called the Socialist State. But nobody seems to realize how very near all the industrial countries are to it. At any moment it may appear in the simple form of compulsory arbitration; for compulsory arbitration dealing with private employers is by definition slavery. When workmen receive unemployment pay, and at the same time arouse more and more irritation by going on strike, it may seem very natural to give them the unemployment pay for good and forbid them the strike for good; and the combination of those two things is by definition slavery. And Trotsky can beat any Trust magnate as a strike-breaker; for he does not even pretend that his compulsory labour is a free bargain. If Trotsky and the Trust magnate come to a working compromise, that compromise will be a Servile State. But it will also be the supreme and by far the most constructive and conclusive result of the industrial movement in history; of the power of machinery or money; of the huge populations of the modern cities; of scientific inventions and resources; of all the things before which the agricultural society of the Southern Confederacy went down. But even those who cannot see that commercialism may end in the triumph of slavery can see that the Northern victory has to a great extent ended in the triumph of commercialism. And the point at the moment is that this did definitely mean, even at the time, the triumph of one American type over another American type; just as much as any European war might mean the triumph of one European type over another. A victory of England over France would be a victory of merchants over peasants; and the victory of Northerners over Southerners was a victory of merchants over squires. So that that very unity, which Mr. Wells contrasts so favourably with war, was not only itself due to a war, but to a war which had one of the most questionable and even perilous of the results of war. That result was a change in the balance of power, the predominance of a particular partner, the exaltation of a particular example, the eclipse of excellent traditions when the defeated lost their international influence. In short, it made exactly the same sort of difference of which we speak when we say that 1870 was a disaster to Europe, or that it was necessary to fight Prussia lest she should Prussianize the whole world. America would have been very different if the leadership had remained with Virginia. The world would have been very different if America had been very different. It is quite reasonable to rejoice that the issue went as it did; indeed, as I have explained elsewhere, for other reasons I do on the whole rejoice in it. But it is certainly not self-evident that it is a matter for rejoicing. One type of American state conquered and subjugated another type of American state; and the virtues and value of the latter were very largely lost to the world. So if Mr. Wells insists on the parallel of a United States of Europe, he must accept the parallel of a Civil War of Europe. He must suppose that the peasant countries crush the industrial countries or *vice versa*; and that one or other of them becomes the European tradition to the neglect of the other. The situation which seems to satisfy him so completely in America is, after all, the situation which would result in Europe if the German Empire, let us say, had entirely arrested the special development of the Slavs; or if the influence of France had really broken off short under the blow from Britain. The Old South had qualities of humane civilization which have not sufficiently survived; or at any rate have not sufficiently spread. It is true that the decline of the agricultural South has been considerably balanced by the growth of the agricultural West. It is true, as I have occasion to emphasize in another place, that the West does give the New America something that is nearly a normal peasantry, as a pendant to the industrial towns. But this is not an answer; it is rather an augmentation of the argument. In so far as America is saved it is saved by being patchy; and would be ruined if the Western patch had the same fate as the Southern patch. When all is said, therefore, the advantages of American unification are not so certain that we can apply them to a world unification. The doubt could be expressed in a great many ways and by a great many examples. For that matter, it is already being felt that supremacy of the Middle West in politics is inflicting upon other localities exactly the sort of local injustice that turns provinces into nations struggling to be free. It has already inflicted what amounts to religious persecution, or the imposition of an alien morality, on the wine-growing civilization of California. In a word, the American system is a good one as governments go; but it is too large, and the world will not be improved by making it larger. And for this reason alone I should reject this second method of uniting England and America; which is not only Americanizing England, but Americanizing everything else.

But the essential reason is that a type of culture came out on top in America and England in the nineteenth century, which cannot and would not be tolerated on top of the world. To unite all the systems at the top, without improving and simplifying their social organization below, would be to tie all the tops of the trees together where they rise above a dense and poisonous jungle, and make the jungle darker than before. To create such a cosmopolitan political platform would be to build a roof above our own heads to shut out the sunlight, on which only usurers and conspirators clad in gold could walk about in the sun. This is no moment when industrial intellectualism can inflict such an artificial oppression upon the world. Industrialism itself is coming to see dark days, and its future is very doubtful. It is split from end to end with strikes and struggles for economic life, in which the poor not only plead that they are starving, but even the rich can only plead that they are bankrupt. The peasantries are growing not only more prosperous but more politically effective; the Russian moujik has held up the Bolshevist Government of Moscow and Petersburg; a huge concession has been made by England to Ireland; the League of Nations has decided for Poland against Prussia. It is not certain that industrialism will not wither even in its own field; it is certain that its intellectual ideas will not be allowed to cover every field; and this sort of cosmopolitan culture is one of its ideas. Industrialism itself may perish;

or on the other hand industrialism itself may survive, by some searching and scientific reform that will really guarantee economic security to all. It may really purge itself of the accidental maladies of anarchy and famine; and continue as a machine, but at least as a comparatively clean and humanely shielded machine; at any rate no longer as a man-eating machine. Capitalism may clear itself of its worst corruptions by such reform as is open to it; by creating humane and healthy conditions for labour, and setting the labouring classes to work under a lucid and recognized law. It may make Pittsburg one vast model factory for all who will model themselves upon factories; and may give to all men and women in its employment a clear social status in which they can be contented and secure. And on the day when that social security is established for the masses, when industrial capitalism has achieved this larger and more logical organization and found peace at last, a strange and shadowy and ironic triumph, like an abstract apology, will surely hover over all those graves in the Wilderness where lay the bones of so many gallant gentlemen; men who had also from their youth known and upheld such a social stratification, who had the courage to call a spade a spade and a slave a slave.

16

A New Martin Chuzzlewit

The aim of this book, if it has one, is to suggest this thesis; that the very worst way of helping Anglo-American friendship is to be an Anglo-American. There is only one thing lower, of course, which is being an Anglo-Saxon. It is lower, because at least Englishmen do exist and Americans do exist; and it may be possible, though repulsive, to imagine an American and an Englishman in some way blended together. But if Angles and Saxons ever did exist, they are all fortunately dead now; and the wildest imagination cannot form the weakest idea of what sort of monster would be made by mixing one with the other. But my thesis is that the whole hope, and the only hope, lies not in mixing two things together, but rather in cutting them very sharply asunder. That is the only way in which two things can succeed sufficiently in getting outside each other to appreciate and admire each other. So long as they are different and yet supposed to be the same, there can be nothing but a divided mind and a staggering balance. It may be that in the first twilight of time man and woman walked about as one quadruped. But if they did, I am sure it was a quadruped that reared and bucked and kicked up its heels. Then the flaming sword of some angel divided them, and they fell in love with each other.

Should the reader require an example a little more within historical range, or a little more subject to critical tests, than the above prehistoric anecdote (which I need not say was revealed to me in a vision) it would be easy enough to supply them both in a hypothetical and a historical form. It is obvious enough in a general way that if we begin to subject diverse countries to an identical test, there will not only be rivalry, but what is far more deadly and disastrous, superiority. If we institute a competition between Holland and Switzerland as to the relative grace and agility of their mountain guides, it will be clear that the decision is disproportionately easy; it will also be clear that certain facts about the configuration of Holland have escaped our international eye. If we establish a comparison between them in skill and industry in the art of building dykes against the sea, it will be equally clear that the injustice falls the other way; it will also be clear that the situation of Switzerland on the map has received insufficient study. In both cases there will not only be rivalry but very unbalanced and unjust rivalry; in both cases, therefore there will not only be enmity but very bitter or insolent enmity. But so long as the two are sharply divided there can be no enmity because there can be no rivalry. Nobody can argue about whether the Swiss climb mountains better than the Dutch build dykes; just as nobody can argue about whether a triangle is more triangular than a circle is round.

This fancy example is alphabetically and indeed artificially simple; but, having used it for convenience, I could easily give similar examples not of fancy but of fact. I had occasion recently to attend the Christmas festivity of a club in London for the exiles of one of the Scandinavian nations. When I entered the room the first thing that struck my eye, and greatly raised my spirits, was that the room was dotted with the colours of peasant costumes and the specimens of peasant craftsmanship. There were, of course, other costumes and other crafts in evidence; there were men dressed like myself (only better) in the garb of the modern middle classes; there was furniture like the furniture of any other room in London. Now, according to the ideal formula of the ordinary internationalist, these things that we had in common ought to have moved me to a sense of the kinship of all civilization. I ought to have felt that as the Scandinavian gentleman wore a collar and tie, and I also wore a collar and tie, we were brothers and nothing could come between us. I ought to have felt that we were standing for the same principles of truth because we were wearing the same pair of trousers; or rather, to speak with more precision, similar pairs of trousers. Anyhow, the pair of trousers, that cloven pennon, ought to have floated in fancy over my head as the banner of Europe or the League of Nations. I am constrained to confess that no such rush of emotions overcame me; and the topic of trousers did not float across my mind at all. So far as those things were concerned, I might have remained in a mood of mortal enmity, and cheerfully shot or stabbed the best dressed gentleman in the room. Precisely what did warm my heart with an abrupt affection for that northern nation was the very thing that is utterly and indeed lamentably lacking in my own nation. It was something corresponding to the one great gap in English history, corresponding to the one great blot on English civilization. It was the spiritual presence of a peasantry, dressed according to its own dignity, and expressing itself by its own creations.

The sketch of America left by Charles Dickens is generally regarded as something which is either to be used as a taunt or covered with an apology. Doubtless it was unduly critical, even of the America of that day; yet curiously enough it may well be the text for a true reconciliation at the present day. It is true that in this, as in other things, the Dickensian exaggeration is itself exaggerated. It is also true that, while it is over-emphasized, it is not allowed for. Dickens tended too much to describe the United States as a vast lunatic asylum; but partly because he had a natural inspiration and imagination suited to the description of lunatic asylums. As it was his finest poetic fancy that created a lunatic over the garden wall, so it was his fancy that created a lunatic over the western sea. To read some of the complaints, one would fancy that Dickens had deliberately invented a low and farcical America to be a contrast to his high and exalted England. It is suggested that he showed America as full of rowdy bullies like Hannibal Chollop, or ridiculous windbags like Elijah Pogram, while England was full of refined and sincere spirits like Jonas Chuzzlewit, Chevy Slime, Montague Tigg, and Mr. Pecksniff. If *Martin Chuzzlewit* makes America a lunatic asylum, what in the world does it make England? We can only say a criminal lunatic asylum. The truth is, of course, that Dickens so described them because he had a genius for that sort of description; for the making of almost maniacal grotesques of the same type as Quilp or Fagan. He made these Americans absurd because he was an artist in absurdity; and no artist can help finding hints everywhere for his own peculiar art. In a word, he created a laughable Pogram for the same reason that he created a laughable Pecksniff; and that was only because no other creature could have created them.

It is often said that we learn to love the characters in romances as if they were characters in real life. I wish we could sometimes love the characters in real life as we love the characters in romances. There are a great many human souls whom we should accept more kindly, and even appreciate more clearly, if we simply thought of them as people in a story. *Martin Chuzzlewit* is itself indeed an unsatisfactory and even unfortunate example; for it is, among its author's other works, a rather unusually harsh and hostile story. I do not suggest that we should feel towards an American friend that exact shade or tint of tenderness that we feel towards Mr. Hannibal Chollop. Our enjoyment of the foreigner should rather resemble our enjoyment of Pickwick than our enjoyment of Pecksniff. But there is this amount of appropriateness even in the particular example; that Dickens did show in both countries how men can be made amusing to each other. So far the point is not that he made

214

fun of America, but that he got fun out of America. And, as I have already pointed out, he applied exactly the same method of selection and exaggeration to England. In the other English stories, written in a more amiable mood, he applied it in a more amiable manner; but he could apply it to an American too, when he was writing in that mood and manner. We can see it in the witty and withering criticism delivered by the Yankee traveller in the musty refreshment room of Mugby Junction; a genuine example of a genuinely American fun and freedom satirizing a genuinely British stuffiness and snobbery. Nobody expects the American traveller to admire the refreshments at Mugby Junction; but he might admire the refreshment at one of the Pickwickian inns, especially if it contained Pickwick. Nobody expects Pickwick to like Pogram; but he might like the American who made fun of Mugby Junction. But the point is that, while he supported him in making fun, he would also think him funny. The two comic characters could admire each other, but they would also be amused at each other. And the American would think the Englishman funny because he was English; and a very good reason too. The Englishman would think the American amusing because he was American; nor can I imagine a better ground for his amusement.

Now many will debate on the psychological possibility of such a friendship founded on reciprocal ridicule, or rather on a comedy of comparisons. But I will say of this harmony of humours what Mr. H. G. Wells says of his harmony of states in the unity of his World State. If it be truly impossible to have such a peace, then there is nothing possible except war. If we cannot have friends in this fashion, then we shall sooner or later have enemies in some other fashion. There is no hope in the pompous impersonalities of internationalism.

And this brings us to the real and relevant mistake of Dickens. It was not in thinking his Americans funny, but in thinking them foolish because they were funny. In this sense it will be noticed that Dickens's American sketches are almost avowedly superficial; they are descriptions of public life and not private life. Mr. Jefferson Brick had no private life. But Mr. Jonas Chuzzlewit undoubtedly had a private life; and even kept some parts of it exceeding private. Mr. Pecksniff was also a domestic character; so was Mr. Quilp. Mr. Pecksniff and Mr. Quilp had slightly different ways of surprising their families; Mr. Pecksniff by playfully observing "Boh!" when he came home; Mr. Quilp by coming home at all. But we can form no picture of how Mr. Hannibal Chollop playfully surprised his family; possibly by shooting at them; possibly by not shooting at them. We can only say that he would rather surprise us by having a family at all. We do not know how the Mother of the Modern Gracchi managed the Modern Gracchi; for her maternity was rather a public than a private office. We have no romantic moonlit scenes of the love-making of Elijah Pogram, to balance against the love story of Seth Pecksniff. These figures are all in a special sense theatrical; all facing one way and lit up by a public limelight. Their ridiculous characters are detachable from their real characters, if they have any real characters. And the author might perfectly well be right about what is ridiculous and wrong about what is real. He might be as right in smiling at the Pograms and the Bricks as in smiling at the Pickwicks and the Boffins. And he might still be as wrong in seeing Mr. Pogram as a hypocrite as the great Buzfuz was wrong in seeing Mr. Pickwick as a monster of revolting heartlessness and systematic villainy. He might still be as wrong in thinking Jefferson Brick a charlatan and a cheat as was that great disciple of Lavater, Mrs. Wilfer, in tracing every wrinkle of evil cunning in the face of Mrs. Boffin. For Mr. Pickwick's spectacles and gaiters and Mrs. Boffin's bonnets and boudoir are after all superficial jokes; and might be equally well seen whatever we saw beneath them. A man may smile and smile and be a villain; but a man may also make us smile and not be a villain. He may make us smile and not even be a fool. He may make us roar with laughter and be an exceedingly wise man.

Now that is the paradox of America which Dickens never discovered. Elijah Pogram was far more fantastic than his satirist thought; and the most grotesque feature of Brick and Chollop was hidden from him. The really strange thing was that Pogram probably did say, "Rough he may be. So air our bars. Wild he may be. So air our buffalers," and yet was a perfectly intelligent and public-spirited citizen while he said it. The extraordinary thing is that Jefferson Brick may really have said, "The libation of freedom must sometimes be quaffed in blood," and yet Jefferson Brick may have served freedom, resisting unto blood. There really has been a florid school of rhetoric in the United States which has made it quite possible for serious and sensible men to say such things. It is amusing simply as a difference of idiom or costume is always amusing; just as English idiom and English costume are amusing to Americans. But about this kind of difference there can be no kind of doubt. So sturdy not to say stuffy a materialist as Ingersoll could say of so shoddy not to say shady a financial politician as Blaine, "Like an arméd warrior, like a pluméd knight, James G. Blaine strode down the hall of Congress, and flung his spear full and true at the shield of every enemy of his country and every traducer of his fair name." Compared with that, the passage about bears and buffaloes, which Mr. Pogram delivered in defense of the defaulting post-master, is really a very reasonable and appropriate statement. For bears and buffaloes are wild and rough and in that sense free; while pluméd knights do not throw their lances about like the assegais of Zulus. And the defaulting post-master was at least as good a person to praise in such a fashion as James G. Blaine of the Little Rock Railway. But anybody who had treated Ingersoll or Blaine merely as a fool and a figure of fun would have very rapidly found out his mistake. But Dickens did not know Brick or Chollop long enough to find out his mistake. It need not be denied that, even after a full understanding, he might still have found things to smile at or to criticize. I do not insist on his admitting that Hannibal Chollop was as great a hero as Hannibal, or that Elijah Pogram was as true a prophet as Elijah. But I do say very seriously that they had something about their atmosphere and situation that made possible a sort of heroism and even a sort of prophecy that were really less natural at that period in that Merry England whose comedy and common sense we sum up under the name of Dickens. When we joke about the name of Hannibal Chollop, we might remember of what nation was the general who dismissed his defeated soldiers at Appomatox with words which the historian has justly declared to be worthy of Hannibal: "We have fought through this war together. I have done my best for you." It is not fair to forget Jefferson, or even Jefferson Davis, entirely in favour of Jefferson Brick.

For all these three things, good, bad, and indifferent, go together to form something that Dickens missed, merely because the England of his time most disastrously missed it. In this case, as in every case, the only way to measure justly the excess of a foreign country is to measure the defect of our own country. For in this matter the human mind is the victim of a curious little unconscious trick, the cause of nearly all international dislikes. A man treats his own faults as original sin and supposes them scattered everywhere with the seed of Adam. He supposes that men have then added their own foreign vices to the solid and simple foundation of his own private vices. It would astound him to realize that they have actually, by their strange erratic path, avoided his vices as well as his virtues. His own faults are things with which he is so much at home that he at once forgets and assumes them abroad. He is so faintly conscious of them in himself that he is not even conscious of the absence of them in other people. He assumes that they are there so that he does not see that they are not there. The Englishman takes it for granted that a Frenchman will have all the English faults. Then he goes on to be seriously angry with the Frenchman for having dared to complicate them by the French faults. The notion that the Frenchman has the French faults and *not* the English faults is a paradox too wild to cross his mind.

He is like an old Chinaman who should laugh at Europeans for wearing ludicrous top-hats and curling up their pig-tails inside them; because obviously all men have pig-tails, as all monkeys have tails. Or he is like an old Chinese lady who should justly deride the high-heeled shoes of the West, considering them a needless addition to the sufficiently tight and secure bandaging of the foot; for, of course, all women bind up their feet, as all women bind up their hair. What these

218

Celestial thinkers would not think of, or allow for, is the wild possibility that we do not have pig-tails although we do have top-hats, or that our ladies are not silly enough to have Chinese feet, though they are silly enough to have high-heeled shoes. Nor should we necessarily have come an inch nearer to the Chinese extravagances even if the chimney-pot hat rose higher than a factory chimney or the high heels had evolved into a sort of stilts. By the same fallacy the Englishman will not only curse the French peasant as a miser, but will also try to tip him as a beggar. That is, he will first complain of the man having the surliness of an independent man, and then accuse him of having the servility of a dependent one. Just as the hypothetical Chinaman cannot believe that we have top-hats but not pig-tails, so the Englishman cannot believe that peasants are not snobs even when they are savages. Or he sees that a Paris paper is violent and sensational; and then supposes that some millionaire owns twenty such papers and runs them as a newspaper trust. Surely the Yellow Press is present everywhere to paint the map yellow, as the British Empire to paint it red. It never occurs to such a critic that the French paper is violent because it is personal, and personal because it belongs to a real and responsible person, and not to a ring of nameless millionaires. It is a pamphlet, and not an anonymous pamphlet. In a hundred other cases the same truth could be illustrated; the situation in which the black man first assumes that all mankind is black, and then accuses the rest of the artificial vice of painting their faces red and yellow, or the hypocrisy of white-washing themselves after the fashion of whited sepulchres. The particular case of it now before us is that of the English misunderstanding of America; and it is based, as in all these cases, on the English misunderstanding of England.

For the truth is that England has suffered of late from not having enough of the free shooting of Hannibal Chollop; from not understanding enough that the libation of freedom must sometimes be quaffed in blood. The prosperous Englishman will not admit this; but then the prosperous Englishman will not admit that he has suffered from anything. That is what he is suffering from. Until lately at least he refused to realize that many of his modern habits had been bad habits, the worst of them being contentment. For all the real virtue in contentment evaporates, when the contentment is only satisfaction and the satisfaction is only self-satisfaction. Now it is perfectly true that America and not England has seen the most obvious and outrageous official denials of liberty. But it is equally true that it has seen the most obvious flouting of such official nonsense, far more obvious than any similar evasions in England. And nobody who knows the subconscious violence of the American character would ever be surprised if the weapons of Chollop began to be used in that most lawful lawlessness. It is perfectly true that the libation of freedom must sometimes be drunk in blood, and never more (one would think) than when mad millionaires forbid it to be drunk in beer. But America, as compared with England, is the country where one can still fancy men obtaining the libation of beer by the libation of blood. Vulgar plutocracy is almost omnipotent in both countries; but I think there is now more kick of reaction against it in America than in England. The Americans may go mad when they make laws; but they recover their reason when they disobey them. I wish I could believe that there was as much of that destructive repentance in England; as indeed there certainly was when Cobbett wrote. It faded gradually like a dying fire through the Victorian era; and it was one of the very few realities that Dickens did not understand. But any one who does understand it will know that the days of Cobbett saw the last lost fight for English democracy; and that if he had stood at that turning of the historic road, he would have wished a better fate to the frame-breakers and the fury against the first machinery, and luck to the Luddite fires.

Anyhow, what is wanted is a new Martin Chuzzlewit, told by a wiser Mark Tapley. It is typical of something sombre and occasionally stale in the mood of Dickens when he wrote that book, that the comic servant is not really very comic. Mark Tapley is a very thin shadow of Sam Weller. But if Dickens had written it in a happier mood, there might have been a truer meaning in Mark Tapley's happiness. For it is true that this illogical good humour amid unreason and disorder is one of the real virtues of the English people. It is the real advantage they have in that adventure all over the world, which they were recently and reluctantly induced to call an Empire. That receptive ridicule remains with them as a secret pleasure when they are colonists—or convicts. Dickens might have written another version of the great romance, and one in which America was really seen gaily by Mark instead of gloomily by Martin. Mark Tapley might really have made the best of America. Then America would have lived and danced before us like Pickwick's England, a fairyland of happy lunatics and lovable monsters, and we might still have sympathized as much with the rhetoric of Lafayette Kettle as with the rhetoric of Wilkins Micawber, or with the violence of Chollop as with the violence of Boythorn. That new Martin Chuzzlewit will never be written; and the loss of it is more tragic than the loss of Edwin Drood. But every man who has travelled in America has seen glimpses and episodes in that untold tale; and far away on the Red-Indian frontiers or in the hamlets in the hills of Pennsylvania, there are people whom I met for a few hours or for a few moments, whom I none the less sincerely like and respect because I cannot but smile as I think of them. But the converse is also true; they have probably forgotten me; but if they remember they laugh.

17

The Spirit of America

I suggest that diplomatists of the internationalist school should spend some of their money on staging farces and comedies of cross-purposes, founded on the curious and prevalent idea that England and America have the same language. I know, of course, that we both inherit the glorious tongue of Shakespeare, not to mention the tune of the musical glasses; but there have been moments when I thought that if we spoke Greek and they spoke Latin we might understand each other better. For Greek and Latin are at least fixed, while American at least is still very fluid. I do not know the American language, and therefore I do not claim to distinguish between the American language and the American slang. But I know that highly theatrical developments might follow on taking the words as part of the English slang or the English language. I have already given the example of calling a person "a regular guy," which in the States is a graceful expression of respect and esteem, but which on the stage, properly handled, might surely lead the way towards a divorce or duel or something lively. Sometimes coincidence merely clinches a mistake, as it so often clinches a misprint. Every proof-reader knows that the worst misprint is not that which makes nonsense but that which makes sense; not that which is obviously wrong but that which is hideously right. He who has essayed to write "he got the book," and has found it rendered mysteriously as "he got the boob" is pensively resigned. It is when it is rendered quite lucidly as "he got the boot" that he is moved to a more passionate mood of regret. I have had conversations in which this sort of accident would have wholly misled me, if another accident had not come to the rescue. An American friend of mine was telling me of his adventures as a cinema-producer down in the south-west where real Red Indians were procurable. He said that certain Indians were "very bad actors." It passed for me as a very ordinary remark on a very ordinary or natural deficiency. It would hardly seem a crushing criticism to say that some wild Arab chieftain was not very good at imitating a farmyard; or that the Grand Llama of Thibet was rather clumsy at making paper boats. But the remark might be natural in a man travelling in paper boats, or touring with an invisible farmyard for his menagerie. As my friend was a cinema-producer, I supposed he meant that the Indians were bad cinema actors. But the phrase has really a high and austere moral meaning, which my levity had wholly missed. A bad actor means a man whose actions are bad or morally reprehensible. So that I might have embraced a Red Indian who was dripping with gore, or covered with atrocious crimes, imagining there was nothing the matter with him beyond a mistaken choice of the theatrical profession. Surely there are here the elements of a play, not to mention a cinema play. Surely a New England village maiden might find herself among the wigwams in the power of the formidable and fiendish "Little Blue Bison," merely through her mistaken sympathy with his financial failure as a Film Star. The notion gives me glimpses of all sorts of dissolving views of primeval forests and flamboyant theatres; but this impulse of irrelevant theatrical production must be curbed. There is one example, however, of this complication of language actually used in contrary senses, about which the same figure can be used to illustrate a more serious fact.

Suppose that, in such an international interlude, an English girl and an American girl are talking about the fiancé of the former, who is coming to call. The English girl will be haughty and aristocratic (on the stage), the American girl will of course have short hair and skirts and will be cynical; Americans being more completely free from cynicism than any people in the world. It is the great glory of Americans that they are not cynical; for that matter, English aristocrats are hardly ever haughty; they understand the game much better than that. But on the stage, anyhow, the American girl may say, referring to her friend's fiancé, with a cynical wave of the cigarette, "I suppose he's bound to come and see you." And at this the blue blood of the Vere de Veres will boil over; the English lady will be deeply wounded and insulted at the suggestion that her lover only comes to see her because he is forced to do so. A staggering stage quarrel will then ensue, and things will go from bad to worse; until the arrival of an Interpreter who can talk both English and American. He stands between the two ladies waving two pocket dictionaries, and explains the error on which the quarrel turns. It is very simple; like the seed of all tragedies. In English "he is bound to come and see you" means that he is obliged or constrained to come and see you. In American it does not. In American it means that he is bent on coming to see you, that he is irrevocably resolved to do so, and will surmount any obstacle to do it. The two young ladies will then embrace as the curtain falls.

Now when I was lecturing in America I was often told, in a radiant and congratulatory manner, that such and such a person was bound to come and hear me lecture. It seemed a very cruel form of conscription, and I could not understand what authority could have made it compulsory. In the course of discovering my error, however, I thought I began to understand certain American ideas and instincts that lie behind this

American idiom. For as I have urged before, and shall often urge again, the road to international friendship is through really understanding jokes. It is in a sense through taking jokes seriously. It is quite legitimate to laugh at a man who walks down the street in three white hats and a green dressing-gown because it is unfamiliar; but after all the man has *some* reason for what he does; and until we know the reason we do not understand the story, or even understand the joke. So the outlander will always seem outlandish in custom or costume; but serious relations depend on our getting beyond the fact of difference to the things wherein it differs. A good symbolical figure for all this may be found among the people who say, perhaps with a self-revealing simplicity, that they are bound to go to a lecture.

If I were asked for a single symbolic figure summing up the whole of what seems eccentric and interesting about America to an Englishman, I should be satisfied to select that one lady who complained of Mrs. Asquith's lecture and wanted her money back. I do not mean that she was typically American in complaining; far from it. I, for one, have a great and guilty knowledge of all that amiable American audiences will endure without complaint. I do not mean that she was typically American in wanting her money; quite the contrary. That sort of American spends money rather than hoards it; and when we convict them of vulgarity we acquit them of avarice. Where she was typically American, summing up a truth individual and indescribable in any other way, is that she used these words: "I've risen from a sick-bed to come and hear her, and I want my money back."

The element in that which really amuses an Englishman is precisely the element which, properly analysed, ought to make him admire an American. But my point is that only by going through the amusement can he reach the admiration. The amusement is in the vision of a tragic sacrifice for what is avowedly a rather trivial object. Mrs. Asquith is a candid lady of considerable humour; and I feel sure she does not regard the experience of hearing her read her diary as an ecstasy for which the sick should thus suffer martyrdom. She also is English; and had no other claim but to amuse Americans and possibly to be amused by them. This being so, it is rather as if somebody said: "I have risked my life in fire and pestilence to find my way to the music hall," or, "I have fasted forty days in the wilderness sustained by the hope of seeing Totty Toddles do her new dance." And there is something rather more subtle involved here. There is something in an Englishman which would make him feel faintly ashamed of saying that he had fasted to hear Totty Toddles, or risen from a sick-bed to hear Mrs. Asquith. He would feel it was undignified to confess that he had wanted mere amusement so much; and perhaps that he had wanted anything so much. He would not like, so to speak, to be seen rushing down the street after Totty Toddles, or after Mrs. Asquith, or perhaps after anybody. But there is something in it distinct from a mere embarrassment at admitting enthusiasm. He might admit the enthusiasm if the object seemed to justify it; he might perfectly well be serious about a serious thing. But he cannot under stand a person being proud of serious sacrifices for what is not a serious thing. He does not like to admit that a little thing can excite him; that he can lose his breath in running, or lose his balance in reaching, after something that might be called silly.

Now that is where the American is fundamentally different. To him the enthusiasm itself is meritorious. To him the excitement itself is dignified. He counts it a part of his manhood to fast or fight or rise from a bed of sickness for something, or possibly for anything. His ideal is not to be a lock that only a worthy key can open, but a "live wire" that anything can touch or anybody can use. In a word, there is a difference in the very definition of virility and therefore of virtue. A live wire is not only active, it is also sensitive. Thus sensibility becomes actually a part of virility. Something more is involved than the vulgar simplification of the American as the irresistible force and the Englishman as the immovable post. As a fact, those who speak of such things nowadays generally mean by something irresistible something simply immovable, or at least something unalterable, motionless even in motion, like a cannon ball; for a cannon ball is as dead as a cannon. Prussian militarism was praised in that way—until it met a French force of about half its size on the banks of the Marne. But that is not what an American means by energy; that sort of Prussian energy is only monotony without repose. American energy is not a soulless machine; for it is the whole point that he puts his soul into it. It is a very small box for so big a thing; but it is not an empty box. But the point is that he is not only proud of his energy, he is proud of his excitement. He is not ashamed of his emotion, of the fire or even the tear in his manly eye, when he tells you that the great wheel of his machine breaks four billion butterflies an hour.

That is the point about American sport; that it is not in the least sportive. It is because it is not very sportive that we sometimes say it is not very sporting. It has the vices of a religion. It has all the paradox of original sin in the service of aboriginal faith. It is sometimes untruthful because it is sincere. It is sometimes treacherous because it is loyal. Men lie and cheat for it as they lied for their lords in a feudal conspiracy, or cheated for their chieftains in a Highland feud. We may say that the vassal readily committed treason; but it is equally true that he readily endured torture. So does the American athlete endure torture. Not only the self-sacrifice but the solemnity of the American athlete is like that of the American Indian. The athletes in the States have the attitude of the athletes among the Spartans, the great historical nation without a sense of humour. They suffer an ascetic régime not to be matched in any monasticism and hardly in any militarism. If any tradition of these things remains in a saner age, they will probably be remembered as a mysterious religious order of fakirs or dancing dervishes, who shaved their heads and fasted in honour of Hercules or Caster and Pollux. And that is really the spiritual atmosphere though the Gods have vanished; and the religion is subconscious and therefore irrational. For the problem of the modern world is that is has continued to be religious when it has ceased to be rational. Americans really would starve to win a cocoa-nut shy. They would fast or bleed to win a race of paper boats on a pond. They would rise from a sick-bed to listen to Mrs. Asquith.

But it is the real reason that interests me here. It is certainly not that Americans are so stupid as not to know that cocoa-nuts are only cocoa-nuts and paper boats only made of paper. Americans are, on an average, rather more intelligent than Englishmen; and they are well aware that Hercules is a myth and that Mrs. Asquith is something of a mythologist. It is not that they do not know that the object is small in itself; it is that they do really believe that the enthusiasm is great in itself. They admire people for being impressionable. They admire people for being excited. An American so struggling for some disproportionate trifle (like one of my lectures) really feels in a mystical way that he is right, because it is his whole morality to be keen. So long as he wants something very much, whatever it is, he feels he has his conscience behind him, and the common sentiment of society behind him, and God and the whole universe behind him. Wedged on one leg in a hot crowd at a trivial lecture, he has self-respect; his dignity is at rest. That is what he means when he says he is bound to come to the lecture.

Now the Englishman is fond of occasional larks. But these are not larks; nor are they occasional. It is the essential of the Englishman's lark that he should think it a lark; that he should laugh at it even when he does it. Being English myself, I like it; but being English myself, I know it is connected with weaknesses as well as merits. In its irony there is condescension and therefore embarrassment. This patronage is allied to the patron, and the patron is allied to the aristocratic tradition of society. The larks are a variant of laziness because of leisure; and the leisure is a variant of the security and even supremacy of the gentleman. When an undergraduate at Oxford smashes half a hundred windows, he is well aware that the incident is merely a trifle. He can be trusted to explain to his parents and guardians that it was merely a trifle. He does not say, even in the American sense, that he was bound to smash the windows. He does not say that he had risen from a sick-bed to smash the windows. He does not especially think he has risen at all; he knows he has descended (though with delight, like one diving or sliding down the banisters) to something flat and farcical and full of the

229

English taste for the bathos. He has collapsed into something entirely commonplace; though the owners of the windows may possibly not think so. This rather in describable element runs through a hundred English things, as in the love of bathos shown even in the sound of proper names; so that even the yearning lover in a lyric yearns for somebody named Sally rather than Salome, and for a place called Wapping rather than a place called Westermain. Even in the relapse into rowdiness there is a sort of relapse into comfort. There is also what is so large a part of comfort; carelessness. The undergraduate breaks windows, because he does not care about windows, not because he does care about more fresh air like a hygienist, or about more light like a German poet. Still less does he heroically smash a hundred windows because they come between him and the voice of Mrs. Asquith. But least of all does he do it because he seriously prides himself on the energy apart from its aim, and on the will-power that carries it through. He is not "bound" to smash the windows, even in the sense of being bent upon it. He is not bound at all but rather relaxed; and his violence is not only a relaxation but a laxity. Finally, this is shown in the fact that he only smashes windows when he is in the mood to smash windows; when some fortunate conjunction of stars and all the tints and nuances of nature whisper to him that it would be well to smash windows. But the American is always ready, at any moment, to waste his energies on the wilder and more suicidal course of going to lectures. And this is because to him such excitement is not a mood but a moral ideal. As I note in another connection, much of the English mystery would be clear to Americans if they understood the word "mood." Englishmen are very moody, especially when they smash windows. But I doubt if many Americans understand exactly what we mean by the mood; especially the passive mood.

It is only by trying to get some notion of all this that an Englishman can enjoy the final crown and fruit of all international friendship; which is really liking an American to be American. If we only think that parts of him are excellent because parts of him are English, it would be far more sensible to stop at home and possibly enjoy the society of a whole complete Englishman. But anybody who does understand this can take the same pleasure in an American being American that he does in a thunderbolt being swift and a barometer being sensitive. He can see that a vivid sensibility and vigilance really radiate outwards through all the ramifications of machinery and even of materialism. He can see that the American uses his great practical, powers upon very small provocation; but he can also see that there is a kind of sense of honour, like that of a duellist, in his readiness to be provoked. Indeed, there is some parallel between the American man of action, however vulgar his aims, and the old feudal idea of the gentleman with a sword at his side. The gentleman may have been proud of being strong or sturdy; he may too often have been proud of being thick-headed; but he was not proud of being thick-skinned. On the contrary, he was proud of being thin-skinned. He also seriously thought that sensitiveness was a part of masculinity. It may be very absurd to read of two Irish gentlemen trying to kill each other for trifles, or of two Irish-American millionaires trying to ruin each other for trash. But the very pettiness of the pretext and even the purpose illustrates the same conception; which may be called the virtue of excitability. And it is really this, and not any rubbish about iron will-power and masterful mentality, that redeems with romance their clockwork cosmos and its industrial ideals. Being a live wire does not mean that the nerves should be like wires; but rather that the very wires should be like nerves.

Another approximation to the truth would be to say that an American is really not ashamed of curiosity. It is not so simple as it looks. Men will carry off curiosity with various kinds of laughter and bravado, just as they will carry off drunkenness or bankruptcy. But very few people are really proud of lying on a door-step, and very few people are really proud of longing to look through a key hole. I do not speak of looking through it, which involves questions of honour and self-control; but few people feel that even the desire is dignified. Now I fancy the American, at least by comparison with the Englishman, does feel that his curiosity is consistent with his dignity, because dignity is consistent with vivacity. He feels it is not merely the curiosity of Paul Pry, but the curiosity of Christopher Columbus. He is not a spy but an explorer; and he feels his greatness rather grow with his refusal to turn back, as a traveller might feel taller and taller as he neared the source of the Nile or the North-West Passage. Many an Englishman has had that feeling about discoveries in dark continents; but he does not often have it about discoveries in daily life. The one type does believe in the indignity and the other in the dignity of the detective. It has nothing to do with ethics in the merely external sense. It involves no particular comparison in practical morals and manners. It is something in the whole poise and posture of the self; of the way a man carries himself. For men are not only affected by what they are; but still more, when they are fools, by what they think they are; and when they are wise, by what they wish to be.

There are truths that have almost become untrue by becoming untruthful. There are statements so often stale and insincere that one hesitates to use them, even when they stand for something more subtle. This point about curiosity is not the conventional complaint against the American interviewer. It is not the ordinary joke against the American child. And in the same way I feel the danger of it being identified with the cant about "a young nation" if I say that it has some of the attractions, not of American childhood, but of real childhood. There is some truth in the tradition that the children of wealthy Americans tend to be too precocious and luxurious. But there is a sense in which we can really say that if the children are like adults, the adults are like children. And that sense is in the very best sense of childhood. It is something which the modern world does not understand. It is something that modern Americans do not understand, even when they possess it; but I think they do possess it.

The devil can quote Scripture for his purpose; and the text of Scripture which he now most commonly quotes is, "The kingdom of heaven is within you." That text has been the stay and support of more

Pharisees and prigs and self-righteous spiritual bullies than all the dogmas in creation; it has served to identify self-satisfaction with the peace that passes all understanding. And the text to be quoted in answer to it is that which declares that no man can receive the kingdom except as a little child. What we are to have inside is the childlike spirit; but the childlike spirit is not entirely concerned about what is inside. It is the first mark of possessing it that one is interested in what is outside. The most childlike thing about a child is his curiosity and his appetite and his power of wonder at the world. We might almost say that the whole advantage of having the kingdom within is that we look for it somewhere else.

18

The Spirit of England

Nine times out of ten a man's broad-mindedness is necessarily the narrowest thing about him. This is not particularly paradoxical; it is, when we come to think of it, quite inevitable. His vision of his own village may really be full of varieties; and even his vision of his own nation may have a rough resemblance to the reality. But his vision of the world is probably smaller than the world. His vision of the universe is certainly much smaller than the universe. Hence he is never so inadequate as when he is universal; he is never so limited as when he generalizes. This is the fallacy in the many modern attempts at a creedless creed, at something variously described as essential Christianity or undenominational religion or a world faith to embrace all the faiths in the world. It is that every sectarian is more sectarian in his unsectarianism than he is in his sect. The emancipation of a Baptist is a very Baptist emancipation. The charity of a Buddhist is a very Buddhist charity, and very different from Christian charity. When a philosophy embraces everything it generally squeezes everything, and squeezes it out of shape; when it digests it necessarily assimilates. When a theosophist absorbs Christianity it is rather as a cannibal absorbs Christian missionaries. In this sense it is even possible for the larger thing to be swallowed by the smaller; and for men to move about not only in a Clapham sect but in a Clapham cosmos under Clapham moon and stars.

But if this danger exists for all men, it exists especially for the Englishman. The Englishman is never so insular as when he is imperial; except indeed when he is international. In private life he is a good friend and in practical politics generally a very good ally. But theoretical politics are more practical than practical politics. And in theoretical politics the Englishman is the worst ally the world ever saw. This is all the more curious because he has passed so much of his historical life in the character of an ally. He has been in twenty great alliances and never understood one of them. He has never been farther away from European politics than when he was fighting heroically in the thick of them. I myself think that this splendid isolation is sometimes really splendid; so long as it is isolation and does not imagine itself to be imperialism or internationalism. With the idea of being international, with the idea of being imperial, comes the frantic and farcical idea of being impartial. Generally speaking, men are never so mean and false and hypocritical as when they are occupied in being impartial. They are performing the first and most typical of all the actions of the devil; they are claiming the throne of God. Even when it is not hypocrisy but only mental confusion, it is always a confusion worse and worse confounded. We see it in the impartial historians of the Victorian Age, who now seem far more Victorian than the partial historians. Hallam wrote about the Middle Ages; but Hallam was far less mediaeval than Macaulay; for Macaulay was at least a fighter. Huxley had more mediaeval sympathies than Herbert Spencer for the same reason that Huxley was a fighter. They both fought in many ways for the limitations of their own rationalistic epoch; but they were nearer the truth than the men who simply assumed those limitations as rational. The war of the controversionalists was a wider thing than the peace of the arbiters. And in the same way the Englishman never cuts a less convincing figure before other nations than when he tries to arbitrate between them.

I have by this time heard a great deal about the necessity of saving Anglo-American friendship, a necessity which I myself feel rather too strongly to be satisfied with the ambassadorial and editorial style of achieving it. I have already said that the worst style of all is to be Anglo-American; or, as the more illiterate would express, to be Anglo-Saxon. I am more and more convinced that the way for the Englishman to do it is to be English; but to know that he is English and not everything else as well. Thus the only sincere answer to Irish nationalism is English nationalism, which is a reality; and not English imperialism, which is a reactionary fiction, or English internationalism, which is a revolutionary one.

For the English are reviled for their imperialism because they are not imperialistic. They dislike it, which is the real reason why they do it badly; and they do it badly, which is the real reason why they are disliked when they do it. Nobody calls France imperialistic because she has absorbed Brittany. But everybody calls England imperialistic because she has not absorbed Ireland. The Englishman is fixed and frozen for ever in the attitude of a ruthless conqueror; not because he has conquered such people, but because he has not conquered them; but he is always trying to conquer them with a heroism worthy of a better cause. For the really native and vigorous part of what is unfortunately called the British Empire is not an empire at all, and does not consist of these conquered provinces at all. It is not an empire but an adventure; which is probably a much finer thing. It was not the power of making strange countries similar to our own, but simply the pleasure of seeing strange countries because they were different from our own. The adventurer did indeed, like the third son, set out to seek his fortune, but not primarily to alter other people's fortunes; he wished to trade with people rather than to rule them. But as the other people remained different from him, so did he remain different from them. The adventurer saw a thousand strange things and remained a stranger. He was the Robinson Crusoe on a hundred desert islands; and on each he remained as insular as on his own island.

What is wanted for the cause of England to-day is an Englishman with enough imagination to love his country from the outside as well as the inside. That is, we need somebody who will do for the English what has never been done for them, but what is done for any outlandish peasantry or even any savage tribe. We want people who can make England attractive; quite apart from disputes about whether England is strong or weak. We want somebody to explain, not that England is everywhere, but what England is anywhere; not that England is or is not really dying, but why we do not want her to die. For this purpose the official and conventional compliments or claims can never get any farther than pompous abstractions about Law and Justice and Truth; the ideals which England accepts as every civilized state accepts them, and violates as every civilized state violates them. That is not the way in which the picture of any people has ever been painted on the sympathetic imagination of the world. Enthusiasts for old Japan did not tell us that the Japs recognized the existence of abstract morality; but that they lived in paper houses or wrote letters with paint-brushes. Men who wished to interest us in Arabs did not confine themselves to saying that they are monotheists or moralists; they filled our romances with the rush of Arab steeds or the colours of strange tents or carpets. What we want is somebody who will do for the Englishman with his front garden what was done for the Jap and his paper house; who shall understand the Englishman with his dog as well as the Arab with his horse. In a word, what nobody has really tried to do is the one thing that really wants doing. It is to make England attractive as a nationality, and even as a small nationality.

For it is a wild folly to suppose that nations will love each other because they are alike. They will never really do that unless they are really alike; and then they will not be nations. Nations can love each other as men and women love each other, not because they are alike but because they are different. It can easily be shown, I fancy, that in every case where a real public sympathy was aroused for some unfortunate foreign people, it has always been accompanied with a particular and positive interest in their most foreign customs and their most foreign externals. The man who made a romance of the Scotch Highlander made a romance of his kilt and even of his dirk; the friend of the Red Indians was interested in picture writing and had some tendency to be interested in scalping. To take a more serious example, such nations as Serbia had been largely commended to international consideration by the study of Serbian epics, or Serbian songs. The epoch of negro emancipation was also the epoch of negro melodies. Those who wept over Uncle Tom also laughed over Uncle Remus. And just as the admiration for the Redskin almost became an apology for scalping, the mysterious fascination of the African has sometimes almost led us into the fringes of the black forest of Voodoo. But the sort of interest that is felt even in the scalp-hunter and the cannibal, the torturer and the devil-worshipper, that sort of interest has never been felt in the Englishman.

And this is the more extraordinary because the Englishman is really very interesting. He is interesting in a special degree in this special manner; he is interesting because he is individual. No man in the world is more misrepresented by everything official or even in the ordinary sense national. A description of English life must be a description of private life. In that sense there is no public life. In that sense there is no public opinion. There have never been those prairie fires of public opinion in England which often sweep over America. At any rate, there have never been any such popular revolutions since the popular revolutions of the Middle Ages. The English are a nation of amateurs; they are even a nation of eccentrics. An Englishman is never more English than when he is considered a lunatic by the other Englishmen. This can be clearly seen in a figure like Dr. Johnson, who has become national not by being normal but by being extraordinary. To express this mysterious people, to explain or suggest why they like tall hedges, heavy breakfasts, crooked roads and small gardens with large fences, and why they alone among Christians have kept quite consistently the great Christian glory of the open fireplace, here would be a strange and stimulating opportunity for any of the artists in words, who study the souls of strange peoples. That would be the true way to create a friendship between England and America, or between England and anything else; yes, even between England and Ireland. For this justice at least has already been done to Ireland; and as an indignant patriot I demand a more equal treatment for the two nations.

I have already noted the commonplace that in order to teach internationalism we must talk nationalism. We must make the nations as nations less odious or mysterious to each other. We do not make men love each other by describing a monster with a million arms and legs but by describing the men as men, with their separate and even solitary emotions. As this has a particular application to the emotions of the Englishman, I will return to the topic yet further. Now Americans have a power that is the soul and success of democracy, the power of spontaneous social organization. Their high spirits, their humane ideals, are really creative, they abound in unofficial institutions; we might almost say in unofficial officialism. Nobody who has felt the presence of all the leagues and guilds and college clubs will deny that Whitman was national when he said he would build states and cities out of the love of comrades. When all this communal enthusiasm collides with the Englishman, it too often seems literally to leave him cold. They say he is reserved; they possibly think he is rude. And the Englishman, having been taught his own history all wrong, is only too likely to take the criticism as a compliment. He admits that he is reserved because he is stern and strong; or even that he is rude because he is shrewd and candid. But as a fact he is not rude and not especially reserved; at least reserve is not the meaning of his reluctance. The real difference lies, I think, in the fact that American high spirits are not only high but level; that the hilarious American spirit is like a plateau, and the humorous English spirit like a ragged mountain range.

The Englishman is moody; which does not in the least mean that the Englishman is morose. Dickens, as we all feel in reading his books, was boisterously English. Dickens was moody when he wrote *Oliver Twist*; but he was also moody when he wrote *Pickwick*. That is, he was in another and much healthier mood. The mood was normal to him in the sense that nine times out of ten he felt and wrote in that humorous and hilarious mood. But he was, if ever there was one, a man of moods; and all the more of a typical Englishman for being a man of moods. But it was because of this almost entirely, that he had a misunderstanding with America.

In America there are no moods, or there is only one mood. It is the same whether it is called hustle or uplift; whether we regard it as the heroic love of comrades or the last hysteria of the herd instinct. It has been said of the typical English aristocrats of the Government offices that they resemble certain ornamental fountains and play from ten till four; and it is true that an Englishman, even an English aristocrat, is not always inclined to play any more than to work. But American sociability is not like the Trafalgar fountains. It is like Niagara. It never stops, under the silent stars or the rolling storms. There seems always to be the same human heat and pressure behind it; it is like the central heating of hotels as explained in the advertisements and announcements. The temperature can be regulated; but it is not. And it is always rather overpowering for an Englishman, whose mood changes like his own mutable and shifting sky. The English mood is very like the English weather; it is a nuisance and a national necessity.

If anyone wishes to understand the quarrel between Dickens and the Americans, let him turn to that chapter in *Martin Chuzzlewit*, in which young Martin has to receive endless defiles and deputations of total strangers each announced by name and demanding formal salutation. There are several things to be noticed about this incident. To begin with, it did not happen to Martin Chuzzlewit; but it did happen to

Charles Dickens. Dickens is incorporating almost without alteration a passage from a diary in the middle of a story; as he did when he included the admirable account of the prison petition of John Dickens as the prison petition of Wilkins Micawber. There is no particular reason why even the gregarious Americans should so throng the portals of a perfectly obscure steerage passenger like young Chuzzlewit. There was every reason why they should throng the portals of the author of *Pickwick* and *Oliver Twist*. And no doubt they did. If I may be permitted the aleatory image, you bet they did. Similar troops of sociable human beings have visited much more insignificant English travellers in America, with some of whom I am myself acquainted. I myself have the luck to be a little more stodgy and less sensitive than many of my countrymen; and certainly less sensitive than Dickens. But I know what it was that annoyed him about that unending and unchanging stream of American visitors; it was the unending and unchanging stream of American sociability and high spirits. A people living on such a lofty but level tableland do not understand the ups and downs of the English temperament; the temper of a nation of eccentrics or (as they used to be called) of humorists. There is something very national in the very name of the old play of *Every Man in His Humour*. But the play more often acted in real life is "Every Man Out of His Humour." It is true, as Matthew Arnold said, that an Englishman wants to do as he likes; but it is not always true even that he likes what he likes. An Englishman can be friendly and yet not feel friendly. Or he can be friendly and yet not feel hospitable. Or he can feel hospitable and yet not welcome those whom he really loves. He can think, almost with tears of tenderness, about people at a distance who would be bores if they came in at the door.

American sociability sweeps away any such subtlety. It cannot be expected to understand the paradox or perversity of the Englishman, who thus can feel friendly and avoid friends. That is the truth in the suggestion that Dickens was sentimental. It means that he probably felt most sociable when he was solitary. In all these attempts to describe the indescribable, to indicate the real but unconscious differences between the two peoples, I have tried to balance my words without the irrelevant bias of praise and blame. Both characteristics always cut both ways. On one side this comradeship makes possible a certain communal courage, a democratic derision of rich men in high places, that is not easy in our smaller and more stratified society. On the other hand the Englishman has certainly more liberty, if less equality and fraternity. But the richest compensation of the Englishman is not even in the word "liberty" but rather in the word "poetry." That humour of escape or seclusion, that genial isolation, that healing of wounded friendship by what Christian Science would call absent treatment, that is the best atmosphere of all for the creation of great poetry; and out of that came "bare ruined choirs where late the sweet birds sang" and "thou wast not made for death, immortal bird." In this sense it is indeed true that poetry is emotion remembered in tranquillity; which may be extended to mean affection remembered in loneliness. There is in it a spirit not only of detachment but even of distance; a spirit which does desire, as in the old English rhyme, to be not only over the hills but also far away. In other words, in so far as it is true that the Englishman is an exception to the great truth of Aristotle, it is because he is not so near to Aristotle as he is to Homer. In so far as he is not by nature a political animal, it is because he is a poetical animal. We see it in his relations to the other animals; his quaint and almost illogical love of dogs and horses and dependants whose political rights cannot possibly be defined in logic. Many forms of hunting or fishing are but an excuse for the same thing which the shameless literary man does without any excuse. Sport is speechless poetry. It would be easy for a foreigner, by taking a few liberties with the facts, to make a satire about the sort of silent Shelley who decides ultimately to shoot the skylark. It would be easy to answer these poetic suggestions by saying that he himself might be responsible for ruining the choirs where late the sweet birds sang, or that the immortal bird was likely to be mortal when he was out with his gun. But these international satires are never just; and the real relations of an Englishman and an English bird are far more delicate. It would be equally easy and equally unjust to suggest a similar satire against American democracy; and represent Americans merely as birds of a feather who can do nothing but flock together. But this would leave out the fact that at least it is not the white feather; that democracy is capable of defiance and of death for an idea. Touching the souls of great nations, these criticisms are generally false because they are critical.

But when we are quite sure that we rejoice in a nation's strength, then and not before we are justified in judging its weakness. I am quite sure that I rejoice in any democratic success without *arrière pensée*; and nobody who knows me will credit me with a covert sneer at civic equality. And this being granted, I do think there is a danger in the gregariousness of American society. The danger of democracy is not anarchy; on the contrary, it is monotony. And it is touching this that all my experience has increased my conviction that a great deal that is called female emancipation has merely been the increase of female convention. Now the males of every community are far too conventional; it was the females who were individual and criticized the conventions of the tribe. If the females become conventional also, there is a danger of individuality being lost. This indeed is not peculiar to America; it is common to the whole modern industrial world, and to everything which substitutes the impersonal atmosphere of the State for the personal atmosphere of the home. But it is emphasized in America by the curious contradiction that Americans do in theory value and even venerate the individual. But individualism is still the foe of individuality. Where men are trying to compete with each other they are trying to copy each other. They become featureless by "featuring" the same part. Personality, in becoming a conscious ideal, becomes a common ideal. In this respect perhaps there is really something to be learnt from the Englishman with his turn or twist in the direction of private life. Those who have travelled in such a fashion as to see all the American hotels and none of the American houses are sometimes driven to the excess of saying that the Americans have no private life. But even if the exaggeration has a hint of truth, we must balance it with the corresponding truth; that the English have no public life. They on their side have still to learn the meaning of the public thing, the republic; and how great are the dangers of cowardice and corruption when the very State itself has become a State secret.

The English are patriotic; but patriotism is the unconscious form of nationalism. It is being national without understanding the meaning of a nation. The Americans are on the whole too self-conscious, kept moving too much in the pace of public life, with all its temptations to superficiality and fashion; too much aware of outside opinion and with too much appetite for outside criticism. But the English are much too unconscious; and would be the better for an increase in many forms of consciousness, including consciousness of sin. But even their sin is ignorance of their real virtue. The most admirable English things are not the things that are most admired by the English, or for which the English admire themselves. They are things now blindly neglected and in daily danger of being destroyed. It is all the worse that they should be destroyed, because there is really nothing like them in the world. That is why I have suggested a note of nationalism rather than patriotism for the English; the power of seeing their nation as a nation and not as the nature of things. We say of some ballad from the Balkans or some peasant costume in the Netherlands that it is unique; but the good things of England really are unique. Our very isolation from continental wars and revolutionary reconstructions have kept them unique. The particular kind of beauty there is in an English village, the particular kind of humour there is in an English public-house, are things that cannot be found in lands where the village is far more simply and equally governed, or where the vine is far more honourably served and praised. Yet we shall not save them by merely sinking into them with the conservative sort of contentment, even if the commercial capacity of our plutocratic reforms would allow us to do so. We must in a sense get far away from England in order to behold her; we must rise above patriotism in order to be practically patriotic; we must have some sense of more varied and remote things before these vanishing virtues can be seen suddenly for what they are; almost as one might fancy that a man would have to rise to the dizziest heights of the divine understanding before he saw, as from a peak far above a whirlpool, how precious is his perishing soul.

19

The Future of Democracy

The title of this final chapter requires an apology. I do not need to be reminded, alas, that the whole book requires an apology. It is written in accordance with a ritual or custom in which I could see no particular harm, and which gives me a very interesting subject, but a custom which it would be not altogether easy to justify in logic. Everybody who goes to America for a short time is expected to write a book; and nearly everybody does. A man who takes a holiday at Trouville or Dieppe is not confronted on his return with the question, "When is your book on France going to appear?" A man who betakes himself to Switzerland for the winter sports is not instantly pinned by the statement, "I suppose your History of the Helvetian Republic is coming out this spring?" Lecturing, at least my kind of lecturing, is not much more serious or meritorious than ski-ing or sea-bathing; and it happens to afford the holiday-maker far less opportunity of seeing the daily life of the people. Of all this I am only too well aware; and my only defence is that I am at least sincere in my enjoyment and appreciation of America, and equally sincere in my interest in its most serious problem, which I think a very serious problem indeed; the problem of democracy in the modern world. Democracy may be a very obvious and facile affair for plutocrats and politicians who only have to use it as a rhetorical term. But democracy is a very serious problem for democrats. I certainly do not apologize for the word democracy; but I do apologize for the word future. I am no Futurist; and any conjectures I make must be taken with the grain of salt which is indeed the salt of the earth; the decent and moderate humility which comes from a belief in free will. That faith is in itself a divine doubt. I do not believe in any of the scientific predictions about mankind; I notice that they always fail to predict any of the purely human developments of men; I also notice that even their successes prove the same truth as their failures; for their successful predictions are not about men but about machines. But there are two things which a man may reasonably do, in stating the probabilities of a problem, which do not involve any claim to be a prophet. The first is to tell the truth, and especially the neglected truth, about the tendencies that have already accumulated in human history; any miscalculation about which must at least mislead us in any case. We cannot be certain of being right about the future; but we can be almost certain of being wrong about the future, if we are wrong about the past. The other thing that he can do is to note what ideas necessarily go together by their own nature; what ideas will triumph together or fall together. Hence it follows that this final chapter must consist of two things. The first is a summary of what has really happened to the idea of democracy in recent times; the second a suggestion of the fundamental doctrine which is necessary for its triumph at any time.

The last hundred years have seen a general decline in the democratic idea. If there be anybody left to whom this historical truth appears a paradox, it is only because during that period nobody has been taught history, least of all the history of ideas. If a sort of intellectual inquisition had been established, for the definition and differentiation of heresies, it would have been found that the original republican orthodoxy had suffered more and more from secessions, schisms and backslidings. The highest point of democratic idealism and conviction was towards the end of the eighteenth century, when the American Republic was "dedicated to the proposition that all men are equal." It was then that the largest number of men had the most serious sort of conviction that the political problem could be solved by the vote of peoples instead of the arbitrary power of princes and privileged orders. These men encountered various difficulties and made various compromises in relation to the practical politics of their time; in England they preserved aristocracy; in America they preserved slavery. But though they had more difficulties, they had less doubts. Since their time democracy has been steadily disintegrated by doubts; and these political doubts have been contemporary with and often identical with religious doubts. This fact could be followed over almost the whole field of the modern world; in this place it will be more appropriate to take the great American example of slavery. I have found traces in all sorts of intelligent quarters of an extraordinary idea that all the Fathers of the Republic owned black men like beasts of burden because they knew no better, until the light of liberty was revealed to them by John Brown and Mrs. Beecher Stowe. One of the best weekly papers in England said recently that even those who drew up the Declaration of Independence did not include negroes in its generalization about humanity. This is quite consistent with the current convention, in which we were all brought up; the theory that the heart of humanity broadens in ever larger circles of brotherhood, till we pass from embracing a black man to adoring a black beetle. Unfortunately it is quite inconsistent with the facts of American history. The facts show that, in this problem of the Old South, the eighteenth century was *more* liberal than the nineteenth century. There was *more* sympathy for the negro in the school of Jefferson than in the school of Jefferson Davis. Jefferson, in the dark estate of his simple

Deism, said the sight of slavery in his country made him tremble, remembering that God is just. His fellow Southerners, after a century of the world's advance, said that slavery in itself was good, when they did not go farther and say that negroes in themselves were bad. And they were supported in this by the great and growing modern suspicion that nature is unjust. Difficulties seemed inevitably to delay justice, to the mind of Jefferson; but so they did to the mind of Lincoln. But that the slave was human and the servitude inhuman—that was, if anything, clearer to Jefferson than to Lincoln. The fact is that the utter separation and subordination of the black like a beast was a *progress*; it was a growth of nineteenth-century enlightenment and experiment; a triumph of science over superstition. It was "the way the world was going," as Mathew Arnold reverentially remarked in some connection; perhaps as part of a definition of God. Anyhow, it was not Jefferson's definition of God. He fancied, in his far-off patriarchial way, a Father who had made all men brothers; and brutally unbrotherly as was the practice, such democratical Deists never dreamed of denying the theory. It was not until the scientific sophistries began that brotherhood was really disputed. Gobineau, who began most of the modern talk about the superiority and the inferiority of racial stocks, was seized upon eagerly by the less generous of the slave-owners and trumpeted as a new truth of science and a new defence of slavery. It was not really until the dawn of Darwinism, when all our social relations began to smell of the monkey-house, that men thought of the barbarian as only a first and the baboon as a second cousin. The full servile philosophy has been a modern and even a recent thing; made in an age whose invisible deity was the Missing Link. The Missing Link was a true metaphor in more ways than one; and most of all in its suggestion of a chain.

By a symbolic coincidence, indeed, slavery grew more brazen and brutal under the encouragement of more than one movement of the progressive sort. Its youth was renewed for it by the industrial prosperity of Lancashire; and under that influence it became a commercial and competitive instead of a patriarchal and customary thing. We may say with no exaggerative irony that the unconscious patrons of slavery were Huxley and Cobden. The machines of Manchester were manufacturing a great many more things than the manufacturers knew or wanted to know; but they were certainly manufacturing the fetters of the slave, doubtless out of the best quality of steel and iron. But this is a minor illustration of the modern tendency, as compared with the main stream of scepticism which was destroying democracy. Evolution became more and more a vision of the break-up of our brotherhood, till by the end of the nineteenth century the genius of its greatest scientific romancer saw it end in the anthropophagous antics of the Time Machine. So far from evolution lifting us above the idea of enslaving men, it was providing us at least with a logical and potential argument for eating them. In the case of the American negroes, it may be remarked, it does at any rate permit the preliminary course of roasting them. All this materialistic hardening, which replaced the remorse of Jefferson, was part of the growing evolutionary suspicion that savages were not a part of the human race, or rather that there was really no such thing as the human race. The South had begun by agreeing reluctantly to the enslavement of men. The South ended by agreeing equally reluctantly to the emancipation of monkeys.

This is what had happened to the democratic ideal in a hundred years. Anybody can test it by comparing the final phase, I will not say with the ideal of Jefferson, but with the ideal of Johnson. There was far more horror of slavery in an eighteenth-century Tory like Dr. Johnson than in a nineteenth-century democrat like Stephen Douglas. Stephen Douglas may be mentioned because he is a very representative type of the age of evolution and expansion; a man thinking in continents, like Cecil Rhodes, human and hopeful in a truly American fashion, and as a consequence cold and careless rather than hostile in the matter of the old mystical doctrines of equality. He "did not care whether slavery was voted up or voted down." His great opponent Lincoln did indeed care very much. But it was an intense individual conviction with Lincoln exactly as it was with Johnson. I doubt if the spirit of the age was not much more behind Douglas and his westward expansion of the white race. I am sure that more and more men were coming to be in the particular mental condition of Douglas; men in whom the old moral and mystical ideals had been undermined by doubt but only with a negative effect of indifference. Their positive convictions were all concerned with what some called progress and some imperialism. It is true that there was a sincere sectional enthusiasm against slavery in the North; and that the slaves were actually emancipated in the nineteenth century. But I doubt whether the Abolitionists would ever have secured Abolition. Abolition was a by-product of the Civil War; which was fought for quite other reasons. Anyhow, if slavery had somehow survived to the age of Rhodes and Roosevelt and evolutionary imperialism, I doubt if the slaves would ever have been emancipated at all. Certainly if it had survived till the modern movement for the Servile State, they would never have been emancipated at all. Why should the world take the chains off the black man when it was just putting them on the white? And in so far as we owe the change to Lincoln, we owe it to Jefferson. Exactly what gives its real dignity to the figure of Lincoln is that he stands invoking a primitive first principle of the age of innocence, and holding up the tables of an ancient law, *against* the trend of the nineteenth century; repeating, "We hold these truths to be self-evident; that all men are created equal, that they are endowed by their Creator, etc.," to a generation that was more and more disposed to say something like this: "We hold these truths to be probable enough for pragmatists; that all things looking like men were evolved somehow, being endowed by heredity and environment with no equal rights, but very unequal wrongs," and so on. I do not believe that creed, left to itself, would ever have founded a state; and I am pretty certain that, left to itself, it would never have overthrown a slave state. What it did do, as I have said, was to produce some very wonderful literary and artistic flights of sceptical imagination. The world did have new visions, if they were visions of monsters in the moon and Martians striding about like spiders as tall as the sky, and the workmen and capitalists becoming two separate species, so that one could devour the other as gaily and greedily as a cat devours a bird. No one has done justice to the meaning of Mr. Wells and his original departure in fantastic fiction; to these nightmares that were the last apocalypse of the nineteenth century. They meant that the bottom had fallen out of the mind at last, that the bridge of brotherhood had broken down in the modern brain, letting up from the chasms this infernal light like a dawn. All had grown dizzy with degree and relativity; so that there would not be so very much difference between eating dog and eating darkie, or between eating darkie and eating dago. There were different sorts of apes; but there was no doubt that we were the superior sort.

Against all this irresistible force stood one immovable post. Against all this dance of doubt and degree stood something that can best be symbolized by a simple example. An ape cannot be a priest, but a negro can be a priest. The dogmatic type of Christianity, especially the Catholic type of Christianity, had riveted itself irrevocably to the manhood of all men. Where its faith was fixed by creeds and councils it could not save itself even by surrender. It could not gradually dilute democracy, as could a merely sceptical or secular democrat. There stood, in fact or in possibility, the solid and smiling figure of a black bishop. And he was either a man claiming the most towering spiritual privileges of a man, or he was the mere buffoonery and blasphemy of a monkey in a mitre. That is the point about Christian and Catholic democracy; it is not that it is necessarily at any moment more democratic, it is that its indestructible minimum of democracy really is indestructible. And by the nature of things that mystical democracy was destined to survive, when every other sort of democracy was free to destroy itself. And whenever democracy destroying itself is suddenly moved to save itself, it always grasps at a rag or tag of that old tradition that alone is sure of itself. Hundreds have heard the story about the mediaeval demagogue who went about repeating the rhyme

When Adam delved and Eve span,
Who was then the gentleman?

Many have doubtless offered the obvious answer to the question, "The Serpent." But few seem to have noticed what would be the more modern answer to the question, if that innocent agitator went about propounding it. "Adam never delved and Eve never span, for the simple reason that they never existed. They are fragments of a Chaldeo-Babylonian mythos, and Adam is only a slight variation of Tag-Tug, pronounced Uttu. For the real beginning of humanity we refer you to Darwin's *Origin of Species*." And then the modern man would go on to justify plutocracy to the mediaeval man by talking about the Struggle for Life and the Survival of the Fittest; and how the strongest man seized authority by means of anarchy, and proved himself a gentleman by behaving like a cad. Now I do not base my beliefs on the theology of John Ball, or on the literal and materialistic reading of the text of Genesis; though I think the story of Adam and Eve infinitely less absurd and unlikely than that of the prehistoric "strongest man" who could fight a hundred men. But I do note the fact that the idealism of the leveller could be put in the form of an appeal to Scripture, and could not be put in the form of an appeal to Science. And I do note also that democrats were still driven to make the same appeal even in the very century of Science. Tennyson was, if ever there was one, an evolutionist in his vision and an aristocrat in his sympathies. He was always boasting that John Bull was evolutionary and not revolutionary, even as these Frenchmen. He did not pretend to have any creed beyond faintly trusting the larger hope. But when human dignity is really in danger, John Bull has to use the same old argument as John Ball. He tells Lady Clara Vere de Vere that "the gardener Adam and his wife smile at the claim of long descent"; their own descent being by no means long. Lady Clara might surely have scored off him pretty smartly by quoting from "Maud" and "In Memoriam" about evolution and the eft that was lord of valley and hill. But Tennyson has evidently forgotten all about Darwin and the long descent of man. If this was true of an evolutionist like Tennyson, it was naturally ten times truer of a revolutionist like Jefferson. The Declaration of Independence dogmatically bases all rights on the fact that God created all men equal; and it is right; for if they were not created equal, they were certainly evolved unequal.

There is no basis for democracy except in a dogma about the divine origin of man. That is a perfectly simple fact which the modern world will find out more and more to be a fact. Every other basis is a sort of sentimental confusion, full of merely verbal echoes of the older creeds. Those verbal associations are always vain for the vital purpose of constraining the tyrant. An idealist may say to a capitalist, "Don't you sometimes feel in the rich twilight, when the lights twinkle from the distant hamlet in the hills, that all humanity is a holy family?" But it is equally possible for the capitalist to reply with brevity and decision, "No, I don't," and there is no more disputing about it further than about the beauty of a fading cloud. And the modern world of moods is a world of clouds, even if some of them are thunderclouds.

For I have only taken here, as a convenient working model, the case of negro slavery; because it was long peculiar to America and is popularly associated with it. It is more and more obvious that the line is no longer running between black and white but between rich and poor. As I have already noted in the case of Prohibition, the very same arguments, of the inevitable suicide of the ignorant, of the impossibility of freedom for the unfit, which were once applied to barbarians brought from Africa are now applied to citizens born in America. It is argued even by industrialists that industrialism has produced a class submerged below the status of emancipated mankind. They imply that the Missing Link is no longer missing, even from England or the Northern States, and that the factories have manufactured their own monkeys. Scientific hypotheses about the feeble-minded and the criminal type will supply the masters of the modern world with more and more excuses for denying the dogma of equality in the case of white labour as well as black. And any man who knows the world knows perfectly well that to tell the millionaires, or their servants, that they are disappointing the sentiments of Thomas Jefferson, or disregarding a creed composed in the eighteenth century, will be about as effective as telling them that they are not observing the creed of St. Athanasius or keeping the rule of St. Benedict.

The world cannot keep its own ideals. The secular order cannot make secure any one of its own noble and natural conceptions of secular perfection. That will be found, as time goes on, the ultimate argument for a Church independent of the world and the secular order. What has become of all those ideal figures from the Wise Man of the Stoics to the democratic Deist of the eighteenth century? What has become of all that purely human hierarchy or chivalry, with its punctilious pattern of the good knight, its ardent ambition in the young squire? The very name of knight has come to represent the petty triumph of a profiteer, and the very word squire the petty tyranny of a landlord. What has become of all that golden liberality of the Humanists, who found on the high tablelands of the culture of Hellas the very balance of repose in beauty that is most lacking in the modern world? The very Greek language that they loved has become a mere label for snuffy and snobbish dons, and a mere cock-shy for cheap and half-educated utilitarians, who make it a symbol of superstition and reaction. We have lived to see a time when the heroic legend of the Republic and the Citizen, which seemed to Jefferson the eternal youth of the world, has begun to grow old in its turn. We cannot recover the earthly estate of knighthood, to which all the colours and complications of heraldry seemed as fresh and natural as flowers. We can not re-enact the intellectual experiences of the Humanists, for whom the Greek grammar was like the song of a bird in spring. The more the matter is considered the clearer it will seem that these old experiences are now only alive, where they have found a lodgment in the Catholic tradition of Christendom, and made themselves friends for ever. St. Francis is the only surviving troubadour. St. Thomas More is the only surviving Humanist. St. Louis is the only surviving knight.

It would be the worse sort of insincerity, therefore, to conclude even so hazy an outline of so great and majestic a matter as the American democratic experiment, without testifying my belief that to this also the same ultimate test will come. So far as that democracy becomes or remains Catholic and Christian, that democracy will remain democratic. In so far as it does not, it will become wildly and wickedly undemocratic. Its rich will riot with a brutal indifference far beyond the feeble feudalism which retains some shadow of responsibility or at least of patronage. Its wage-slaves will either sink into heathen slavery, or seek relief in theories that are destructive not merely in method but in aim; since they are but the negations of the human appetites of property and personality. Eighteenth-century ideals, formulated in eighteenth-century language, have no longer in themselves the power to hold all those pagan passions back. Even those documents depended upon Deism; their real strength will survive in men who are still Deists. And the men who are still Deists are more than Deists. Men will more and more realize that there is no meaning in democracy if there is no meaning in anything; and that there is no meaning in anything if the universe has not a centre of significance and an authority that is the author of our rights. There is truth in every ancient fable, and there is here even something of it in the fancy that finds the symbol of the Republic in the bird that bore the bolts of Jove. Owls and bats may wander where they will in darkness, and for them as for the sceptics the universe may have no centre; kites and vultures may linger as they like over carrion, and for them as for the plutocrats existence may have no origin and no end; but it was far back in the land of legends, where instincts find their true images, that the cry went forth that freedom is an eagle, whose glory is gazing at the sun.

THE END